A PRACTICAL GUIDE TO CRIMINAL JUSTICE

A PRACTICAL GUIDE TO CRIMINAL JUSTICE

CURATED INTRODUCTORY READINGS

FIRST EDITION

Edited By Audra Cronen Tignor

University of West Alabama

cognella®
SAN DIEGO

Bassim Hamadeh, CEO and Publisher

Michelle Piehl, Senior Project Editor

Susana Christie, Senior Developmental Editor

Celeste Paed, Associate Production Editor

Asfa Arshi, Graphic Design Assistant

Trey Soto, Licensing Specialist

Natalie Piccotti, Director of Marketing

Kassie Graves, Senior Vice President, Editorial

Jamie Giganti, Director of Academic Publishing

Printed in the United States of America.

CONTENTS

INTRODUCTION

> In matters of truth and justice, there is no difference between large and small problems, for issues concerning the treatment of people are all the same.
>
> Albert Einstein

This textbook was created to give the student a practical guide that introduces them to the criminal justice system. Throughout the chapters, there will be readings that detail the inner workings of the criminal justice system, firsthand experiences, definitions, and challenging questions.

The chapters were hand-picked to give the student a varied idea of what the criminal justice system entails. As a criminal justice student, I always wanted to read relative yet thought-provoking texts, but most books were just filled with heavy definitions without giving real-life examples. I wanted to bring these examples and challenging ideas to the students without them having to take the extra time.

In the first chapter, "Basics of Criminal Justice," the reading "Crime in Society" by Jocelyn Pollock gives us the fundamentals of criminal justice: types of crimes, individual's roles in defining crime, patterns of crime, and how we manage crime. This chapter helps to provide insight to the reader on how society determines what we know about crime and how we see it reflected around us. This chapter will explain the essential definitions of crime, the sources we use to collect data on crimes committed, our perception of crime around us, and how other countries' crime rates compare to the United States.

In the second chapter, "Policing," the reading "Police and Policing" by Bradley D. Edwards and Lawrence F. Travis III describes policing history and reform, police functions, police management, policing styles, and counterterrorism and homeland security. This chapter dives deep into introductory basics and generalized policing.

Throughout the third chapter, "Court of Law," the reading "The Courts" by Mia R. Ortiz dives into the US court system's history, evolution, and the individuals in the court room and an analysis of the system. The reading expands on individuals' rights and due process, profiles of the criminal defendant, and the offender's trajectory throughout the system. The analysis then focuses on the growing problems within the court system that affect our society today.

The fourth chapter, "Corrections," includes the reading "A History of Incarceration in the United States" by Marilyn D. McShane, which concentrates on the history of the US prison system, reformation, and problems within the system. The reading highlights many acts that have been passed to allow offenders a better life within the prison walls. Understanding prison history will help to work to solve the problems within our prison system today.

In the fifth chapter, "Juvenile Justice," is the reading "Policing and Juveniles" by John T. Whitehead and Steven P. Lab. The reading focuses on juvenile statistics, community or problem-solving policing, attitudes toward the police, and recent issues in juvenile justice. The authors guide us through the chapter with an explanation of definitions such as "broken windows" policing, police effectiveness, and the school-to-prison pipeline.

The final chapter, "Current Issues in Criminal Justice," explores current issues in criminal justice through the reading "Societal Justice" by Virginia Murphy-Berman. This reading focuses on justice within our society and how it can be perceived, but also how it is defined on a universal level. The reading focuses on our understanding of human rights and its application in the world.

CHAPTER 1

Basics of Criminal Justice

Crime in Society

Joycelyn Pollock

Joycelyn Pollock, "Crime in Society," *Crime and Criminal Justice in America*, pp. 31–65. Copyright © 2017 by Taylor & Francis Group. Reprinted with permission.

[Reading] Preview

- What Is Crime?
- What Is the Role of Legislators, Victims, Police, and Prosecutors in Defining Crimes?
- What Sources Do We Use to Find Out About the Patterns of Crime?
- What Crimes Are People Most Frequently Arrested for?
- What Do We Know About Homicide?
- What Has Been the Pattern of Crime Over the Years? Has It Declined?
- Does The Public Have an Accurate Perception About the Prevalence of Crime?
- How Do the Crime Rates of the United States Compare to Other Countries?
- Focus On Data: Is There a Ferguson Effect? Is There a Current Crime Wave?
- Summary
- Critical Thinking Exercises

What Is Crime?

What is crime? This seems like an easy question, and it is, in a way. However, the answer is not necessarily murder, robbery, or rape. Those may be examples of crime, but the definition of **crime** is simply "an action that is prohibited by law." For instance, the definition of simple **assault** in one state is as follows:

1. Intentionally, knowingly, or recklessly causes bodily injury to another, including the person's spouse.

2. Intentionally or knowingly threatens another with imminent bodily injury, including the person's spouse.
3. Intentionally or knowingly causes physical contact with another when the person knows or should reasonably believe that the other will regard the contact as offensive or provocative.[1]

So, if you pushed or even hugged someone who you knew would consider it to be provocative or offensive, you have committed simple assault. This is a Class A misdemeanor unless some other conditions are met; therefore, it is not a very "serious" crime. Most simple assaults are not brought to the attention of the criminal justice system. However, many other, more serious crimes are also never reported. This creates what is known as the **dark figure of crime**, which is crime that does not find its way into official numbers. Crimes such as domestic violence, acquaintance rape, and even theft, are more likely than other crimes to be part of this dark figure of crime.

Because the dark figure of crime is so high, it makes theorizing about who commits crime difficult. We do not know if the offenders who never come to the attention of authorities are similar to those who do. We do not know if these unknown offenders have similar motivations and patterns of criminal offending. Studies that are based only on known offenders may be faulty in that they are not able to present findings on all offenders—only those we know about. It is important to ask relevant questions about crime, e.g. has homicide increased or not; but, it is also important to note the weaknesses of our data sources when trying to understand crime patterns.

What Is the Role of Legislators, Victims, Police, and Prosecutors in Defining Crime?

Crime is called a "constructed reality" because it is created by the definitions and perceptions of the legislators, perpetrators, observers, victims, and formal system actors (such as police and prosecutors). Take for instance, the following scenario: Person A shoves Person B. Is it a crime? It might be simple assault if Person A did it intentionally, believing it to be offensive to Person B. Is it prosecutable? It might be, only if Person B reports it to police or perhaps if a police officer happened to be close enough to see it and chose to arrest. Will it be prosecuted? A variety of factors affect the decision to prosecute, including the wishes of the victim, the resources of the prosecutor's office, the nature of the evidence and, some would say, perhaps the race and ethnicity of the offender and/or victim.

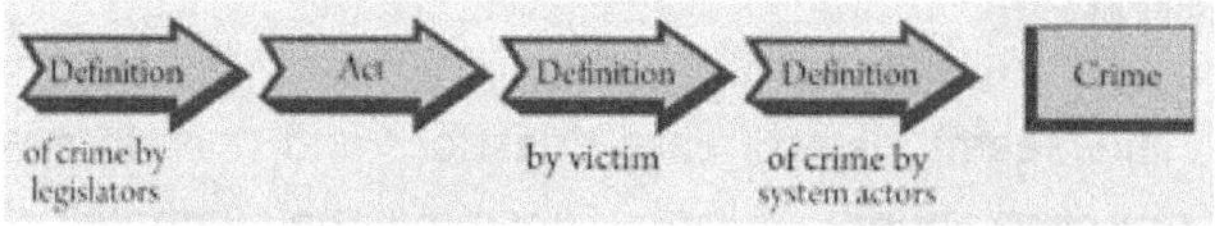

FIGURE 1.1 Crime: A "Constructed Reality"

1. Texas Penal Code. Retrieved 4/10/2007 from http://tlo2.tlc.state.tx.us/statutes/docs/PE/content/htm/pe.005.00.000022.00.htm#22.01.00.

Before we can punish any act as a crime, a law has to be created by legislation. [M]ost of our laws come from common law; however, state and federal legislators are constantly fine-tuning our criminal codes and adding new laws or changing existing laws. Recent changes in some states have legalized possession of small amounts of marijuana, and the carrying of guns on college campuses. Other changes in some states' laws have criminalized talking on your cellphone while driving, and posting nude pictures of someone on social media sites without their permission. [S]tates are free to create new crimes as long as they do not violate individuals' federal constitutional rights. It is not at all unusual to have one state legislature pass a new law that criminalizes behavior that is still legal in other states or vice versa.

According to statistics, in 2014, 431,000 people were injured and 3,179 were killed in car accidents involving distracted drivers, which has prompted many states to pass laws banning texting or cellphone use while driving.

Before a crime can be counted by officials, it must be reported by the victim. Why might someone *not* report a crime to authorities? The most common reason is that they believe police can't do anything about it, but they might also interpret the event as a private matter and not a crime. Domestic violence victims sometimes do not want the involvement of the police, even though they are obviously victims of assault. Rape victims also may not report their own victimization, sometimes because they do not want formal intervention, but sometimes because they do not interpret the event as a crime. Studies have shown that female victims who are raped in "date-rape" scenarios by someone they know in circumstances where the lack of consent may be somewhat ambiguous sometimes do not define what occurred as a crime. If the victim does not perceive the event as a crime, or does not want formal system intervention, then the event is never reported to police and does not appear in our crime statistics.[2] In 2007, only 40 percent of all criminal victimizations were reported to police. Robberies with injury and auto theft were reported by 85 percent of victims, but only a quarter of some other types of crimes were reported to police.[3] In Figure 1.2, we display 2013 figures, but also show those for 2004. We see that the percentage of individuals who report their victimization to the police has decreased in many crime categories since 2004, but has increased in some crime categories.

2. See H. Cleveland, M. Koss and J. Lyons, "Rape tactics from the survivor's perspective." *Journal of Interpersonal Violence* 14(5) (1999): 532–548.
3. *Sourcebook of Criminal Justice Statistics 2010.* Retrieved 9/9/2010 from http://www.albany.edu/sourcebook/pdf/13332007.pdf.

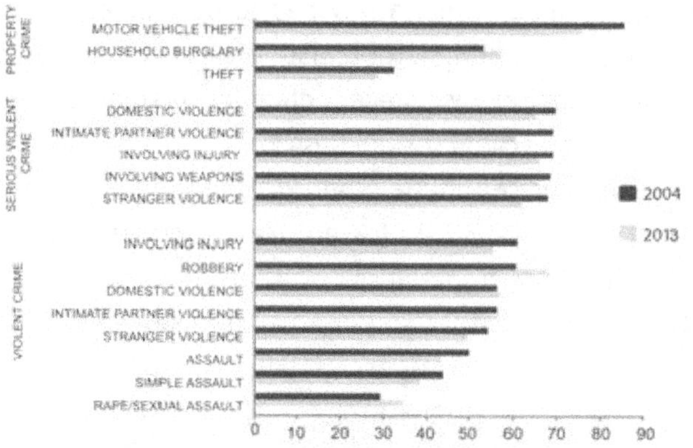

*Important footnotes regarding methodology omitted. See source.

FIGURE 1.2 Percent of Victimizations Reported to Police, by Type of Crime, 2004 and 2013*

Source: J. Truman and L. Langton, 2014. Criminal Victimization, 2013. Washington, DC: Bureau of Justice Statistics, DOJ. Retrieved from: http://www.bjs.gov/content/pub/pdf/cv13.pdf

To find the most current statistics regarding victim reporting, go to the website of the Bureau of Justice Statistics. The 2014 report can be found at: http://www.bjs.gov/content/pub/pdf/cv14.pdf.

Even if the victim calls police, there may not be an arrest. Police do not arrest in a large percentage of cases where an arrest is legally justified; perhaps in as many as half of all cases. Although arrests are usually made in serious felony cases, or in situations in which victims demand an arrest, even assaults may be dealt with informally rather than by initiating a formal report or arrest.[4] Obviously, arrest statistics represent only the cases in which police officers receive a report and decide to make an arrest. These numbers represent only a small portion of the total number of criminal incidents.

Before we can ask [the reading's] question "Why do people commit crime?" we need to become familiar with the patterns and characteristics of crime. We use a number of sources that provide crime data. These are not perfect and each has inherent weaknesses, but they are the source of everything we think we know about crime in this country.

What Sources Do We Use to Find Out About the Patterns of Crime?

The two most common sources of crime data are the Uniform Crime Reports (which includes both reports to police and arrests) and the National Crime Victimization Survey. It is important to note that everything

4. See C. Mendias and E. Kobe, "Engagement of policing ideals and the relationship to the exercise of discretionary powers." *Criminal Justice and Behavior* 33 (2006): 70–77.

that we think we know about crime is derived primarily from these sources; thus, if there is some bias (inaccuracy) in the way these sources present the patterns of crime, then what we think we know is not necessarily accurate. It is important to know when you are looking at crime statistics whether the numbers reflect "reports to police," "arrests," or respondents reporting in a victimization survey. Each reflects slightly different realities of crime.

The Uniform Crime Reports

The most well-known and used source of crime statistics in this country is the **Uniform Crime Reports**. This collection of local crime reports and arrest data began in 1929 and is now produced by the Federal Bureau of Investigation. The numbers come either directly from local law enforcement agencies or from a state agency that collects the data from local agencies and delivers it in a centralized format. About 98 percent of law enforcement agencies submit crime data to the FBI.[5]

You can find the UCR at https://www.fbi.gov/about-us/cjis/ucr/ucr

The Uniform Crime Reports present crime reports in terms of **rates** as well as raw numbers. The rates you will see in the Uniform Crime Reports are the number of crimes divided by the population and then multiplied to display by a standard number. You can compute a rate (per 100,000) using the following mathematical formula. The rate tells you how many crimes took place for each 100,000 people.

$$\text{Rate} = (\text{Number of Crimes} \div \text{Population}) \times 100{,}000$$

The advantage of a rate is that it allows us to compare patterns of crime in very different populations. For instance, with rates, we can compare the same city in two different periods, even if the city's population has dramatically changed. We can also compare two different cities, even if one is very large and the other very small. Knowing, for instance, the raw number of burglaries in New York City; Portland, Oregon; Austin, Texas; and Los Angeles, California, tells us something, but it doesn't tell us the relative risk of victimization in these cities because they do not have similar populations. The only way to compare the crime of two different

5. N. James, *How Crime in the United States Is Measured*. Washington, DC: Congressional Research Service (CRS), 2008.

populations is to compute the rate of each city, then compare the rates. In 2013, the *numbers* of reported burglaries and the *rates* for these cities looked like this:[6]

City	Population	Number of Burglaries	Rate
New York City	8,396,126	16,606	197
Portland	609,136	4,128	678
Austin	859,180	6,550	752
Los Angeles	3,878,725	15,728	405

Who would have thought that there were more burglaries per 100,000 people in Portland, Austin, and Los Angeles than in New York City? Compare other big cities which also show quite different rates for burglary.

City	**Population**	**Number of Burglaries**	**Rate**
Houston	2,180,606	23,733	1088
Chicago	2,720,554	17,775	653

The FBI cautions against anyone using these numbers to compare the crime risk between cities because there are so many variables that go into them, including police departments' recording practices, urban density, victim reporting practices, and so on. If city limits extend out into the suburbs, the crime rate will be lower because crime occurs less often in suburban than in urban areas. Any or all of these factors may help to explain why New York's burglary rates are so much lower than other cities. New York City also may have a low rate of burglaries because of a higher percentage of buildings with security, a lower percentage of occupied dwellings than other metropolitan areas, or a number of other factors that affects the number of burglaries in that geographic area. Even though we want to be cautious when comparing rates across cities, an examination of these rates do tell us that just because New Yorkers report over 16,000 burglaries and citizens of Austin report only about 6,500 does not mean necessarily that an individual has a greater risk of being burgled in New York City.

It is very important to have an accurate population base for rates to mean anything. If the population base is inaccurate, then so too will be the rate. If, for instance, the population base is out of date and the actual population has grown considerably, then the crimes (which inevitably would increase with a larger population) will be divided by an artificially small population indicating that the rate of crime in that locale (the amount of crime per person) is higher than what it actually is. In contrast, if the population used is inaccurate in the other direction and shows a much larger population than what actually exists (perhaps because people have been moving away from that area), and the crime rate is computed using this

6. Federal Bureau of Investigation, *Crime in the United States, 2013*, Table 6, Crime in the United States by State, by City, 2013. Retrieved 9/12/2007 from https://www.fbi.gov/about-us/cjis/ucr/crime-in-the-u.s/2013/crime-in-the-u.s.-2013/tables/6tabledatadecpdf/table-6.

inaccurately high population, then the crime rate will appear to be lower than it actually is. Usually, the FBI uses the most recent census numbers for the area, but these numbers may be vulnerable to rapid fluctuations in population/migration.

Crime reports are gathered from law enforcement agencies via a standard reporting form so that, for instance, larceny means the same thing in all states whether or not state laws differ in defining the dollar amount that would change larceny from a misdemeanor to a felony. Because these are standard definitions, they may or may not conform to the state's definition for that particular crime.

The UCR provides the total number of reported crimes for the eight **index crimes**: murder and non-negligent manslaughter, forcible rape, robbery, aggravated assault, burglary, larceny-theft, motor vehicle theft, and arson. Violent crimes include the first four crimes and property crimes include the last four crimes. These index crimes are also presented as rates per 100,000. In Figure 1.3a and b, we see the UCR rates for violent and property crimes across several decades. Note that all crime categories show dramatic declines in the crimes reported to the police.

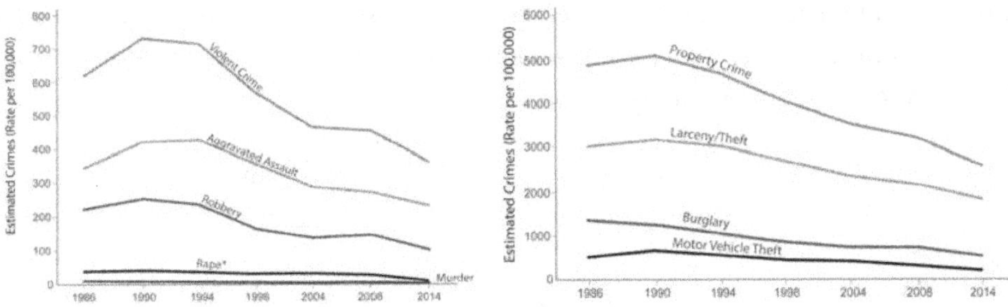

FIGURES 1.3A AND B Uniform Crime Reports—Violent Crime and Property Crime, 1986–2014. *The definition of rape changed for reporting purposes and the 2014 report included both the "legacy" rape rates (with the word forcible included) as shown here, but also a rate of 36.6 for the new definition: The revised UCR definition of rape is: "penetration, no matter how slight, of the vagina or anus with any body part or object, or oral penetration by a sex organ of another person, without the consent of the victim."

Source: UCR, Table 1, Crime in the United States, Table 1. By Volume and Rate, 1986–2005. Retrieved from www.fbi.gov/ucr/05cius/data/table/_01/html. Crime in the United States, 2008, Table 1. By Volume and Rate, 1989–2008. Retrieved from www.fbi.gov/ucr/cius2008/data/table_01.html. Crime in the United States, 2014. Table 1. By Volume and Rate. Retrieved from https://www.fbi.gov/about-us/cjis/ucr/crime-in-the-u.s/2014/crime-in-the-u.s.-2014/tables/table-1

One of the most oft-cited criticisms of the UCR is that it represents only reported crimes. If someone does not report a criminal victimization to the police, it does not get counted as a crime. Consequently, there is a "dark" figure of crime that never appears in the UCR. The amount of unreported crime varies by the type of crime. We saw in Figure 1.2 that less than half of violent crime victimizations and a little over a third of property crime victimizations are reported to police and, thus, are represented in the UCR. This presents a distinct problem if one uses the UCR as a measure of crime. In fact, it is not a measure of crime, but only a measure of *reported* crime. Another problem is that crimes such as identity theft, cybercrimes, and domestic violence are not easily identified in the traditional UCR because the reporting system is not set up to identify them.

One more potential problem is that some police departments have been exposed as "cooking" their numbers, meaning that they systematically downgrade citizens' reports of crimes in official reports. Scandals in New York City,[7] Chicago, and other cities[8] are troubling reminders that what we think we know about crime is dependent on accurate crime counts. When police departments categorize deaths as "undetermined" despite clear indications of homicide, they are not counted; when they record a robbery as theft instead of robbery, the true nature of the crime is hidden. These troubling incidents potentially make it unwise to utilize the UCR as the only source of understanding crime patterns—at least in specific cities.

The FBI also presents statistics on arrests. Arrest data is presented for 21 crime categories. In addition to the eight index crimes, arrests are also reported for other assaults, forgery, fraud, prostitution, and even curfew violations. The numbers of arrests are by no means a measure of crime, because they capture only the crimes in which a suspect was identified and a decision to arrest was made. Arrest data are presented for 21 crime categories in Figure 1.4, arranged in order of frequency. The graph shows that arrests for most crimes decreased. For some crimes, such as prostitution, changes over time are likely due to changes in decisions to arrest; for other crimes, such as homicide, arrest decisions are less likely to change because of discretionary enforcement. We must always remember that fluctuations in arrest rates may be real differences in such behavior, differences in perception and/or enforcement of the behavior, or differences in counting crimes. In this graph, the last several crimes are displayed separately since they show up as almost non-existent when in the same display as more frequent crimes.

7. J. Eterno and E. Silverman, "The trouble with Compstat: Pressure on NYPD commanders endangered the integrity of crime stats." *New York Daily News*, February 15, 2010. Retrieved 9/15/2010 from http://www.nydailynews.com/opinions/2010/02/15/2010-02-15_the_trouble_with_compstat.html; J. Eterno, A. Verma, E. Silverman, "Police manipulations of crime reporting: Insiders' revelations." *Justice Quarterly*, 2014. Accessed from: doi.org/10.1080/07418825.2014. 980838.
8. D. Bernstein and N. Isackson, "The truth about Chicago's crime rates, Part I and II." *Chicago Magazine* (May, June, 2014) Retrieved 12/9/2015 from http://www.chicagomag.com/Chicago-Magazine/June-2014/Chicago-crime-statistics/.

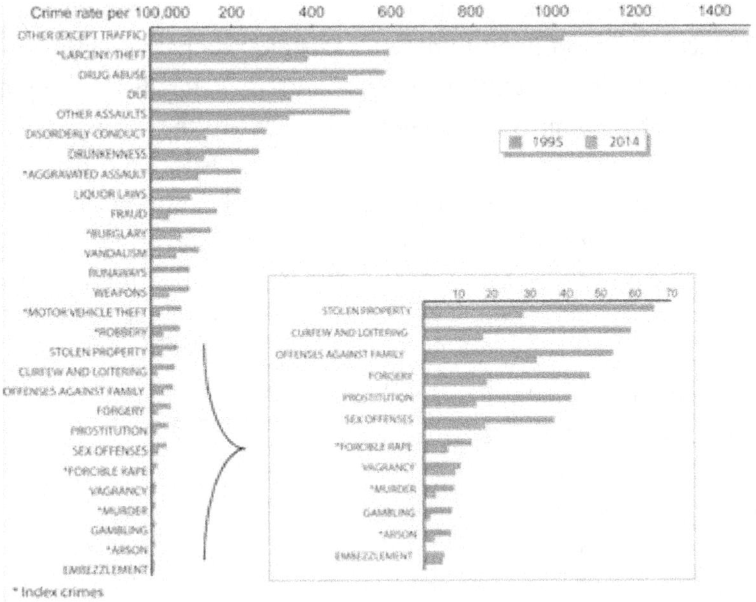

FIGURE 1.4 Uniform Crime Report Arrests, 2014. Note: Murder includes murder and non-negligent manslaughter.

Source: FBI, Crimes in the United States, 2014, Arrest Rates. https://www.fbi.gov/about-us/cjis/ucr/crime-in-the-u.s/2014/crime-in-the-u.s.-2014/tables/table-30

Many crimes go unsolved or are not cleared. Crimes are considered cleared when an arrest is made for an offense. The FBI reports on the number of crimes cleared by arrest with a statistic called the **clearance rate**. The clearance rates vary greatly by crime. In 2004, murder and non-negligent homicide had the highest clearance rate (62.6 percent), while burglary had the lowest clearance rate (12.9 percent).[9] In 2009, the clearance rate for murder and non-negligent homicide increased to 66.6 percent, while motor vehicle theft and burglary declined to 12.4 percent and 12.5 percent, respectively.[10] In 2014, the clearance rate for murder and non-negligent manslaughter slipped to 64.5 percent. The clearance rate for motor vehicle theft and burglary was 12.8 percent and 13.6 percent, respectively.[11]

To see clearance rates, go to http://www.fbi.gov/ucr/cius_04/offenses_cleared/index.html

9. Federal Bureau of Investigation, *Crime in the United States, 2004*. Retrieved 8/1/2006 from http://www.fbi.gov/ucr/cius_04/offenses_cleared/index.html.
10. Federal Bureau of Investigation, *Crime in the United States, 2009*. Retrieved 9/15/2010 from http://www.fbi.gov/ucr/cius2009/offenses/data/table_25.html.
11. Federal Bureau of Investigation, *Crime in the United States, 2014*. Retrieved 12/5/2015 from https://www.fbi.gov/about-us/cjis/ucr/crime-in-the-u.s/2014/crime-in-the-u.s.-2014/tables/table-25.

The FBI has also been collecting crime statistics in a different format to address other recognized problems. The National Incident-Based Reporting System (**NIBRS**) gathers much more detailed information about each criminal incident. While the UCR reporting format is hierarchical, meaning that only the most serious crime is counted, NIBRS requires information to be submitted on each crime within a criminal transaction. Instead of reporting crimes via the eight index offenses, NIBRS will display information on Group A offense categories (22 different crimes) and Group B offenses (11 different crimes). More information is obtained about each offense, including information about the victim and offender. For 22 offense categories, the following information is being collected and will be reported in NIBRS reports, also available on the FBI website:

- Victim, offender, and arrestee data
- Location and time of day of incidents
- Weapon data for select offenses
- Drug, alcohol, and gang involvement in offenses
- Attempted versus completed offenses
- Clearances by incidents
- Relationship of victims to offenders.

NIBRS reports are not comparable to the UCR because the way crimes are counted is different. For instance, a robbery, rape, and murder would only be reported as a murder in the UCR, but as three separate crimes under NIBRS. Law enforcement agencies have been slow to adopt the NIBRS reporting procedures, probably because it is much more detailed, requiring more effort to enter the data. There is also the concern that NIBRS will make it appear that there is an increase in crime because it would report each separate criminal incident instead of the hierarchical reporting system of the UCR. In 2012, about 30 percent of the nation's population was represented by crime statistics reported under NIBRS.[12] Currently only fifteen U.S. states have complete NIBRS agency participation, with an additional 18 states that submit both summary UCR and NIBRS data.[13]

Victimization Studies

Another source of crime statistics comes from victimization surveys. The Bureau of Justice Statistics presents findings from the **National Crime Victimization Survey** (NCVS). Begun in 1973 as the National Crime Survey, the U.S. Bureau of the Census has been interviewing household members in a nationally representative sample. In 1992–93, the survey was redesigned and relabeled as the National Crime Victimization Survey. The redesign effort was intended to obtain more information and include less serious crimes. The items in the survey capture more information than what is available through the UCR. For instance, one question asks

12. Bureau of Justice Statistics, NIBRS. Retrieved 12/5/2015 from BJS website, note on methodology on NIBRS. http://www.bjs.gov/index.cfm?ty=dcdetail&iid=301#_ftnref3.
13. D. Roberts, "Why participating in NIBRS is a good idea." *Police Chief Magazine*, December 2015. Retrieved 12/5/2015 from http://www.policechiefmagazine.org/magazine/index.cfm?fuseaction=display&issue_id=92014&category_ID=4.

the respondent whether the crime was reported to the police. This is the source for our information in Figure 1.2, about how much crime goes unreported. Findings from the National Crime Victimization Survey can be accessed most easily through the Bureau of Justice Statistics, an agency that also presents other statistics about corrections, police, and specific crimes.

For more information, go to http://bjs.gov/

These two sources of crime data may be compared, but it is important to note their differences. The NCVS excludes homicide, arson, commercial crimes, and crimes against children under age twelve (the UCR includes these crimes). The NCVS also does not include any information on victimless crimes such as drug crimes, gambling, or prostitution. The UCR only collects arrest data on simple assault and sexual assaults other than rape, not reported crimes. Further, the NCVS calculates rates on the basis of 1000 *households,* while the UCR calculates rates based on 100,000 *persons*. Thus, it would be a mistake to treat findings from the two sources as comparable statistically. In general, the UCR gives us a broad picture of crime patterns (as reported to police) in the United States, while the NCVS gives us more information about the characteristics of victimizations in certain selected crime categories and reporting trends by victims.

Because the NCVS is based on a random sample of the population and does not collect reports of all victimizations, it is subject to all the potential problems of sampling and survey weaknesses. If any principles of **random sampling** are violated, then the applicability to the general population is in doubt. The sample size of the NCVS has been decreasing over the years, and some observers have begun to worry that the smaller sample size has begun to affect the representativeness of the sample.[14]

The advantage of having both the UCR (reports to police) and the NCVS (survey respondents' reports of victimization) is that, even if not completely comparable, we can note whether the general crime patterns are similar, thus being more confident in the accuracy of either source. Recall that the UCR shows a dramatic decline in crime reports across the last several decades. We can be more confident that the UCR is accurately representing a crime decline because the NCVS also shows dramatic declines in the number of people reporting victimization (whether or not they reported the victimization to the police). We will explore these patterns more closely when we answer the question about crime patterns below.

Self-Report Studies

Another source of crime data is simply to ask the offender. Self-report studies ask individuals to report the crimes they have committed. Obviously, there are problems inherent in such an approach, such as whether the individual is answering honestly or not. Self-reports are generally only obtained from targeted groups,

14. S. Ansari and N. He, "Convergence revisited: A multi-definition, multi-method analysis of the UCR and the NCVS crime series." *Justice Quarterly* 32 (2012): 1–31.

specifically juveniles (who are still in school) and offenders (who are incarcerated). We do not administer self-report surveys door-to-door to samples of citizens. Self-report studies provide interesting information, but the findings must be considered in light of the characteristics of the sample. For instance, self-report studies of juveniles often use measures of behavior that stretch the definition of "crime" to the breaking point by including minor deviances, such as truancy and other forms of juvenile misbehavior. The definitions of wrongdoing are expanded in such studies because the vast majority of students have not committed any criminal acts. Therefore, in order to get sufficient numbers for statistical analysis, the definition of "offender" is expanded. It should be kept in mind when reading these studies that these "offenders" are not necessarily who we think of as criminals.

Part of the reason that student self-report studies have difficulty obtaining sufficient numbers of offenders for statistical analysis when testing crime theories is that by the time they are administered in junior or senior years, many high-risk juveniles have already dropped out or are not in school the day the study is administered. Therefore, the young people most likely to have committed crimes are likely to be absent from the study, and the reports of criminal activity are likely to under-represent the true nature of juvenile crime.

Like school samples, prisoner samples are relatively easy to obtain, but non-representative. Prisoners do not represent all offenders (only those who are caught and sentenced to prison). They also may not admit or may exaggerate their criminal activities. In addition, these surveys are subject to the potential inaccuracies of all surveys in that respondents may forget or misremember when events occurred. Self-report studies are typically used to understand behavior differences between offenders; for instance, the finding that a small percentage of offenders are responsible for a disproportional number of crimes came from offender self-report studies.

Cohort Studies

One other source of crime data is the **cohort study**, which follows a group of subjects over a long period. For instance, one cohort study followed all males born in Philadelphia in 1948.[15] Another longitudinal study conducted by the Harvard Program on Human Development and Criminal Behavior collected data on a cohort sample.[16] Typically, the follow-up period extends throughout childhood and into adulthood. A large number of factors have been identified as influencing criminality, including family factors, genetic factors, school and neighborhood factors, and peer factors. Proponents of longitudinal research argue that this method of data collection can illuminate how causal factors work at various times in one's life.

15. M. Wolfgang, R. Figlio and T. Sellin, *Delinquency in a Birth Cohort.* Chicago: University of Chicago Press, 1978.
16. M. Tonry, L. Ohlin and D. Farrington, *Human Development and Criminal Behavior: New Ways of Advancing Knowledge.* New York: Springer-Verlag, 1991.

What Crimes Are People Most Frequently Arrested For?

When people think of crime, they probably think of robbery, murder, or violent assault. These crimes fill our newspapers and prime-time television, either as drama or reality television. It is important to note, however, that the most common crimes are fairly mundane. Looking again at Figure 1.4, we see that, in reality, the picture of crime is much different than what is reflected in the popular media. Murder, rape, and even robbery arrests are extremely rare. In contrast, the most common arrests are for a wide variety of minor misbehavior ("other"), drug violations (possession and distribution combined), and theft.

Since one of the most frequent types of arrest is for a drug offense, this category bears further scrutiny. In Figure 1.5, we see that over 80 percent of all drug arrests are for possession, and the most common drug for those arrests is marijuana. In fact, about 40 percent of all drug violation arrests are for marijuana possession.[17]

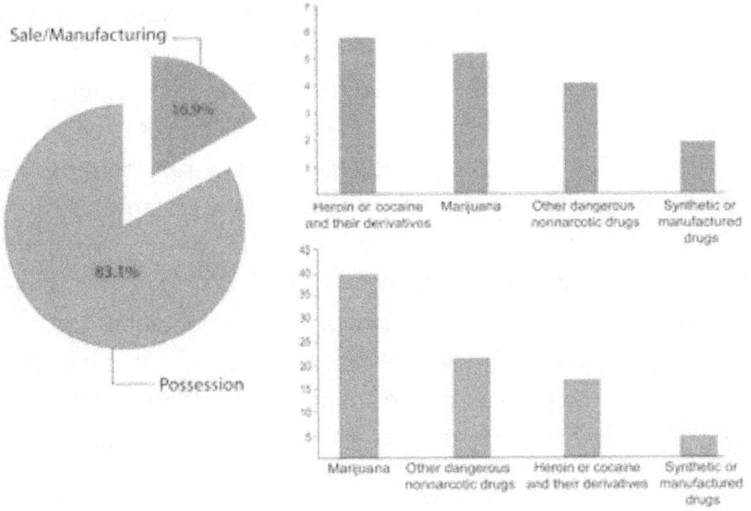

FIGURE 1.5 Arrests for Drug Abuse Violations

Source: FBI, Crimes in the United States, 2014. Arrests, main page. Retrieved 12/9/2015 from https://www.fbi.gov/about-us/cjis/ucr/crime-in-the-u.s/2014/crime-in-the-u.s.-2014/persons-arrested/main

As we noted before, it is important to remember that arrests are not a true reflection of crimes committed; they only represent who is arrested. Reports to police would provide more information about frequency of crimes, but the UCR only offers information on the eight index crimes. Figure 1.6 below presents these reports for 2014. We see that the most frequent crime reports are of larceny/theft, and following far behind are reports of burglaries. Recall, however, that most people report only a fraction of all crimes to police, thus, this picture of crime is also an inaccurate representation of crime.

17. Federal Bureau of Investigation, *Crime in the United States, 2014.* Retrieved from https://www.fbi.gov/about-us/cjis/ucr/crime-in-the-u.s/2014/crime-in-the-u.s.-2014/persons-arrested/main.

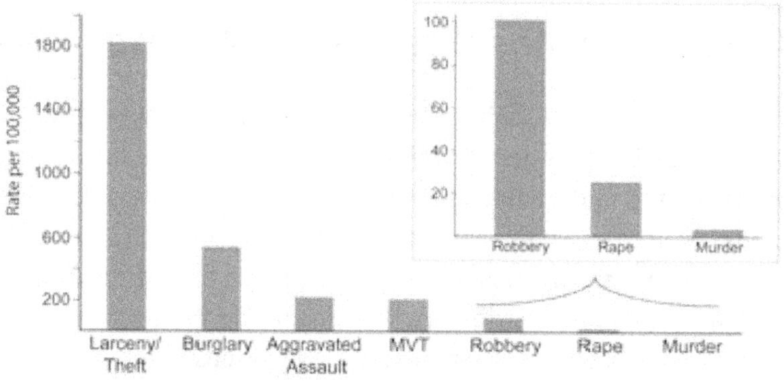

FIGURE 1.6 Crime Reports Rate, 2014

Source: FBI, Crime in the United States, 2014. https://www.fbi.gov/about-us/cjis/ucr/crime-in-the-u.s/2014/crime-in-the-u.s.-2014/tables/table-1

Victimization surveys are closer to approximating the true prevalence of crime, but they are not comparable to the crime categories of the UCR or arrest tables. Recall that the most frequent arrests are for drug violations, but that crime category is not represented at all in the victimization reports. In the latest NCVS report, the most frequently reported victimization was theft (at 6.41 reports per 1,000), followed by burglary (at 1.67 reports per 1,000). Thus, these two crimes appear as the most frequent crimes in both reports to the police (UCR) and reports in the NCVS. In contrast, the least frequently reported victimization was serious intimate partner violence (at 0.05 reports per 1,000), which does not have a crime category parallel in the UCR, and rape/sexual assault (at 0.06 reports per 1,000).[18]

To summarize, our crime sources give us fragmented information about the true prevalence of crime. The most frequent arrests in 2014 were for drug offenses, and the most frequent victim-harming crimes seem to be larceny/theft and burglary, as reported to police and in victimization reports. The constant media focus on violent crimes is highly disproportionate to the true prevalence of crime categories.

What Do We Know About Homicide?

Even though homicide is a very rare occurrence, people are quite rightly more fearful of homicide, rape, aggravated assault, and robbery than property crimes. The rate of homicide has been declining for decades—the murder rate fell by more than half nationally from its peak in 1980, as seen in Figure 1.7. It is also true, however, that some cities have experienced increases in some years.

18. J. Truman and L. Langton, *Criminal Victimization, 2014*. Table 4. Retrieved from http://www.bjs.gov/content/pub/pdf/cv14.pdf.

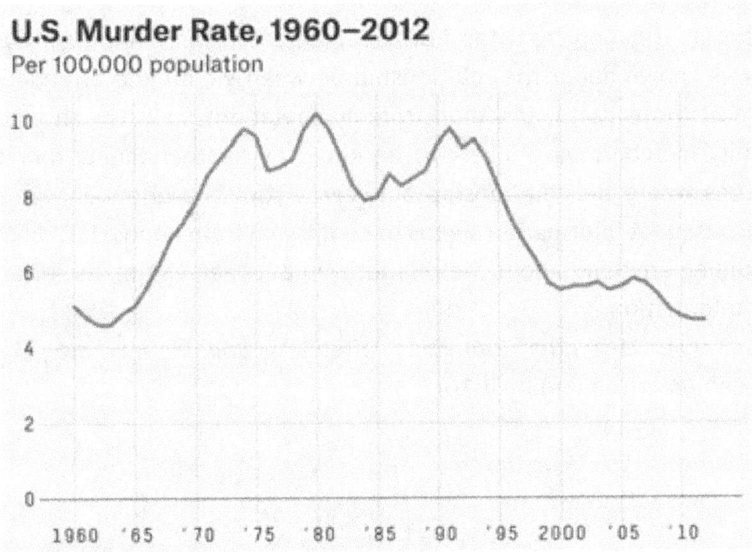

FIGURE 1.7 Homicide Rates Over Time

Source: C. Bialik, "Scare headlines exaggerated the US crime wave." Fivethirtyeight.com. Retrieved 12/12/2015 from https://fivethirtyeight.com/features/scare-headlines-exaggerated-the-u-s-crime-wave

We can obtain more detailed information about homicides from the supplemental homicide reports of the FBI. Figure 1.8 shows that the most recent report indicates that homicides are most likely to be single victim and single offender.

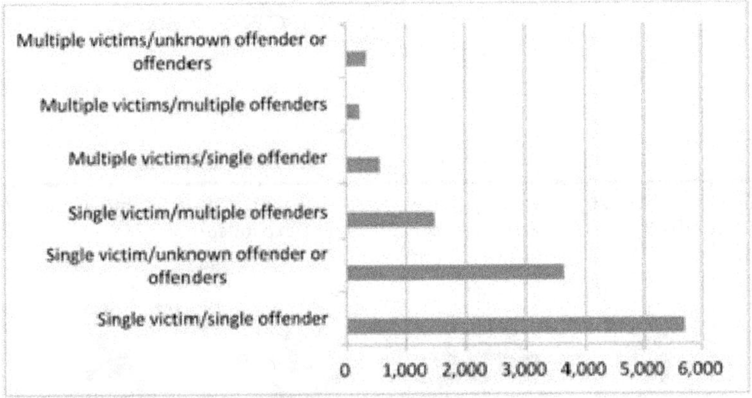

FIGURE 1.8 Murder: Victim/Offender Situation

Source: Crime in the U.S., 2014, Table 4.

You can explore the statistics on homicide by going to a data analysis tool offered by the Office of Juvenile Justice and Delinquency: http://www.ojjdp.gov/ojstatbb/ezashr/asp/off_selection.asp

Figure 1.9 displays information from the FBI's supplemental information on homicides. We see that, in 2012, information was known about the relationship between victim and offender in only slightly more than half of all cases. Of those cases, the most common relationship between victim and offender was acquaintance. The family members most likely to be killed by another family member were wives. Only 12 percent of the victims where the relationship between victim and offender was known were killed by strangers. However, because that information seems to be missing from almost half of all homicides, we must be cautious about assuming anything about the relationship between victim and offender from those cases where we do have the information.

Using 2013 data, it is clear that homicide offenders *and* victims are likely to be male and disproportionately African American (Figure 1.10).

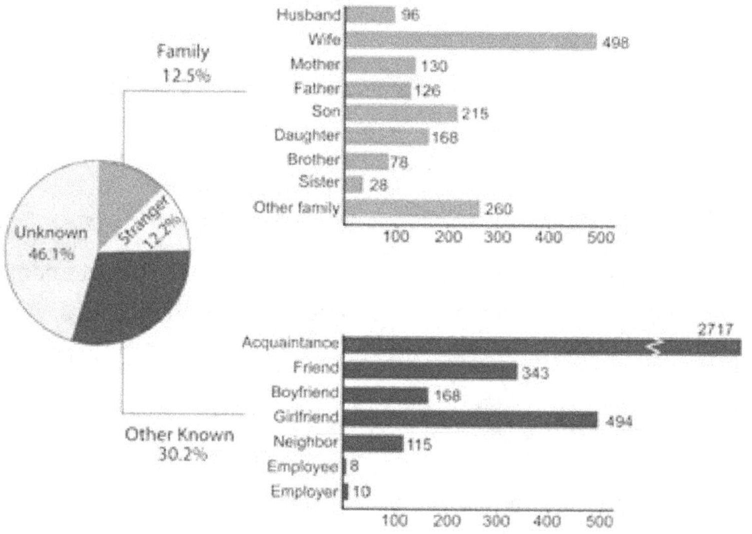

FIGURE 1.9 Relationship between Homicide Victims and Offenders

Source: FBI. Retrieved 1/4/2016 from https://www.fbi.gov/about-us/cjis/ucr/crime-in-the-u.s/2012/crime-in-the-u.s.-2012/offenses-known-to-law-enforcement/expanded-homicide/expandhomicidemain

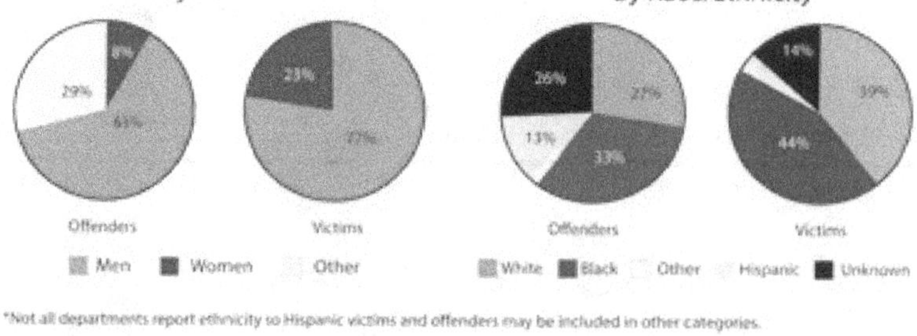

FIGURE 1.10 Homicide Offenders/Victims

Source: Crime in the United States, 2014, Table 3; 4; Table 6.

It is important to note that these percentages are of total homicide numbers. Rates (per 100,000) would look much different since African Americans comprise only about 13 percent of the total population; thus, the fact that 44 percent of all murder victims are African American is a truly astounding figure. Data analysis from the time period of the most dramatic decline in homicide illustrated the fact that between the mid-1990s and late 2000s, the most dramatic declines in homicide also took place with African American men (see Figure 1.11).[19]

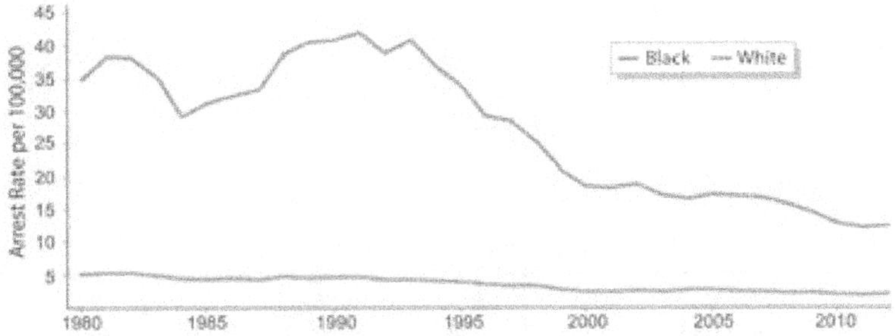

FIGURE 1.11 Homicide Declines by Race, 1985–2012

Source: Crime in the United States, 2014, Table 3; 4; Table 6.

It is important to note that when there are changes in the number of homicides, not all racial/ethnic and gender groups are equally at risk. Homicides have increased in some urban areas, but, similar to past patterns, not everyone is equally vulnerable.

What Has Been the Pattern of Crime Over the Years? Has It Declined?

Recall from the above discussion that the UCR has recorded dramatic declines in all crime categories in the last twenty years. This could be due to a true decrease in criminal activity, or it could be due to less people reporting their victimization. The way to know for sure is to compare victimization reports to crime reports. [T]riangulating data utilizes different sources to compare facts. We can be more confident that we have truly experienced a decline in crime because the UCR, the National Crime Victimization Survey, and arrest tables all show a steady overall decline since the early 1990s. Figure 1.12 illustrates this consensus. Although there was a bit of an increase in 2012, the decline continued afterwards.

19. See, for instance, J. Cancino and J. Pollock, "Gender, race, and ethnicity: An analysis of homicide rates and trends in San Antonio, 1990–2004." Paper presented at the American Society of Criminology Meeting, Los Angeles, CA (2006, November).

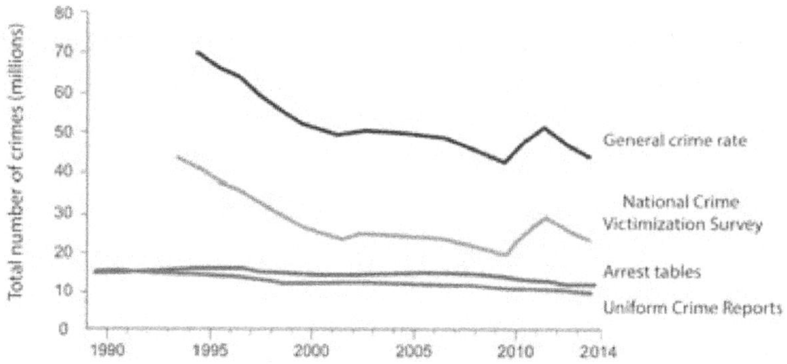

FIGURE 1.12 Composite View of Decline in Crime, 1990–2014

Source: Bureau of Justice Statistics, Criminal Victimization Survey, 1994–2014. Online Sourcebook of Criminal Justice Statistics, Table 3, Estimated number and rate of offenses known to police, 1990–2014. UCR, Crime in the United States, 1995–2014.

Does the Public Have an Accurate Perception About the Prevalence of Crime?

There is no doubt that our crime rates are about as low as they have been since the 1970s, but does the public know that? The short answer is no. A Gallup poll indicates that about 70 percent of Americans think there is more crime in the U.S. now than there was a year ago. In fact, in most years, the majority of Americans think crime was higher than the year before, but they have been wrong. The only year the minority of citizens (41 percent) thought crime had declined was in 2001.

It is also interesting to note that women are more likely to think crime has risen. Conservatives (80 percent) are more likely than liberals (57 percent), and those in rural towns are more likely than urban residents to think crime has risen. Figure 1.13 shows these differences. In 2015, nearly six in ten Americans (59 percent) said U.S. crime is an "extremely" or "very" serious problem—up slightly from 55 percent in 2014.[20]

20. Gallup poll. Retrieved from: http://www.gallup.com/poll/186308/americans-say-crime-rising.aspx?utm_source=alert&utm_medium=email&utm_content=morelink&utm_campaign=syndication.

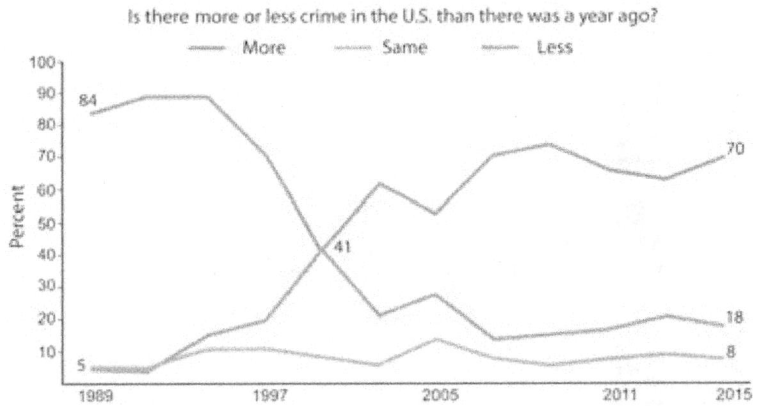

FIGURE 1.13 Public Perceptions of Crime in the U.S., 1989–2015

Source: Gallup Poll. Retrieved 1/4/2015 from http://www.gallup.com/poll/186308/americans-say-crime-rising.aspx?utm_source=alert&utm_medium=email&utm_content=morelink&utm_campaign=syndication

How Do the Crime Rates of the United States Compare to Other Countries?

There is a widespread perception that one of the reasons the United States leads the world in incarceration rates is because there is more crime here than in similar Western countries such as the United Kingdom, France, or Canada. This is true only for homicide. Property crime rates in the United States are roughly comparable to those of other countries. It should be pointed out that comparing crimes cross-culturally is difficult because definitions and reporting practices that affect crime statistics vary. The United Nations Office of Drugs and Crime, however, has collected and makes available crime rates as reported by member nations in order to make some tentative comparisons. In the latest report available, about 138 countries are represented. In Figure 1.14 below, certain selected countries and crimes are displayed.

Homicide is perhaps the most consistently reported crime and offers the most reliable comparison. The homicide rate per 100,000 of the United States is about 3.8. That is down from previous years, but still higher than many European countries, Canada, and Australia. On the other hand, the rate of homicide in the U.S. is much lower than Mexico's or other countries in South America and Africa. Mexico's robbery rate is extremely high compared to other countries. France has a higher robbery rate than the U.S. and Australia has a higher burglary rate. While we must be careful with these statistics because it is unknown how accurate or consistent reporting is across all the countries, it does indicate that the crime rate in the U.S. is not wildly disproportionate to other Western, industrialized countries, except for the homicide rate.

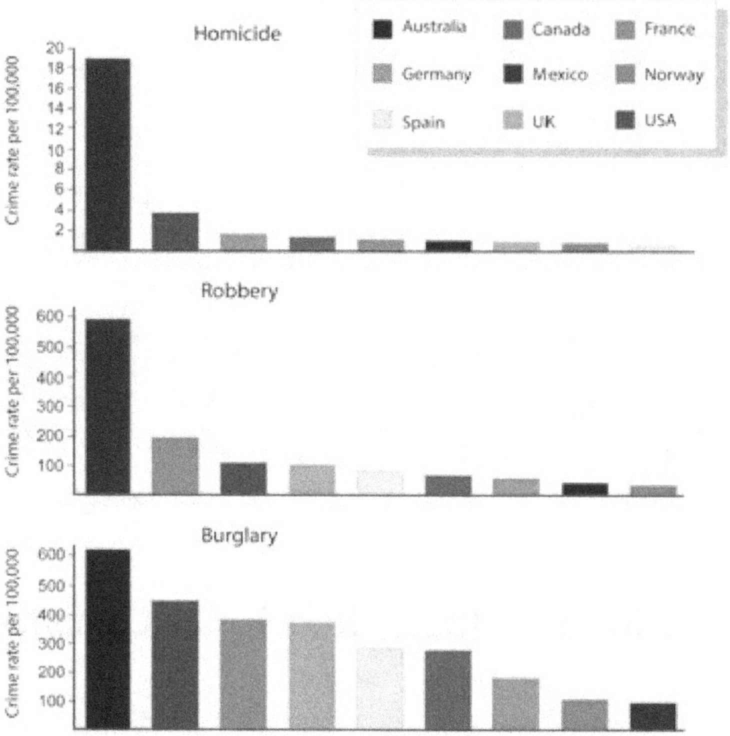

FIGURE 1.14 Selected Crimes in Selected Countries: Homicide, Robbery, Burglary

Source: United Nations Office of Drugs and Crimes, Crime Data tool, retrieved 12/9/2015 from https://data.unodc.org/#state:14

To explore for yourself some of these statistics, go to https://data.unodc.org/#state:14

Before we leave this [reading] on crime statistics, we will offer a discussion that illustrates how important accurate data and reasonable data interpretation can be when discussing current events. A current controversy playing out in newspapers and other public arenas today is whether there has been a "**Ferguson Effect**" on American policing that has resulted in "**de-policing**" which, in turn, has led to a spike in homicides and violent crimes in major cities. The Focus on Data section below examines this question.

Focus on Data: Is There a Ferguson Effect? Is There a Current Crime Wave?

In the summer and fall of 2014, the shooting of young Black men by police officers led to a number of violent protests in several American cities, most notably in Ferguson, Missouri and Baltimore, Maryland. Some argued that the public scrutiny and criticism of police led to a change in police behavior, dubbed the

"Ferguson Effect," which referred to police officers choosing not to engage with citizens for fear of being labeled racist or violent. This "de-policing," as it was also called, then, arguably, led to a spike in homicide.

FIGURE 1.15 Demonstrators marking the one-year anniversary of the shooting of Michael Brown confront police during a protest in Ferguson, Missouri. Some have argued that criticism of police, both in the media and through protests, has led to the "Ferguson Effect."

Source: Getty

Beginning in 2015, major news outlets began reporting on big-city crime spikes. Eventually the *Washington Post*, *New York Times*, NPR, CNN, BBC, *USA Today*, Reuters, *Time*, and other major news outlets had "crime spike" stories. In August of 2015, the Major Cities Chiefs Association (MCCA) reported increased homicides as a problem. In contrast, others (*New York Daily News*, Brennan Center, Marshall Project) argued that there was no evidence yet to indicate alarm was warranted. Let's look at the facts.

Heather MacDonald's much publicized article in the *Wall Street Journal* reported that gun violence was up 60 percent in Baltimore with May 2015 as the most violent month the city had seen in fifteen years. A list of cities with percentage increases [was] offered, including Milwaukee (180 percent by May 17 over the same period the previous year), St. Louis (25 percent), Atlanta (32 percent), Chicago (17 percent), and New York (13 percent). Then she argued that city-wide statistics masked much larger neighborhood increases such as 500 percent in one East Harlem neighborhood. Because the first six months of 2014 continued a twenty-year pattern of decline, her argument was that the increases in the first six months of 2015 were due to a surge of lawlessness because of people's agitation against police departments and media focus on the events. MacDonald noted the "Ferguson Effect" (a term evidently coined by St. Louis police chief Sam Dotson) was the phenomenon of police officers disengaging from discretionary enforcement activity, with a resulting feeling of empowerment by criminals. She pointed to the fact that arrests in St. Louis city and county had dropped a third since the shooting of Michael Brown in August, while homicides surged 47 percent and robberies were up 82 percent through November 2014. Other cities also showed a decline in arrests; for instance, she reported that Baltimore had 56 percent fewer arrests by May 2015 compared to 2014. In New York City, stop-and-frisk policies led to a lawsuit and intense media scrutiny; consequently, stops dropped 95 percent from the 2011 high according to MacDonald. She further argued that aggressive policing has led to urban reclamation and saved thousands of Black lives and warned that continued criticism of police would lead to losing the gains in crime reduction that had been achieved in the last twenty years.[21] There are [three] arguments to this position:

1. Homicides and other crimes in American cities are increasing.
2. Police officers are not policing in the way they have in previous years, meaning they are less likely to engage in "pro-active" policing such as stop-and-frisks and arrests for minor crimes due to the public and media scrutiny and criticism that has arisen since the summer of 2014.
3. The reduction in pro-active policing, if it exists, caused the increase in homicides and other crime, if the increase exists.

1) Are Homicides and Other Crimes in American Cities Increasing?

Unfortunately, the UCR and the FBI's Supplemental Homicide Report are not as current as we would need to answer this question. It usually takes six months to a year before crime reports are available for public consumption. The latest FBI data (UCR) for 2014 indicate that there was a 2 percent decrease in homicide rates per 100,000 nationwide, however, the pattern was different between cities and suburban and rural areas. In the largest cities (over 1 million), there was a 2.2 percent *increase* in homicides per 100,000, but a 16 percent *decrease* in non-metropolitan counties. Thus, contrary to MacDonald's proposition that the first months of 2015 were an aberration due to changing circumstances after the Michael Brown shooting, homicides had already begun to increase in cities (as opposed to suburban and rural areas) in 2014.

Recent analyses of 2015 homicides for the largest American cities showed that there was probably about a 17 percent increase in homicides in the first six months of 2015 compared to the first six months of 2014—a dramatic increase, but this increase seems to be confined to only some cities.[22] In fact, the pattern is highly skewed: ten cities account for two-thirds of the increase. These cities are characterized by: higher poverty, a falling population, and high unemployment.[23] The National Institute of Justice published an analysis of the increase (using data collected by the *New York Times* and *Washington Post*) and showed that from 2014 to 2015, 127 more people were killed in Baltimore (a 59 percent increase); 61 more people were killed in Milwaukee from the year before (a 73 percent increase); 57 more people killed in Cleveland (a 91 percent increase) and 34 more people killed in Nashville (an 83 percent increase).[24]

21. H. MacDonald, "The new nationwide crime wave." *The Wall Street Journal*, May 29, 2015. Retrieved 12/12/2015 from http://www.wsj.com/articles/the-new-nationwide-crime-wave-1432938425.
22. R. Rosenfeld, *Documenting and Explaining the 2015 Homicide Rise: Research Directions*. Washington, DC: NIJ, OJP, June 2016, p. 6.
23. J. Gravwert and J. Cullen, *Crime in 2015: A Final Analysis*. Washington, DC: Brennan Center, April 2016.
24. R. Rosenfeld, *Documenting and Explaining the 2015 Homicide Rise: Research Directions*. Washington, DC: NIJ, OJP, June 2016, p. 8.

Note that, even with over 200 murders in 2015, that number is dramatically lower than the high in 1993 when New York City recorded 1,946 murders.[25] UCR trend data shows that homicide and violent crime has been declining for the last twenty years.

News headlines that refer to large percentage increases in murder rates in specific cities usually neglect to mention that large percentage increases happen more easily with small base numbers. A 50 percent increase in murders sounds ominous, but a 50 percent increase of twelve is six additional homicides. Homicide numbers, because they have been quite small in the last decade, can be influenced by such things as an intra-familial multiple murder, or police recording practices, such as reclassifying cases from undetermined to homicide, or other reporting changes. In fact, several journalists, in articles analyzing crime increases in certain cities such as Chicago, New York, and Los Angeles, have suggested that at least part of the increase might be due to changes in reporting practices after major scandals that exposed police departments as not recording crime reports accurately. For instance, Domanick reported that violent crime in Los Angeles rose more than 20 percent during the first half of 2015, with felony assaults up 26 percent and robberies up 19 percent and suggested that the increase might be due, in part, to a *Los Angeles Times* investigation of the department's crime numbers for the first half of 2014, which discovered the misclassification of 1,200 violent felony assaults as misdemeanors, thus making it appear that serious violent crime was going down when, in fact, it went up by 14 percent.[26] A similar article describing Chicago's crime reporting described how, by categorizing a death as "undetermined," despite clear indices of murder, the number of homicides were artificially reduced.[27] While some amount of misrepresenting the seriousness of crimes probably would not significantly influence percentage increase numbers of burglary because the base numbers are so large, such practices could definitely result in significant increases or decreases in crime categories that involve smaller numbers such as homicide and robbery.

Table 1.1.1. Rising Murder Rates in Big Cities, 2014–2015

City	***Absolute Increase***	***% Increase***	***Cumulative % of Total Increase***
Baltimore	127	58.5	15.5
Chicago	61	15.0	22.9
Houston	61	25.2	30.3
Milwaukee	61	72.6	37.8
Cleveland	57	90.5	44.7
Washington DC	57	54.3	51.6

25. D. Hamill, "Keeping a running score of New York's homicide rate seems a bit ridiculous." *New York Daily News*, June 28, 2015. Retrieved 12/15/2015 from http://www.nydailynews.com/new-york/murder-statistics-don-show-return-bad-old-daysarticle-1.2273859.
26. J. Domanick, "Why L.A.'s crime rise is no surprise." *Los Angeles Times* (August 27, 2015). Retrieved 12/12/2015 from http://www.latimes.com/opinion/op-ed/la-oe-domanick-los-angeles-rising-crime-20150827-story.html.
27. D. Bernstein and N. Isackson, "The truth about Chicago's crime rates, Part I and II." *Chicago Magazine* (May, June) Retrieved 12/9/2015 from http://www.chicagomag.com/Chicago-Magazine/June-2014/Chicago-crime-statistics/.

Nashville	34	82.9	55.8
Philadelphia	32	12.9	59.7
Kansas City	29	37.2	63.2
St. Louis	29	18.2	66.7

Source: City police departments, reported in M. Davey and M. Smith. "Murder Rates Rising Sharply in Many Cities." New York Times (September 1, 2015), p. A1.

While the MacDonald article presented data from cities that had increased homicides, others have noted that the pattern is not uniform across American cities. An analysis by FiveThirtyEight.com utilized city data, news reports, and other sources to construct a table with 60 cities and homicide numbers for 2015 compared to the same time period in 2014.[28] In 26 cities, homicides were up by 20 percent or more from a year ago, but the number of homicides was down in nineteen other cities.

More generally, crime analysts will warn against year to year comparisons of homicide, or any crime, because year-to-year rates fluctuate. The better way to understand data is by looking at longer periods of time. When we examine murder trends we see that, although there may be year-to-year increases, the general trend has been downward, in this set of tables from a report produced by the Brennan Center.[29]

28. C. Bialik, "Scare headlines exaggerated the US crime wave." Fivethirtyeight.com. Retrieved 12/12/2015 from https://fivethirtyeight.com/features/scare-headlines-exaggerated-the-u-s-crime-wave/.

29. M. Friedman, "Just facts: America's non-existent 'spike in crime.'" Brennan Center for Justice (August 10, 2015). Retrieved 12/12/2015 from https://www.brennancenter.org/blog/americas-non-existent-spike-crime.

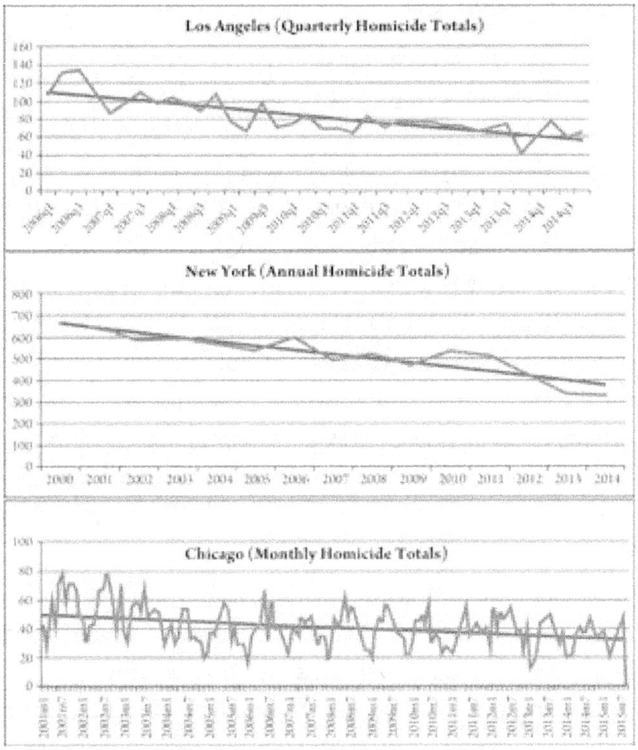

FIGURE 1.16 Homicide Patterns in Selected Cities: Los Angeles, New York, Chicago

Source: M. Friedman. "Just facts: America's non-existent 'spike in crime.'" Brennan Center for Justice (August 10, 2015). Retrieved 12/12/2015 from https://www.brennancenter.org/blog/americas-non-existent-spike-crime.

Moving from homicide to all violent crime, the UCR reported that nationwide violent crime reports to police were down by 0.2 percent and property crime declined by 4.3 percent in 2014.[30] The latest National Crime Victimization Survey, released in August 2015, reported no significant change in violent crime victimization, and property crime victimization fell from 131.4 per 1,000 to 118.1 per 1,000 in 2014.[31]

In summary, many American cities, but not all, have seen recent increases in homicides. Further, it may be that the increases are occurring in large cities, not in smaller towns and suburban areas. The FBI had reported a small increase in large metropolitan areas in 2014 so this increase began at least as early as 2014. Further, analysts point to trend data to show that year-to-year fluctuations have occurred continuously even throughout the twenty-year decline in homicide and other violent crimes.

30. Federal Bureau of Investigation, *Crime in the United States, 2014.* Tables 12. Retrieved 12/12/2015 from https://www.fbi.gov/about-us/cjis/ucr/crime-in-the-u.s/2014/crime-in-the-u.s.-2014.
31. Bureau of Justice Statistics, *Criminal Victimization, 2014.* Office of Justice Programs. Retrieved 12/12/2015 from http://www.bjs.gov/content/pub/pdf/cv14.pdf.

2) Are Police Officers Not Policing in the Way They Have in Previous Years? If So, Is This Due to the Public and Media Scrutiny and Criticism That Have Arisen Since the Summer of 2014?

MacDonald reported fairly dramatic declines in arrests in some cities, arguing this was evidence of "de-policing." Interestingly, fewer arrests can be presented as a decline in crime or a decline in policing, depending on one's perspective. While MacDonald reported dramatic declines, criminologists have pointed to other cities that have not shown declines in arrests.[32] Misdemeanor arrests, traffic tickets, and investigative stops are subject to more discretionary decision making by officers than felony arrests, therefore, all three should be considered to determine if "de-policing" is occurring.

New York City has definitely seen a dramatic drop in the number of stop-and-frisks undertaken by New York City police officers, but the decline had begun earlier than the summer and fall of 2014 when the protests in Ferguson, Missouri and Baltimore, Maryland occurred. A report by the John Jay College of Criminal Justice indicated that between 2011 and 2014 the total number of arrests for felonies and misdemeanors, criminal summonses, and stop-and-frisks fell by more than 800,000, or 31 percent. Street stops declined from a high of 685,000 in 2011 to under 46,000 in 2014, a 93 percent decline in only three years. The declines were mostly in poorer and minority neighborhoods where they had grown the fastest over the previous decade. The decline in stops occurred because of a court ruling in 2013 that found such stops unconstitutional as well as a growing public outcry that the stops were unfairly targeting minority and poor residents who had the misfortune to live in certain areas of the city. Despite the multi-year decline in such stops, crime reports continued to decline as well. In 2014, rates of both violent and nonviolent crime in New York City were lower than the year before, and were almost 90 percent lower than they were in 1980.[33]

Stop-and-Frisk. The NYPD was sued over its controversial stop-and-frisks, which have since declined substantially.

Another city that saw arrests and investigative stops decline was Seattle. In May of 2014 it was reported that police enforcement of lower-level crimes, traffic offenses and infractions dropped dramatically, including a 49 percent decline in misdemeanor criminal arrests between 2005 and 2013. While service calls had increased by 9 percent between the first quarter of 2010 and first quarter of 2014, independent officer-initiated activity had dropped by 44 percent, from 15 percent of their time in 2011 to only 8 percent of their time in the same quarter in 2014. Officer checks of suspicious people and suspicious vehicles

32. L. Bui, A. Phillip and W. Lowery, "Around St. Louis, bloodshed rises in year since Michael Brown was killed." *Washington Post*, August 11, 2015. Retrieved from http://www.washingtonpost.com/national/around-st-louis-bloodshed-rises-in-year-sincemichael-brown-was-killed/2015/08/11/b0ea430c-405c-11e5-bfe3-ff1d8549bfd2_story.html?hpid=z7
33. New York Times Editorial Board, "New York policing, by the numbers." *New York Times*, December 28, 2015, p. A18.

dropped by 80 percent. Bookings into the jail fell by 51 percent between 2006 and 2013. Between 2007 and 2013, infractions filed in Seattle Municipal Court fell 71 percent, covering unlawful activity such as liquor violations, public urination, and noise problems. Because the Seattle Police Department was investigated by the Department of Justice and entered into a consent decree that required substantial changes in policies and practices to address alleged racism and use of force abuses, the dramatic decline was attributed to "de-policing."[34] Others pointed to alternative explanations such as programs of diversion. Recall, also, that Washington legalized small amounts of marijuana effective December 2012, which must have had a significant effect on the number of police investigative stops and misdemeanor arrests. More importantly, however, there has not yet been a connection shown between decreased police actions and UCR index crimes or victimization reports. Unfortunately, the time lag that occurs in our ability to access this information will prevent any immediate analysis.

We can count arrests, stops, and traffic tickets, and we can document whether or not totals are higher, lower, or the same as the year before, but we can't say for certain why such police actions have declined because we have no way of knowing whether or not the number of underlying acts have changed, other factors have affected the decision (e.g. charging practices of the prosecutor's office or changes in the law), or the officers have changed their policing practices (e.g. less likely to arrest or stop-and-frisk). As noted above, court orders requiring the NYPD to change their stop-and-frisk practices and Washington's legalization of marijuana possession have probably more to do with the observed changes than police officers changing their decision-making practices on patrol in these cities than "de-policing."

Anecdotal evidence has been offered (e.g., quotes from individual officers or police administrators) that police officers felt scrutinized and unfairly criticized after the public protests in 2014 and 2015 and reacted by "de-policing." One small study that surveyed officers in a small police department found that officers reported a decline in motivation to do their job and work with the community because of public criticism, but that they did not change their decisions. Further the decline in motivation evidently was also influenced by administrative and managerial practices of the police department, not simply the "Ferguson Effect."[35]

3) Is the Reduction in Pro-Active Policing (If It Exists), the Cause of the Increase in Homicides and Other Crime (If There Is Significant Increase)?

Proposed explanations for the increase in violent crime, including homicides, in some cities have included (in addition to the Ferguson Effect) a rise in heroin use; increased gang violence; entrenched poverty and hopelessness; release of career criminals from prison (who have served their 25–30-year sentences from the high-crime years of the 1980s); more guns, especially automatic weapons like the AK-47; and, as noted before, simply yearly fluctuations in a two-decade decline. What we do know about these homicides is that

34. S. Miletich, "Report cites plunge in SPD enforcement of low-level crime." *Seattle Times*, May 24, 2014. Retrieved 1/3/2016 from http://www.seattletimes.com/seattle-news/report-cites-plunge-in-spd-enforcement-of-low-level-crime/.
35. Scott E. Wolfe and Justin Nix, "The alleged 'Ferguson Effect' and police willingness to engage in community partnership." *Law and Human Behavior*, 2015; DOI: 10.1037/lhb0000164.

they are often gang-related and occur most often in poverty-stricken areas of the city. The only academic study thus far that has addressed this question specifically looked at violent crimes in 81 cities in the year before and the year after the Michael Brown shooting in Ferguson and concluded that the only crime that showed a significant change in direction (from decease to increase) in the second time period was robbery. The study's authors cautioned that even documenting the increase could not "prove" that the increase was due to de-policing because there might be many other factors that affect the increase in robbery.[36] Also, as noted earlier, there have been previous upticks in homicide and violent crime in some cities periodically in the last several decades, even within a general trend of decreasing homicide rates over those years.

A recent study paper from the National Institute of Justice also offered the hypotheses of the growth of heroin markets, an increase in the number of parolees in the community, and a loss of "legitimacy" in Black communities as explanations for the increase in homicide in some American cities.[37] There is no doubt that heroin/opiate deaths have increased, but part of the well-known heroin epidemic is legally obtained opiates through prescriptions so there is no data as yet to prove that illegal heroin markets are fueling the homicide increase. Also, there has been no increase in the number of drug arrests. An increase in the number of parolees contributing to the homicide increase would require a knowledge of whether or not perpetrators were on parole—data we do not have yet for 2015, even for those arrested (and recall that a certain portion of homicides are not ever solved). As for the hypothesis that a legitimacy crisis in the minority community toward the police is causing an increase in homicide, Rosenfeld, in the NIJ analysis referred to above, pointed out that the cities with the largest homicide increases also had higher percentages of Blacks, and public opinion polls show that Blacks have historically low confidence in policing today. He argued that it is a difficult methodolgical problem to determine to what extent a rise is homicides is due to a loss of legitimacy of police and the justice system and suggested ethnographic research.[38] Another possibility is to look at the motivations for killings since part of the loss of legitimacy argument is that people who do not trust the justice system engage in retaliatory behavior. A good question to ask might be: what portion of homicides in these cities are due to retaliation? Also, is the proportion of retaliatory homicides correlated with a decrease in trust in police? We don't have motivation data yet for 2015 (although it will eventually be available in Suppmental Homicide Reports from the FBI).

To conclude, there is no evidence of a trend of increasing homicides at this point. We don't know if the recent increase in some cities will continue nor do we know whether it will spread to more cities. An increase in 2006 spurred similar concern, which proved to be unnecessary since the increase evaporated and the decline in homicides and other violent crimes continued their multi-decade decline after a couple of years.[39] As for "de-policing," there is some quantitative evidence that police discretionary actions (investigative

36. D. Pyrooz, S. Decker, S. Wolfe and J. Shjarback, "Was there a Ferguson Effect on crime rates in large US cities?" *Journal of Criminal Justice* 46 (2016): 1–16.

37. R. Rosenfeld, *Documenting and Explaining the 2015 Homicide Rise: Research Directions*. Washington, DC: NIJ, OJP, June 2016.

38. R. Rosenfeld, *Documenting and Explaining the 2015 Homicide Rise: Research Directions*. Washington, DC: NIJ, OJP, June 2016.

39. R. Rosenfeld, *Documenting and Explaining the 2015 Homicide Rise: Research Directions*. Washington, DC: NIJ, OJP, June 2016.

detentions, traffic tickets, and misdemeanor arrests) have declined in some cities, but not the cities that have experienced the most dramatic increase in homicides.

The proposed explanations for the increase in homicides in some American cities offered instead of a "Ferguson Effect" include: growing heroin markets, an increase in parolees returning from prison, and a loss of legitimacy of police and the justice system in the Black community leading to retaliatory and vigilante justice. Absence of current data make any study of these hypotheses difficult.

SUMMARY

What Is Crime? What Is the Role of Legislators, Victims, Police, and Prosecutors in Defining Crimes?

Crime is a "constructed reality" created by legislators who define acts as crimes, acts of the perpetrator, the perceptions of the victim and decision to report to authorities, and decisions by system actors (e.g., the decision to arrest). Only a portion of all crimes find their way into official statistics.

What Sources Do We Use to Find Out About the Patterns of Crime?

The Uniform Crime Reports present data on eight index crimes that are reported to police. They can be accessed from the FBI's website, which also has data on arrests on a larger number of crime categories. Problems with the UCR include the fact that many people do not report crimes to the police and arrests are not necessarily an accurate representation of crimes committed. We also have the National Crime Victimization Survey, which is a random survey of the population to discover the number of people who have been victimized and some characteristics of their victimization. We also use self-report studies and cohort studies in our study of crime.

What Crimes Are People Most Frequently Arrested For?

The largest category of arrests in 2014 was for drug crimes and possession was the most frequent of these arrests. Larceny/theft is the next most frequent arrest category, along with DUI and non-aggravated assault. The crimes the media focuses on (murder, rape, robbery) are extremely rare.

What Do We Know About Homicide?

Homicide, as most crime, has been on the decline since the mid-1990s. It is important to remember that the relative risk of being a homicide offender or a homicide victim is dramatically dependent on population group. Young Black males are much more likely than other population groups to be both homicide victim and offender.

What Has Been the Pattern of Crime Over the Years? Has It Declined?

All measures of crime (UCR, arrests, and victimization reports) show dramatic declines over the last two decades so that today's crime rates—for both violent and property crimes—are about the same as they were in the 1970s.

Does the Public Have an Accurate Perception About the Prevalence of Crime?

The public seems incredibly unaware of the dramatic declines in crime that have taken place in the last decades. A majority of the public thinks that crime is increasing despite all measures showing declines. It is possible that recent upticks in homicides and violent crimes in cities may be a sign that crime rates may be poised to begin an upward trend.

How Do the Crime Rates of the United States Compare to Other Countries?

While the U.S. has higher murder rates than European countries, other crimes do not show any consistent pattern. In general, property crimes in the U.S. are not higher than many other countries.

CRITICAL THINKING EXERCISES

1. Go to the FBI website for the UCR which is reported in *Crime in the United States*. The 2015 crime statistics have just recently been released at: https://ucr.fbi.gov/crime-in-theu.s/2015/crime-in-the-u.s.-2015. See if homicide and/or violent crime rates are higher than they were in 2014. Write an update to the Focus on Crime section—is there more information available regarding any of the questions raised in the section?
2. Go to the United Nations Office of Drugs and Crime website: https://data.unodc.org/#state:4. Look up the crime rates (not raw numbers) for other crimes to see how the United States compares to other countries. Why do you suppose the homicide rates are so much higher here? How would you test your hypothesis?

Discussion Questions

1. Explain your thoughts on the statement "crime is a constructed reality."
2. The author mentioned the "dark figure of crime." Why do you think that there are so many crimes that are not reported?
3. After reading about the sources we use to gather data of the patterns of crime, which do you believe is the most useful in collecting the data?
4. Do you believe that the media can perpetuate the prevalence of crime in an area? Why or why not?

CHAPTER 2

Policing

Police and Policing

Bradley D. Edwards and Lawrence F. Travis III

Important Terms

community-oriented policing
CompStat
constable
cynicism
legalistic style
order maintenance
paramilitary structure
police specialization
proactive
reactive
service style
shire reeve
watchman style

The most visible image of the formal control applied by the criminal justice system comes in the form of the various police agencies across the United States. A variety of federal, state, municipal, special jurisdiction (housing authority, transit authority, etc.), and private agencies provide law enforcement services. The Bureau of Justice Statistics identified roughly 18,000 local and state police agencies. Combined with federal law enforcement, these agencies combine to employ approximately 885,000 sworn law enforcement officers across the country (Reaves, 2011, 2012).

Approximately 73% of the law enforcement agencies are relatively small, employing 24 or fewer officers (see Figure 2.1). The largest police agencies, however, employ the most officers, meaning that although the typical police organization is small, the typical police officer works in a large agency. Regardless of agency size, most sworn police personnel are assigned to patrol and similar field operations duties. Patrol officers do the bulk of police work in the United States, and the work of patrol officers is varied.

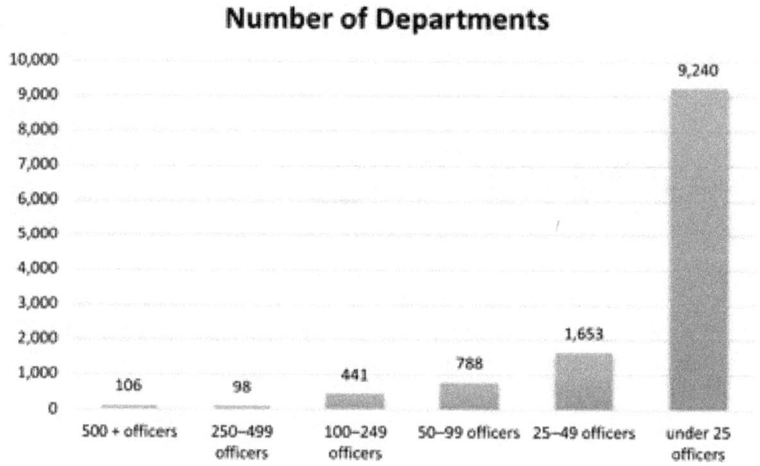

FIGURE 2.1 Distribution of Police Departments, by Size of Department.

Source: Reaves (2015).

Police agencies provide a variety of services to the communities they serve, ranging from travelers' aid through ambulance service. Yet, we continue to think of them as law enforcement. Indeed, enforcing criminal laws is, at most, a part-time activity for most police departments and police officers. The police are what Wilson (1968) called the "agency of last resort." Although we focus here on the law-enforcing duties of police agencies because of our interest in criminal justice, it is also important to remember that other demands are placed on police.

Because police are available 24 hours each day, are mobile, and carry authority, we call on them to resolve many issues and problems. Most of these problems are not, strictly speaking, law-enforcement-oriented in nature (Johnson & Rhodes, 2009). The criminal law is only one of many tools available to police officers and police agencies in their efforts to keep peace in our communities. The police are responsible for dealing with stray children and dogs, lost travelers, injured persons, stranded motorists, traffic accidents, parades, domestic disputes, and crime. It seems that almost any disruptive event can be resolved by "calling the cops" (Payne, Berg, & Sun, 2005). In many cases, people have reported fires to the police first, rather than to the fire department. The police are often called to deal with abandoned cars, but the reason they are called is not because the car may have been involved in a crime. People call the police because the police are the first agency that comes to mind.

People also call the police because they have come to know that the police can (and probably will) do something about the problem. Bittner (1990) observed that the police have a monopoly on the legitimate use of coercive force. The ability to use force and to make people behave in certain ways defines the police role in society. The police are called to deal with a variety of problems that may require force. For example, the police may be called to intervene with a mentally disturbed person who has become disruptive but who may not have committed a crime (Wood, Watson, & Fulambarker, 2017). The police may have no way to help cure the mental disorder, but are nonetheless expected to act in a way that temporarily solves the problem.

Given the scope of police responsibilities (some assigned, some assumed, and some simply evolved), it is clear that law enforcement is only a small part of police duties. Studies of police tasks have revealed that actual crimes consume a small portion of police resources and comprise a small percentage of police tasks. Depending on the definitions used by researchers, the majority of police time is devoted to general patrol, service calls, and paperwork (Cathey & Guerin, 2009; Huey & Ricciardelli, 2015; Famega, 2005). Nonetheless, the public, the media, and the police themselves continue to define policing principally as crime fighting (Surette, 2015). This conception of the police as "crime fighters" developed historically as a response to difficulties encountered in the police role.

The Development of American Policing

The idea of police controlling the behavior of individuals is a relatively recent addition to society. The American colonists did not employ police, and no police forces were created in the United States until the 1840s. In colonial times, law enforcement was the duty of every citizen, and no specialized occupational group had responsibility to ensure public order. As with so much of our justice system, we can trace the origins of public police to our English tradition.

Law Enforcement in England

Most of England had no specialized police force or public office charged with maintaining public order until after the Norman Conquest in 1066 (Critchley, 1972; Stewart-Brown, 1936). At that time, the Normans, having gained control over England and occupying a hostile population, created a centralized governmental structure based on feudalism. High-ranking officers and nobles of William the Conqueror's army received control of large parcels of England. In return, these nobles were to provide a percentage of the production from these lands to the king as taxes, and to supply soldiers in time of war. They also were required to obey the commands of the king and to ensure the "king's peace" in their lands.

To accomplish this administrative task, these nobles further subdivided their lands to lesser officers and nobles, and required them to remit a portion of their profits and to supply a number of soldiers when necessary. The subdivision continued, with each successive rank being required to pay a larger portion of taxes but supply a smaller number of soldiers. The increased taxes represented the need to meet the demands of the king and the higher nobility for income. The lower number of soldiers reflected the increased number of officers who were granted lands. If a duke promised to provide 10,000 soldiers and 5% of profits to the king, he could do it by dividing the land among ten barons. Each baron might be required to provide 1,000 soldiers (10,000 total) and 8% of profits (5% for the king; 3% for the duke). Feudalism provided a structure for government in medieval times.

Essentially rural and agrarian, England was divided into ten family units called tythings. Each tything was responsible for its own tax collection and order maintenance. With the advent of Norman control, new units of 100 families, called shires, were created. Being an occupied country, maintenance of the Norman king's law was problematic, and tax collection was difficult. The office of shire reeve emerged.

The **shire reeve** was responsible for the collection of taxes and the maintenance of the king's peace within the shire, which was usually an area similar to a county or parish in the United States today. The reeve was elected from a list of candidates approved by the lord of the manor. Over time, the shire reeve became known as the sheriff. We can see the resistance of the English to this new structure in the tales of Robin Hood, whose nemesis was the Sheriff of Nottingham.

Each manor also operated a manorial court. To assist in the day-to-day operation of the court functions, they created the office of constable. The lord of the manor selected the **constable** from among qualified property holders. The constable performed the clerical duties of the court and housed prisoners awaiting trial. Over time, these functions expanded to include general peacekeeping.

As villages and towns developed, this rural order-maintenance apparatus proved to be inadequate to the task of law enforcement in congested areas. Traditionally, every citizen was responsible for order maintenance. Drawing on this tradition, town constables were empowered to draft citizens for a watch system. In this system, citizens were required to provide unpaid watch service (typically at night) to patrol for fires and breaches of the peace. As towns grew larger and cities developed, it became increasingly difficult to find either adequate watchmen or persons willing to take the role of constable.

By the early 1800s, English towns and cities were crowded and unruly. The nobility and wealthy citizens traveled with hired guards (footmen) and avoided the more dangerous sections of town. Several experiments with paid watches, "private" law enforcement, and rejuvenated constabulary offices had all failed to provide adequately for order maintenance. One of the most famous of these experiments was the organization of the Bow Street Runners by Henry Fielding. Also known as "thief-takers," this group of men was organized to provide police protection in the Bow Street area of London. There was clearly a need to create a specialized body charged with maintaining the peace.

During the 1820s, Sir Robert Peel, British home secretary, proposed the creation of a police force for England (see Figure 2.2). This force would comprise paid, uniformed, armed, and disciplined officers whose job would be the enforcement of the law, the maintenance of order, and the prevention of crime. Crime prevention was expected to result from the presence of police on the streets. Patrolling police officers would act to deter criminal offenders. Parliament, fearing the effects of such an armed force on the "rights of Englishmen," resisted Peel's idea. In democratic societies, and especially in the Anglo-American tradition, there has always been a tension or conflict between liberty and civility (Lundman, 1980). Our need for order (civility) is in direct conflict with our desire for personal freedom (liberty). The English Parliament had to be convinced that the new police would not unduly threaten English liberty. Peel revised his proposal and, in 1829, Parliament agreed to "experiment" with a Metropolitan Police Force in London. This force would be unarmed, but in every other respect, it would mirror Peel's original plan. If it worked in London, the idea might be expanded. The Metropolitan Police Force of London, created in 1829, was the first modern police force.

The Colonial and Early American Experience

As in many other areas of social life, the American colonists relied on their traditions and experiences from England in developing a social control system. Colonial villages and towns normally had the offices of constable and/or sheriff. The duties of each were similar to those of its English counterpart (Jones & Johnstone, 2012). As towns and cities grew, the Americans experimented with watch systems. In time, it became clear that these less formal systems for order maintenance were inadequate.

Unlike England, however, there was no strong central government in America, and weapons and violence were more commonplace in the New World. Although the American police followed the same general pattern of development, these differences resulted in a modification of the English police structure to suit the situation in America. If anything, Americans were more strongly concerned with liberty, and distrust of centralized governmental power meant that any police would be limited.

FIGURE 2.2 A member of the professional police force organized by Sir Robert Peel. Initially referred to as "Peelers," they later came to be known as "Bobbies."

Metropolitan Police, New Scotland Yard, London

By the 1840s, waves of immigrants began arriving on the shores of America, and industrialization was beginning. The population of American cities swelled, and the cities became unruly and dangerous places. The upper and middle classes viewed the urban poor, especially immigrants, as prerevolutionary. It became common to speak of the immigrant poor in America's congested cities as the "dangerous classes."

To control these "dangerous" people, and to bring order and stability to the cities, Americans began to consider the creation of police forces. On many occasions, the militia or the army was used to quell riots or to break strikes (and would still be used for these purposes in the future), but these were extraordinary circumstances. Many people believed a more permanent solution to the problems of day-to-day disorder was required. The importance of ethnic and cultural conflict to the emergence and development of policing in America cannot be overstated (Barlow & Barlow, 2000).

Knowing about the English experiments and developments, many reformers began to advocate the creation of police forces for the cities. In 1845, New York City created a police force modeled after the Metropolitan Police Force of London, but with several significant differences (Jones & Johnstone, 2012:233–236). The mayor appointed police officers from among candidates recommended by political ward leaders. A Board of Police Commissioners administered the police force. Each officer was to be a resident of the ward in which he would work. Officers objected to wearing uniforms and wanted to be armed.

The New York City Police were created and funded locally. This new American police department had a weak central administration, a municipal organization, and direct political involvement. Over the years, the issues of uniforms and arms were resolved, so that municipal police were both armed and uniformed. Each city created its own police force and organizational structure. In the next 10 years, the New York City Police were followed by the creation of police in most major American cities (see Box 2.1.1). Monkonnen (1981) noted that local police in America were first modeled on the police of London, but that American police agencies quickly grew independent of this original model. It is important to note that the police in America developed in specific cities and towns, with no effort to create a national police force. This ensured that the American police would be under local control and direction.

BOX 2.1.1 MILESTONES IN AMERICAN LAW ENFORCEMENT

1748	Bow Street Runners organized by Henry Fielding
1829	Metropolitan Police Force created in London, England
1838	Boston police created with nine officers
1844	New York City police created with 800 officers
1852	Cincinnati and New Orleans police created
1854	Philadelphia and Boston police establish formal patrol
1855	Orleans police created
1857	Baltimore police created
1893	Organization of the National Chiefs of Police Union
1905	August Vollmer elected marshal of Berkeley, California
1908	Bureau of Investigation (later FBI) created; Berkeley Police School started
1924	J. Edgar Hoover named director of FBI
1930	*Uniform Crime Reports* first published
1931	Police science program started at San Jose State University
1935	FBI National Police Academy opened
1960	O.W. Wilson named Chicago police commissioner
1974	Kansas City preventive patrol experiment initiated
1982	Broken windows theory appears.
1994	Violent Crime Control and Law Enforcement Act passed (created the Office of Community Policing Services)
2001	Terrorists attack the World Trade Center and Pentagon on September 11

The American Police

Similar to New York's, most early police departments in America were not centrally organized and did not have strong leadership. This was in response to a fear of the effect of police on the exercise of rights by individuals (similar to the English Parliament's fears regarding the Metropolitan Police). It was common to employ a "police commission" to govern the department so that no single individual could gain too much power. With the growth of political machines in the cities, however, this weak administrative structure left city police forces open to manipulation and corruption.

Initially, the principal duty of the police was to maintain order. The success of a police officer was most easily established by the absence of disorder on the patrol beat. The fact that officers were recruited from the neighborhoods they were to patrol and were sometimes unwilling to arrest their friends and acquaintances meant that officers tolerated much "deviance," which the upper and middle classes found frightening. Drinking of alcohol, for example, was viewed with suspicion by many city leaders, yet tolerated (even shared) by many officers. The failure of the police to remain free of political influence and corruption, coupled with neighborhood enforcement styles, led to an early call to reform the police.

In the latter part of the nineteenth century, a reform effort to enhance police accountability and to professionalize the police emerged (Travis & Langworthy, 2008; Walker, 1977). Vollmer, perhaps the foremost proponent of police professionalism, led the reform. Vollmer sought higher personnel standards and stronger police leadership. The push for police professionalism continued well into the twentieth century and is still felt (Vogel & Adams, 1983). The police were given strong central administration and a clear crime control mandate. The focus on law enforcement was supposed to circumvent the difficulties that accompanied the more general role of maintaining order (Johnson, 1981). According to many policing historians, the movement to professionalize the police was an effort by middle-class, native-born citizens to gain control over the police and to restrain the growing immigrant population (Toch, 1997).

With the crime control mandate came an equally important definition of the police as serving a crime prevention function. The police were not only expected to detect and apprehend offenders, but police presence on the streets of a city was expected to deter others from committing crimes. From this came the tradition of preventive patrol. The uniformed officer on patrol would not only be better able to detect crime, but the patrol presence would prevent crime as well. Although the technology may have changed from foot patrol to motorized patrol (and perhaps back again), the idea is essentially the same.

The tradition of police as peacekeepers (order maintenance), however, has also remained (Kappeler, 1996). Inasmuch as the definition of the police became (and remains) one of a crime control force, the functions of a modern police department are far broader. The police are the most visible representatives of government in a community, and they represent the legitimate authority of the law. Because they are always (theoretically) present and available, the police have become responsible for handling all sorts of social and legal problems.

The Functions of Police

The role of the police has been broadly classified into three categories. Wilson (1968) suggested that the police are responsible for law enforcement, order maintenance, and service. Further, he argued that, of the three, order maintenance is at once both the most important and the most troublesome. Order maintenance is the main purpose of police. If they do nothing else, the police must ensure that the citizens can go about their daily business safely and efficiently.

Order-maintenance activities include settling disputes, dispersing crowds, keeping sidewalks and streets clear and traffic flowing smoothly, and other important activities. These are troublesome responsibilities because the officer often must operate in the "gray areas" of the law and must choose whether to intervene and, if so, how and with whom (Eck & Spelman, 1987; Wood, Watson, & Fulambarker, 2017).

The service functions of police have evolved over time out of necessity. Citizens ask police to provide a variety of services, from giving directions to travelers to finding missing children. Partly because of a potential link to criminal behavior, police also investigate traffic accidents, provide first aid to victims, and, often, transport the injured to medical facilities. Whatever the reasons, modern police provide a wide variety of services that do not strictly conform to the role of crime control (Rossler & Terrill, 2012).

Law enforcement activities are those that relate directly to the detection and apprehension of criminal offenders. Responding to alarms and citizen complaints of crime, investigating suspicious persons and circumstances, and arresting suspected offenders are all law enforcement activities. Our focus is on the crime control function of police, although it does not comprise the bulk of police tasks. Before turning our attention to the crime control activities of the police, however, we must more fully explore the diverse obligations of contemporary police.

The Police as a Human Services Agency

To understand the role of the police, it is helpful to describe what it is that the police do. Ideally, perhaps, it would be possible to determine what it is that police are supposed to do and, from that, develop a definition of the police role. The problem is that it is not clear what it is that we want the police to do. Historically, the police acquired responsibilities because no other agency existed to perform particular tasks. Today, a variety of social, political, legal, and administrative factors shape the police role.

Whatever it is that the police do, research shows that most of what they do is not criminal law enforcement. Christine Famega (2005) reviewed studies of police officer activity and concluded that only about one-quarter of a patrol officer's time is spent responding to calls for service or dispatches. If you think of your own interactions with the police over the course of your lifetime, how often have you dealt with police officers in nonlaw-enforcement situations? The investigation of traffic accidents and crowd control at parades, demonstrations, sporting events, and the like are important, nonlaw-enforcement services provided by the police.

Many local police agencies, particularly small departments, are consolidated with emergency medical services (EMT) and fire services to create a "public safety" agency (Wilson, Weiss, & Grammich, 2016). Many police departments also serve special functions such as search and rescue, bomb disposal, underwater recovery, and even animal control (Hickman & Reaves, 2006). The driving force behind this movement is the opportunity to provide services more efficiently and the flexibility to better coordinate their responses to emergency situations (Morley & Hadley, 2013). Conversely, some agencies are opting to deconsolidate due to the management difficulties inherent with many consolidated departments (Wilson & Grammich, 2015).

The police serve as a referral center for people in trouble, linking victims, the ill, and others in need of service with available community resources. The police are available all day and every day throughout their jurisdiction. Whether crime, injury, illness, or disputes cause the police to intervene, police problems generally represent problems in living. The sheer scope and variety of situations for which people call the police are evidence of their generic helping activities. Finally, the police, like all governmental agencies, are ultimately responsible to the public (their clients) and the courts.

Historically, as a human services agency, the most important role of the police was that of first aid. Whether the problem is a lost child, domestic disturbance, landlord/tenant dispute, public intoxication, or traffic accident, the police are normally first on the scene. In this role, the police provide first aid by taking charge of the situation, providing immediate help and counseling, and giving referrals for further care (Fritsch, Caeti, Tobolowsky, & Taylor, 2004). It is common, especially in larger police departments, to give officers a directory of social service agencies to which the officers can refer citizens. The fact that the police do not always provide complete human services to resolve the living problems of those with whom they come into contact does not negate the important role of the police in the first stages of human service (Das, 1987).

The Police as a Crime Control Agency

The police control crime in one of two basic ways: reactively or proactively (Black, 1972). These types of policing represent ideal types. A **reactive** police department would only respond (or react) to crime. A **proactive** police department would use its own initiative in aggressively seeking out crimes and criminals. The strictest type of reactive police department would remain at the police station, watching television, cleaning cruisers, and the like, until a complaint of a crime was received or an alarm sounded, when the officers would rush to their cruisers and speed to the scene of the crime. Having investigated or made an arrest, the officers then would return to the station to await their next call.

In contrast, a fully proactive police department would resemble the vice squad. All officers would be in the field seeking out crime. Undercover officers would perform much police work because marked cars and uniforms would forewarn offenders. Traffic officers would establish speed traps rather than patrol stretches of highway. Decoy teams and sting operations would be prevalent.

In reality, of course, one does not find either ideal type. Rather, it is possible to classify police departments as being more or less proactive or reactive. The democratic nature of our society and the municipal organization of the majority of our police forces make police in the United States more reactive than proactive (Travis & Langworthy, 2008). As a society, we prefer to set policing priorities through our complaints and calls. The alternative is for the police to set priorities through deciding how and when to combat crime. Proactive police seeking to prevent crime are required to act on their own initiative to avoid citizen complaints about crime.

The Police as a Peacekeeping Agency

In television and motion picture Westerns, the marshal has responsibility for keeping the peace. At base, peacekeeping means the maintenance of order. The police control disruptions such as fights and riots. They maintain traffic flow and ensure a general level of satisfaction with living in the community. Police protect and enhance orderly social interactions. Wilson (1968:16) argued that order maintenance is at the core of the police task. He wrote:

> The patrolman's role is defined more by his responsibility for maintaining order than by his responsibility for enforcing the law. By "order" is meant the absence of disorder, and by disorder is meant behavior that either disturbs or threatens to disturb the public peace or that involves face-to-face conflict among two or more persons. Disorder, in short, involves a dispute over what is "right" or "seemly" conduct or over who is to blame for conduct that is agreed to be wrong or unseemly.

As Wilson's explanation implies, disorder is often noncriminal. Order-maintenance problems usually involve questions of propriety rather than questions of legality. Youths loitering on a street corner, a neighbor who plays her stereo too loudly, homeless persons congregating in a park, and other noncriminal events are frequently the basis for order-maintenance calls to the police. In these situations, people expect the responding officer to resolve the conflict and thereby restore order.

Most order-maintenance problems fall into a gray area of the law where frequently the officer has no clear legal authority to act. As a matter of practicality, the officer is compelled to do something. Order maintenance is the most common activity of police officers. These tasks often expose officers to physical danger and involve the exercise of discretion by the officer. Order maintenance is the least "consensual" part of the police task (Wilson, 1968). For these reasons, order maintenance is perhaps the most difficult aspect of policing. Jiao (1998) suggested that different communities hold different expectations of their police. He urges police to develop policies and practices based, in large part, on the expectations of the community. Other research has indicated that some police decisions reflect community characteristics. Jackson and Wade (2005) observed that the police are more proactive in their enforcement efforts in neighborhoods characterized by high rates of crime than in low-crime areas. Further, Kane and Cronin (2013) found that order-maintenance policing was more effective at reducing violent crime in areas where informal social controls are lowest. It seems the likelihood of criminal activity influences the decisions of officers to intervene with citizens, as well as the effectiveness of those interventions.

Although there may be a consensus that robbery is intolerable, that police should arrest robbers, that accident victims deserve help, and that the police should help them, there often is no such consensus for order-maintenance questions. In the case of the neighbor with the loud stereo, it is clear that dissension or disagreement exists; one party believes that the stereo is too loud and the other thinks that it is set at an acceptable level. Into this conflict steps the officer. Regardless of the outcome, at least one (if not all) of the parties will be dissatisfied.

Police are also increasingly likely to be a first responder in situations involving mentally ill or developmentally disabled individuals who have either committed a low-level crime or are exhibiting troubling behavior which the public expects to be taken care of (Reuland, Schwarzfeld, & Draper, 2009). These encounters are especially difficult for officers because there is often a lack of legal justification for an arrest or hospitalization. Police departments are increasingly collaborating with community mental health professionals to develop strategies for handling such situations (Edwards & Pealer, 2018).

Difficult as it is, order maintenance is a critical component of policing. Left unattended, minor disputes can escalate into criminal acts (such as assault or vandalism if the complaining neighbor takes the matter of the loud stereo into his or her own hands). Further, the police and the entire justice system must serve the major function of social control. We should be able to go about our daily lives in a relatively smooth and predictable fashion. More than any other police function, order maintenance ensures the routine functioning of society.

As you can see, police officers perform a variety of roles (See Box 2.1.2). In reality, each of the police functions work together in an effort to control crime. The police can work to control crime by enforcement of laws and by prevention. Police efforts to maintain order often have the effect of preventing crime (Braga, Welsh, & Schnell, 2015). Likewise, collaboration with mental health officials can divert mentally ill and developmentally disabled suspects from the criminal justice system so that they can receive the treatment needed to reduce future incidents. Further, as we will discuss in more detail later, the police can (and do) use criminal law to achieve order-maintenance and service functions.

BOX 2.1.2 POLICY DILEMMA: SCHOOL RESOURCE OFFICER

With the increased media attention on school violence, many jurisdictions have placed police officers in the K-12 school setting as a way to maintain a safe environment. These school resource officers are expected to perform many roles, including law enforcement, teacher, counselor, and order maintenance (Lynch, Gainey, & Chappell, 2016; Schlosser, 2014). Johnson (1999) found that the school resource officers did, in fact, lead to a decrease in school violence and disciplinary infractions. Though these officers may help maintain order in the school, critics argue that they, along with the increase in zero-tolerance policies, also contribute to an increased number of juveniles being processed by the criminal justice system (Price, 2009). The fear is that situations which could have previously been handled internally by the school administrators is now resulting in more formal, punitive actions which could lead a juvenile toward further criminal involvement. Are school resource officers placed in the schools in your community? If so, did you experience the school resource officers' involvement in multiple roles?

Police Management

Throughout the past 40 years, research has challenged, and in some cases redefined, the role of police. Walsh and Vito (2004) indicated that police operate within one of three existing models: (1) the rational–legal bureaucratic model, (2) the community, problem-solving model, or (3) the CompStat model. Organizational options were limited when police departments came into being in the mid-1800s. The only organizational model available that allowed control of large groups of personnel was the military model. For this reason above any other, the police often adopted a **paramilitary structure** with ranks and a chain of command. The trappings of a military organization are still a part of American policing in most places (Chappell & Lanza-Kaduce, 2010; King, 2003).

Departments organize patrol units by geography into precincts or districts. In the military model, information flows up the chain of command from the street officers to the police administrator. Orders and commands flow down the chain to the street officers. In theory, the police administrator controls the actions of the officers on the street. Organizationally, this structure enables the police to meet their conflicting functions in a routine manner. Traditional police functions include quickly responding to calls for service, randomly patrolling neighborhoods looking for criminal activity, and investigating crimes which become known to the police.

In practice, the structure of policing is different from the military model. Wilson (1968) noted that, unlike other organizations, street officers have more discretion than administrators do. The reality of police work is that officers on the street must react to a variety of situations. It is not practical for police officers to report every call and await instructions from their superiors.

As policing entered the twentieth century, the advent of the automobile as well as changes in American cities affected the structure of police departments. Although the paramilitary model remained, policing became increasingly bureaucratic. The radio and the telephone allowed more communication between officers and supervisors. In addition, the new communication tools increased demand for police service because a citizen only had to pick up a telephone to request help. However, police began to become overwhelmed by the calls for service generated by the 9-1-1 system. As the former commissioner of the New York City Police Department wrote, "chasing after those thousands of 9-1-1 calls meant putting bandages on the symptoms of the problems generating the calls" (Bratton, 1997:32). At the same time, research began to question the effectiveness of police strategies such as random police patrol and improved response time (Walker, 2015). This research, combined with the increasing crime rate, resulted in the two most widely discussed reforms in policing history: community-oriented policing and CompStat.

Community Policing

Community-oriented policing is an approach to policing that relies on community definitions of police functions and a partnership between the police and the community in the production of public safety. Each police officer is expected to have responsibility for his or her beat area. The officers work with residents to identify problems and implement solutions. This direct link between the officer and the community naturally lessens the bureaucratic control and "chain of command" characteristic of the more formal, specialized police agency (see Box 2.1.3).

BOX 2.1.3 COMMUNITY-ORIENTED POLICING

Programmatic Elements

- Foot patrol
- Bicycle patrol
- Mounted (horse) patrol
- Neighborhood ministations

- Citizen police academies
- Neighborhood Watch
- School resource officers
- D.A.R.E. programs
- Citizen ride-along programs
- Neighborhood police officers
- Prioritizing calls for service
- Geographic mapping

Although community-oriented policing is often discussed as a fundamental philosophical shift in the way police agencies do business, departments reporting the existence of community policing initiatives often point to the implementation of special programs such as these as evidence that they are "doing community policing."

Source: Hickman and Reaves (2006:19, 21).

This trend seeks to actively engage the public, ultimately leading to more effective informal social controls. As Fielding (2005b) described, community policing is a "style of policing in which the police are close to the public, know their concerns from regular everyday contacts, and act on them in accord with the community's wishes" (p. 460). Community-oriented policing, however, is still elusive of definition. Many agencies report that they practice community-oriented policing, but each agency seems to describe something different with this term. Still, community-oriented policing involves an expansion of the police role from reactive crime fighters to proactive problem solvers. In partnership with the community, the police identify community problems that contribute to crime and seek solutions designed to alleviate those problems. Community policing is now a topic of basic police training in most police academies in the United States (Reaves, 2016). See Table 2.1.1 for some statistics on police academy training.

Table 2.1.1 Percent of Police Academies with Training in Community Policing and other Special Topics

	Percent of Academies with Training	**Average Number of Hours Required**
Domestic Violence	98	13
Cultural Diversity/Human Relations	95	12
Mental Illness	95	10
Sexual Assault	92	6
Domestic Preparedness/ Terrorism	85	9
Community Partnership Building	82	10

Conflict Management	82	9
Problem-Solving Approaches	80	12

Source: Reaves (2016).

The rapid acceptance of this new role definition of policing once led some commentators to suggest that community-oriented policing was the new "orthodoxy," or commonly accepted purpose for the police. The police, under community-oriented philosophies, are supposed to be more closely tied to the communities they police, more accessible to the public, and less bureaucratic. The range of issues that are now defined as legitimate police problems is enormous, including street lighting, sanitation removal, recreational and health programming, housing, and almost every other public problem (Fielding, 2005a).

In practice, community-oriented policing has supported decentralized organization in police agencies, alternative patrol strategies and resource allocation, and increased police involvement in civic issues. In theory, the police should be involved in this wide range of problems because they are broadly responsible for public order, and because they are perhaps best organized (jurisdiction-wide, 24-hour availability) to learn about problems, develop solutions, and monitor outcomes. In most places adopting formal community-oriented policing programs, departments assign at least one neighborhood officer to each crime-ridden neighborhood. Permanent assignment to a specific beat is expected to help the officers develop a better understanding of the area and its residents, and to take greater responsibility for public safety and problem solving in the beat. See Figure 2.3.

Kane (2000) found that within a few weeks, officers who were permanently assigned to an area "took ownership" of the beat and began to engage in more proactive, problem-solving efforts. Residents quickly come to appreciate having their own officer. Evidence suggests that community-oriented policing improves citizens' satisfaction with the police (Gill, Weisburd, Telep, Vitter, & Bennett, 2014).

The implementation of community policing has not been easy in all departments and has rarely been implemented completely. Most often, departments have adopted the most visible and easily attainable aspects of community policing without making the fundamental organizational changes needed for community policing to truly become the new policing orthodoxy which it was once envisioned (Magers, 2004). Chappell (2009) identified three primary obstacles to the implementation of community policing: (1) lack of resources, (2) time constraints, and (3) cultural resistance from within the police department. Likewise, Liederbach, Fritsch, Carter, and Bannister (2007) found that whereas citizens valued the community policing in their neighborhoods, many officers still resisted the movement. Smaller police departments seem to have a particularly difficult transition to community policing, as the low turnover rates and infrequent hiring of new officers creates an environment that tends to value traditional techniques over more radical changes (Morabito, 2010).

CompStat

First implemented in New York City, **CompStat** represents a compromise between the decentralized community policing model and the traditional paramilitary-style bureaucracy (Dabney, 2010). This strategy gives the decision-making authority to the middle-level managers such as the district commanders and then redirects resources as needed to assist in solving each district's specific problems (Weisburd, Greenspan, Mastrofski, & Willis, 2008). At its core, CompStat has four components (Police Executive Research Forum, 2013:2):

1. Timely and accurate information and intelligence,
2. Rapid deployment of resources,
3. Effective tactics, and
4. Relentless follow up.

FIGURE 2.3 The Manchester, New Hampshire, Police Department touts its commitment to Community-Oriented Policing (C.O.P.S.) with signs posted around the city.

Ellen S. Boyne

A core component of CompStat is the use of increasingly sophisticated crime analysis and mapping technology (Johnson, 2017; Santos, 2014). These tools allow police managers to have access to important information regarding crime in their community. Police executives then discuss these crime problems at weekly or monthly meetings in an attempt to develop solutions. Middle-level police commanders are then held accountable for implementing the crime reduction strategies to the problems in their districts.

It is important to note that CompStat is, at base, simply a method used to develop solutions to crime problems (Police Executive Research Forum, 2013). Police often use innovative strategies associated with hot spot policing, problem-oriented policing, or community policing to reduce the criminal activity. However, these strategies can be hindered by departmental organizational or cultural issues. For example, a hierarchical culture has been shown to reduce the active participation of low-ranking officers during the CompStat meetings (Bond & Braga, 2015; Willis, Mastrofski, & Weisburd, 2004). Likewise, Dabney (2010) found that the strategies developed during the CompStat meetings were being miscommunicated as they were passed down the chain of command to the street-level officers.

Counterterrorism and Homeland Security

In the aftermath of the terrorist attacks of September 11, 2001, there has been some concern that the increased expectations in terms of security would overshadow the emphasis on community policing. In fact, the use of community policing did decline in the years after the terrorist attacks. However, research shows that many police agencies view community policing and homeland security as complementary strategies (Randol, 2012; Roberts, Roberts, & Liedka, 2012). Community policing can improve community relations, which in turn can improve security. Even so, community policing and terrorism preparedness do at least compete for resources (Lee, 2010).

Several federal and state initiatives involve police in counterterrorism activities. The roles of police and law enforcement agencies in counterterrorism differ by size and type of agency. Many federal law enforcement agencies now operate within the Department of Homeland Security. Some local police departments, especially the largest ones, have counterterrorism units or include counterterrorism efforts within expanding intelligence units. Many observers argue that the most important role of local police in counterterrorism efforts is as producers and consumers of intelligence (O'Connell, 2008).

Perhaps the biggest change in policing since 9/11 has been the growth of intelligence-led policing—the idea of basing police activity on criminal intelligence (Ratcliff, 2016). Great effort has been directed to increase intelligence gathering and information sharing among police departments at various levels. Schaible and Sheffield (2012) found that over 90% of state agencies have allocated more resources to intelligence efforts since 9/11. Much of this effort has been directed toward the increased use of FBI-sponsored Joint Terrorism Task Forces (JTTFs), which allow state and local police agencies to collaborate with federal agencies. Approximately one-third of local law enforcement agencies collaborate with these task forces (Riley, Treverton, Wilson, & Davis, 2005). The creation of state-level fusion centers has perhaps been a more significant development. These centers serve as a clearinghouse of information for the Department of Homeland Security and provide opportunities for agencies at all levels to share information about terrorist or other criminal threats (Chermak, Carter, Carter, McGarrell, & Drew, 2013).

The role of police agencies in counterterrorism preparedness largely depends on the size of the agency. Schafer, Burruss, and Giblin (2009) reported on a study of small municipal police agencies in Illinois. They found that smaller agencies had done relatively little in response to concerns about terrorism. Agencies located close to Chicago or other large cities and larger police departments had done more preparation. Those police chiefs who had done more preparation naturally felt more prepared to respond to acts of terror. Finally, those agencies that perceived a terrorist threat were more likely to prepare to respond.

William Pelfrey (2007) reported a case study of early responses in South Carolina. His research indicated, again, that most local police agencies had done relatively little specifically to prepare for a terrorist attack. Pelfrey found that factors such as the size of the police agency, its technological capacity, and whether it had a Special Weapons and Tactics (SWAT) team predicted its level of preparation. He noted that perhaps not every police agency needed to prepare to combat terrorism.

The small size and limited jurisdiction of most local police departments militate against their having a major role in counterterrorism. It is not clear what we can reasonably expect of the local police concerning terrorism. Reaves (2016) reported that nearly every law enforcement training academy provided some basic training on terrorism to new police recruits. Although there is widespread concern about homeland security in the United States, it has never been a core part of the local police role. The structure of American police reflects their predominantly local focus.

The Structure of American Policing

The structure and organization of law enforcement agencies in the United States show the influences of historical development and the conflicting tasks expected of them. Unlike the police agencies of other countries, most American police agencies exist at a local level. This fragmentation of police service supports the value we place on federalism and local autonomy. Americans do not want national police, and we insist on maintaining a civilian police force that is distinct from the military (Kraska, 1994; Moore, 1987).

The focus of police organization and administration is to standardize the use of civil force (Alpert & Dunham, 1988). The police must weigh the mandate to control behavior against the requirement that they respect individual rights. This double responsibility places a premium on controlling and directing the actions of individual police officers. The bureaucratic response to this concern was the creation of rules and procedures for officers to follow. These departmental policies, or standard operating procedures (SOPs), became a factor determining the actions of individual officers. Although not perfect, the rules affect how officers decide to handle cases (LaFrance & Day, 2013; Mastrofski, Ritti, & Hoffmaster, 1987). Like other organizations, police agencies change slowly in response to external pressures (King, 1999).

Early police officers were sworn into office, issued uniforms and weapons, and sent to the streets. Most states now require training and certification of recruits prior to being assigned to patrol. Beginning in 1972, many police agencies developed field-training programs to evaluate how well new officers apply laws and departmental policies to field situations (McCampbell, 1986). These programs help ensure that police officers know and follow the rules of the police bureaucracy. Today field training is a component of basic police training in the overwhelming majority of American police departments. Over a third (37%) of all police academies require recruits to complete field training as part of the academy program. When not part of the basic academy training, the agency that hired the recruit usually provides field training (Reaves, 2016).

Another development in policing during the twentieth century was specialization. Large police departments, especially those in our biggest cities, use task specialization to assign officers. **Police specialization** divides tasks into special units or divisions. Whereas departments differ among themselves in how they separate and name tasks, Alpert and Dunham (1988:59) identified four basic elements: (1) administration, (2) communication, (3) patrol, and (4) internal review. They observed that many police agencies use divisions that are more precise. Patrol and investigation are two units that include the crime control function of the police. A traffic division and community relations unit may combine with the patrol unit to provide service and order maintenance. Administrative services and internal affairs units assist police administrators in running and controlling the department.

A typical large police department may have several divisions. The investigation unit, for example, may be further divided into homicide, robbery, fraud, vice, and other squads. Regardless of the complexity of the police bureaucracy, most retain the military ranks and chain of command. Figure 2.4 presents a model organizational chart for a specialized police department. This chart shows an organization that has a well-defined hierarchy—there are many steps between the individual patrol officer and the chief of police. Most police departments, however, are small and do not have such a detailed and specialized organization. Still, even the smallest of police departments has a chief of police. An alternative organization, depicted in Figure 2.5, "flattens" this hierarchy, giving patrol officers easier input into policy development and shortened lines of communication. This flatter organizational structure is more consistent with contemporary calls for community-oriented policing (Maguire, Shin, Zhao, & Hassell, 2003; Zhao, Ren, & Lovrich, 2010).

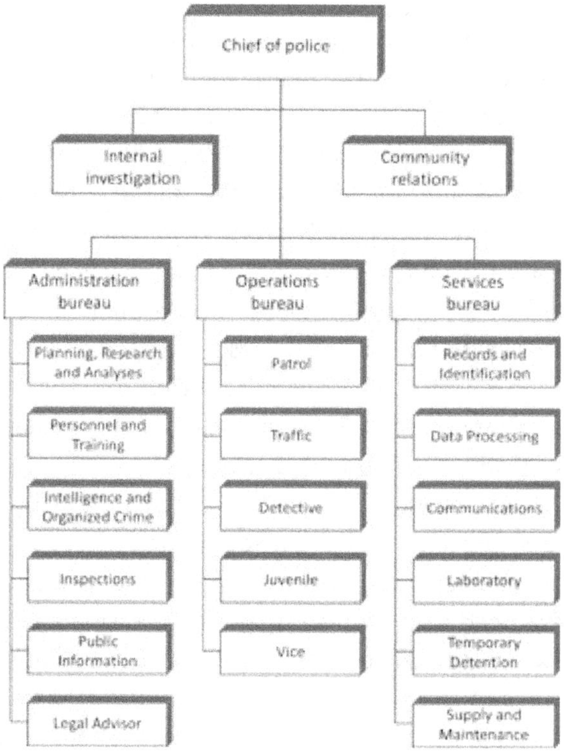

FIGURE 2.4 Organizational Chart for a Police Department.

Source: President's Commission on Law Enforcement and Administration of Justice (1967), Task Force Report: Police (Washington, DC: U.S. Government Printing Office):47.

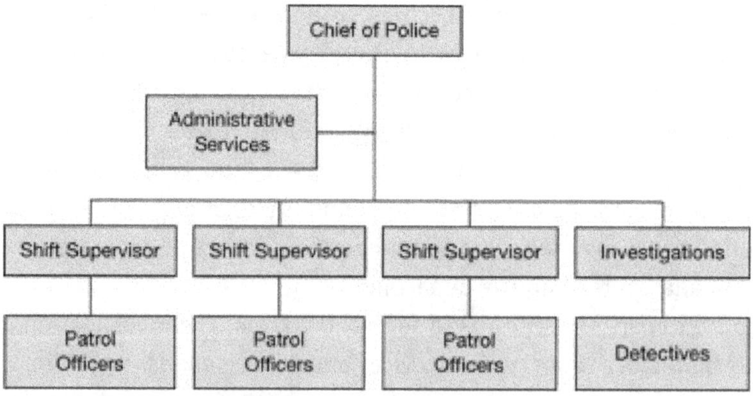

FIGURE 2.5 A Flattened Organizational Structure.

So far, most police organizations have not shown substantial change in their organizational structure. King (2005) suggested that a rigid rank structure is only one part of police hierarchy and that if officers have discretion to make decisions, the police organization can operate in a decentralized fashion while keeping the traditional rank structure.

We must remember that even in the most specialized city police department, patrol officers are generalists. Observers have called patrol the "backbone of policing." Patrol officers still provide the majority of police services. Nearly 70% of officers in local police departments have assignments to patrol (Reaves, 2015). It is unlikely that the decentralized performance of police service by patrol officers will change in the future. What may change is the amount of direction and supervision these generalist patrol officers receive from the central administration.

The degree of specialization in any police department is at least partly the result of the size of the department (Reaves, 2015). Larger departments are more likely to be specialized than are smaller ones. Recall that the majority of police officers work in large, bureaucratic departments, but that most departments are small. This fact of police organization means duplication and inefficiency are part of American policing. Our police serve communities as much as (or more than) they serve in the enforcement of the criminal law. The price we pay for local control of police is inefficiency. To ensure that we have police who are responsive to local needs, we must be willing to tolerate multiple jurisdictions and thousands of separate police agencies.

Understanding Police

Because we are examining the criminal justice system, we will proceed to discuss policing almost exclusively in terms of law enforcement. In doing so, it is easy to forget the other complex demands placed on the police. The purpose of the previous discussion was to recognize and highlight the fact that enforcing the criminal law is only one part of the police function. In dealing with many social problems, the police must develop workable, immediate responses. The multiple goals of policing complicate an analysis of the crime control actions of police departments. Nonetheless, we shall endeavor to focus on the role of the police in the criminal justice system—and that role includes crime control. Several factors influence the practice of policing, but three of the most important are the characteristics of the community, the police organization, and those of the police officer.

Police and Communities

Most policing in the United States happens at a local level. The police serve their various communities. As Wilson (1968) reported, there are varieties of police behavior. It is our goal to understand and explain police behavior as it relates to crime control. We cannot accomplish that goal if we ignore the contributions of community to the decisions of police officers.

Wilson (1968) used the frequency and formality with which officers intervened in the lives of citizens to classify police department styles. Formality refers to the use of the criminal law, whereas frequency refers to the rate at which police interact with citizens. He identified three basic styles of policing: (1) legalistic, (2) service, and (3) watchman. The **legalistic style** involved relatively frequent and formal interventions. In the **service style**, police intervened frequently, but informally (there was little law enforcement). In contrast, in the **watchman style**, police intervened infrequently. For example, in the case of a curfew violation, legalistic policing would involve the police stopping and issuing a citation (formal intervention); the service style would involve a stop followed by a warning (informal intervention); and the watchman style would predict that the officers were likely to ignore the violation (no intervention).

Because these are ideal types, we can expect variety in practice. Sometimes officers in a legalistic-style department will ignore the violation, those in a service-style department will issue a citation, and those in a watchman-style department will stop the citizen. However, the police department as a whole develops a style of policing that is generally characteristic of the organization. Wilson (1968) suggested that these different styles reflect differences in the communities served by the police. Thus, police departments develop policing styles that are appropriate to the desires and needs of the communities in which they work. Although it is difficult to determine exactly what characteristics of communities explain variation in police department styles, it seems clear that local police do exhibit different styles (Liederbach & Travis, 2008). It is also true that neighborhood or community characteristics help explain public perceptions of the police (Luo, Ren, & Zhao, 2017). For example, McNeeley and Grothoff (2016) found that racial tension in certain neighborhoods impacted residents' perception of the police.

Other research has shown that police react to neighborhood or community characteristics. Varano, Schafer, Cancino, and Swatt (2009) found that police were likely to discount the seriousness of several types of crimes depending on the neighborhood in which they occurred. Although police usually report some crimes, such as robbery, as serious crimes, police in lower-class and crime-ridden neighborhoods did not record other crimes, including drug offenses and some assaults. Police tend to identify more problems in disadvantaged neighborhoods and see more crime problems there than do the residents (Sun & Triplett, 2008). Similarly, Sabol, Wu, and Sun (2013) found that police acted more aggressively toward suspects in disadvantaged neighborhoods.

A long tradition of policing research has reported community and neighborhood effects on police actions. It is clear that community characteristics are an important part of the police equation and that explanations of police behavior must include reference to community and neighborhood factors. These community influences are likely to resist change. Zhao and colleagues (2010) found that "incrementalism" best explains community financial support for local police. A tradition of high or low support is a better explanation of current support than is any other. Communities that have supported the police in the past are likely to continue to do so, whereas those that were less supportive will continue to be less supportive. The link between communities and their police is traditional and enduring.

Police Organizations

Beyond recognizing the multiple functions served by police, we must also remain aware of the structure and organization of policing. The actions of police officers and police departments reflect different patterns of organization (Holmes, 1997). Departmental policies and procedures, as well as recruit training, serve as boundaries on police behavior. The diversity of organizational sizes, structures, and policies ensures variety in the practice of policing.

Wilson's (1968) model of police styles explains differences in police organizations resulting from different community characteristics. These organizational differences produce different officer behaviors.

In this model, the organization mediates (or transmits) community characteristics to officer behavior. The greatest influence on what officers do is the product of the police organization.

Phillips and Varano (2008) reported that police officer charging decisions reflect organizational influences. The number and types of charges made in domestic violence cases by local police officers differed from those of state police. The local police decisions reflected their awareness of conditions in the local courts that affected case prosecutions. Nowacki (2015) found officers' use of lethal force related to department size and administrative policy. Smaller departments and those with tighter regulations regarding officer discretion in use of force experienced less lethal force incidents by their officers.

Not surprisingly, the police organization can control and direct the decisions of police officers. Training, regulations, supervision, and discipline all work to constrain the behavior of officers. Beyond these direct controls, much evidence supports the notion that informal understandings and rules exist that structure the decisions and behaviors of officers. Even though individual officers still exercise discretion, their choices are constrained by the organization for which they work.

Selection of Police Officers

The police officer is a very important component of the justice process. In some ways, he or she is the most important component: Police officers decide whom to subject to justice processing, what crimes to investigate, and how vigorously to enforce laws. As the most numerous and most visible agents of criminal justice, police officers are disproportionately responsible for citizens' opinions about the entire justice system. Ultimately, police officers are ordinary people entrusted with extraordinary powers, and they are charged with what some have called "an impossible mandate" (Manning, 1978).

The discretionary nature of the decisions officers make concerning the criminal justice system means that the forces that influence their decisions also influence the workings of the justice system (Brooks, 1989). If a police officer is prejudiced, the system will be prejudiced to some extent. Thus, the characteristics of officers, as well as their relationship to the organization and the citizenry, are important influences on criminal justice system operations. The characteristics of individual officers, including demographic factors (age, gender, race, ethnicity) and experience (education, rank, years on the job, etc.), have been linked to officer decisions (Fridell & Binder, 1992; Harris, 2009; Hassell & Brandi, 2009; LaFrance & Day, 2013; Riksheim & Chermak, 1993).

Because it is believed that individual officer characteristics influence police decisions, the selection and training of police officers is an important topic. Police selection typically involves a number of steps that are designed to produce the best qualified police officers. Research into the police selection process, however, indicates that it is not always effective. Metchik (1999) suggested that our reliance on a "screening out" model aimed at dismissing unsuitable candidates is not as effective as one that seeks to identify and retain good candidates. Similarly, Gaines and Falkenberg (1998) argued that traditional written examinations may not adequately identify the best candidates, and may have the negative effect of excluding female and minority candidates. Henson, Reyns, Klahm, and Frank (2010) reported that selection tests and performance in the academy may be unrelated to performance as a police officer. Likewise, selecting police officers largely based on their education might not have as substantial of an impact as once assumed. Although officers who have a college education might be less likely to resort to the use of force than less educated officers, education does not seem to have an impact on other key discretionary decisions or the frequency of citizen complaints (Bruns & Bruns, 2015; Rydberg & Terrill, 2010; Terrill & Ingram, 2016). Only 15% of local law enforcement agencies have some type of college requirement for entry-level officers (Reaves, 2015).

One of the recent changes in American policing has been the increased hiring of women and minority group members. Some observers feared that women would be unable to endure the danger and rigors of police work (Hale & Wyland, 1993; Potts, 1983). Others believed that the inclusion of women and minorities would improve community relations. Thus far, the data show that female and minority group members make good police officers (Lundman, 2009; Poteyeva & Sun, 2009; Schuck, 2014b). However, only about 12% of sworn officers are female, and about 27% are members of ethnic minority groups (see Figure 2.6). Generally, larger police agencies have greater levels of diversity (Federal Bureau of Investigation, 2016).

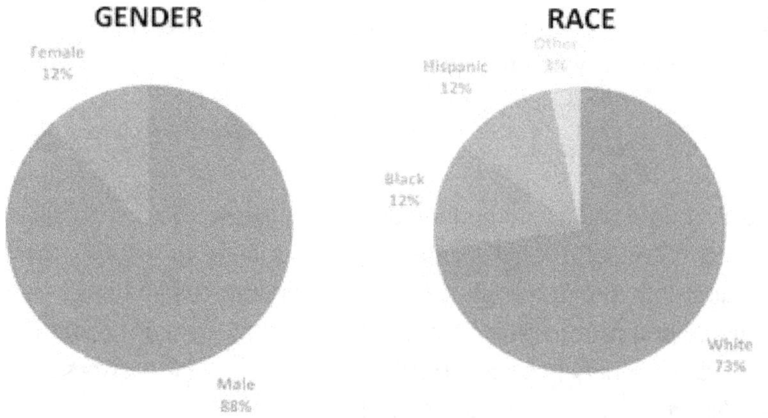

FIGURE 2.6 Gender and Race of Full-Time Police Officers.

Source: Federal Bureau of Investigation (2016).

Challenges to affirmative action policies threaten to limit diversity among police personnel. Cordner and Cordner (2011) surveyed female officers and police chiefs in several police departments in which the female representation was well below the national average. Both groups indicated that the low level of female employment was primarily due to the lack of female applicants. It appears that this was, at least in part, due to the gender-neutral recruitment process. Cordner and Cordner suggested that agencies may need to recruit in a manner that actively encourages female applicants. Overall, only 21% of law enforcement agencies have such recruitment efforts targeting females and minorities (Reaves, 2012). At the same time, there is evidence that traditional officer selection practices such as physical ability testing still work to exclude qualified female and minority candidates (Schuck, 2014a; Lonsway, 2003).

Beyond selecting police officers, training and experience also produce differences among officers, and training frequently is used as a vehicle to change officer attitudes and practices (Caro, 2011). Ingram and Lee (2015) have suggested that officer attitudes are related to job satisfaction. Johnson (2012) found that officers reported lower job satisfaction when they experienced role conflict, defined as discomfort when the required job-related behaviors are inconsistent with the officer's personal beliefs. In short, part of the task in police officer selection and training is to develop a good match between the skills and orientations of officers and the tasks and goals of the police organization.

Police Culture

Many observers have identified a distinct police culture in which officers share a widely accepted set of attitudes, values, and occupational norms. For example, police often isolate themselves from other members of society and maintain loyalty to each other when questioned by outsiders (Paoline, 2003). Officers also tend to be more conservative and conformist, as compared to the rest of society (Ellwanger, 2017). Some have suggested that the policing occupation attracts certain types of people who share similar personality traits. Others argue that the nature of the job changes an average person, thus forming a police personality. Whatever the causes for the police to have this unique culture, it is important to understand the complex set of forces that affects the policing activities of the individual officer.

Just as Wilson (1968) suggested that there are types of police organizations, others have suggested that there are types of police officers. Muir (1977), for example, argued that officers differ in terms of their willingness to use coercive force and their ability to empathize with or understand citizens. These differences result in four distinct types of officers differing in the ways they do policing. Muir used the term "enforcers" to describe those officers who are willing to use force but unable to empathize with citizens. Those comfortable with force and able to empathize he called "professionals." Officers who were unwilling to use force were either "reciprocators," who could empathize with citizens, or "avoiders," who did not understand citizens. More recently, Paoline (2004) identified seven typographies of police officers. Regardless of the specific terminology used, it is reasonable to conclude that police officers probably differ among themselves, and that these differences are relevant to an understanding of their criminal justice decisions (Travis & Langworthy, 2008).

The complexity of the job facing the individual officer is multiplied several times when we analyze the complexity of policing in society on an organizational level. The police officer is a member of an organization and, as such, must be careful to serve the ends of the organization. She or he is also a bureaucrat, and must abide by the rules and regulations of the bureaucracy. Finally, the officer is a member of an occupational group that is larger than his or her individual department. Thus, in any given situation, the behavior of the officer reflects the limits imposed by (1) the department, (2) the goals of the organization, and (3) the prestige of the occupational group. The officer is (at least subliminally) aware that his or her actions will be judged against all of these criteria. Ingram, Paoline, and Terrill (2013) found that officers who work together in the same shifts within a department develop their own police culture.

To this mix of standards, we must add the social context of the situation in which the officer is operating (Corsaro, Frank, & Ozer, 2015; Stein & Griffith, 2017). Many times the goals or expectations of the audiences of a police department conflict with each other and with those of the department. The victim/witness has a set of expectations about how the officer will behave. The officer has expectations about himself or herself and about the victim/witness. Finally, onlookers also have their expectations. The officer is aware of many of these expectations, and they affect his or her behavior. It is increasingly likely that the officer's actions will be captured on some type of video (e.g., body camera, cell phone) for public scrutiny. Although not all calls to which the police respond are dangerous or difficult, there are no simple calls.

Studies of the police show that officers frequently act as if they are cynical (Osborne, 2014). **Cynicism** entails distrust or suspicion. In terms of police, the term refers to a perception or belief that citizens, department leaders, politicians, and other criminal justice officials are not truthful and honest in their dealings with officers. From a police officer's perspective, laws are often created by legislatures who have no background in criminal justice. Further, the officer's job is criticized by a public who have no understanding of the nature of police work (Caplan, 2003). In this sense, cynicism can create a barrier between the officer and the public for which they serve.

Police Officer Stress

The existence and nature of police officer stress has been an important but elusive topic of research for several decades. The evidence about the level of stress experienced by police officers in comparison to those in other occupations is unclear. Policing, as an occupation, contains some unique stressors, such as the chance of killing someone, the threat of attack, and the need to deal with human misery and crime. Police officers also face many of the same stressors faced by other workers, such as rotating shifts, organizational insensitivity, red tape, and the like (Ma et al., 2015; Vila & Kenney, 2002). Investigations of police stress indicate that causes and levels of stress may differ among officers (Gachter, Savage, & Torgler, 2011). Officers whose personality does not fit into the prevailing police culture seem to experience more stress than those who are part of the police culture (Rose & Unnithan, 2015) Research reveals that officers experience stress differently and develop different coping patterns based on their gender, race, level of family support, and length of service (Hassell & Brandi, 2009; Kurtz, 2008; Menard & Arter, 2013). Although police may experience stress as do other people, not all police experience it to the same degree, nor cope with it as well. Some officers respond to stress by leaving the profession (McCarty & Skogan, 2012). Burnout and turnover represent costly problems for police organizations, because replacing officers requires extensive and expensive selection and training processes.

Policing in the Whole System

Returning to our discussion of the location of the criminal justice system within the whole system of American society, Wilson's observations about the police indicate the influence of environmental factors. He saw police agency styles as related to community characteristics. The size, structure, and composition of the community, Wilson (1968) argued, created a "political culture" in which the police exist. Part of this culture defined the limits of police actions that were acceptable in the community. Service-style agencies existed in suburban, middle-class communities. Watchman-style and legalistic agencies operated in heterogeneous (mixed population in terms of social class and ethnicity) cities. The distinction between whether the police would demonstrate a watchman or legalistic style seemed to be related to the type of government in the cities. Those with "professional" governments (city managers) were legalistic; those in "political" governments (strong mayor) were watchman style.

Wilson (1968) did not contend that city governments directly influenced policing practices, but that differences in communities created different environments and that police styles reflected those environments. Thus, the job the police do and the way in which they do it reflects the values and structure of the community in which they exist (Travis & Langworthy, 2008). As a subsystem of the criminal justice and social systems, the police department adapts to its environment, supporting the existing equilibrium. Consider the likely public reaction to a watchman style of policing in a homogeneous, middle-class, suburban community. It is likely that citizens would complain about the failure of the police to enforce the laws, and would demand police reform. On the other hand, a legalistic style would also generate complaints about overzealous enforcement. The service style is most likely to fit the desires and expectations of the citizens in such a community.

Finally, given the essentially democratic nature of government (and policing in particular) in the United States, it is logical that the police reflect the desires of the citizens. After all, if citizens define the police job through their calls for service, the citizens direct the police. The spread of community-oriented policing promises to increase variety in policing. Each large police department can potentially become composed of a large number of distinct "neighborhood" or "community" police. The types of issues that attract police attention, and the ways in which police react to problems, may begin to vary not just between departments but within departments between neighborhoods.

[...]

Review Questions

1. What is meant by calling the police the "agency of last resort"?
2. Briefly trace the development of policing in the United States.
3. Describe how the police can be considered to be a human services agency.
4. How can community policing be considered a revised role for the police?
5. Differentiate between reactive and proactive policing.
6. How do the multiple tasks expected of the police affect them as part of the justice system?
7. What factors influence the decisions and behavior of police officers?

References

Alpert, G., & Dunham, R. (1988). *Policing urban America.* Prospect Heights, IL: Waveland.

Barlow, D., & Barlow, M. (2000). *Police in a multicultural society: An American story.* Prospect Heights, IL: Waveland.

Bittner, E. (1990). *Aspects of police work.* Boston: Northeastern University Press.

Black, D.J. (1972). The mobilization of law. *Journal of Legal Studies, 2*(1), 125–149.

Bond, B.J., & Braga, A.A. (2015). Rethinking the CompStat process to enhance problem-solving responses: Insights from a randomized field experiment. *Police Practice and Research, 16,* 22–35.

Braga, A.A., Welsh, B.C., & Schnell, C. (2015). Can policing disorder reduce crime? A systematic review and meta-analysis. *Journal of Research in Crime and Delinquency, 52*(4), 567–588.

Bratton, W.J. (1997). Crime is down in New York City: Blame the police. In Norman, D. (Ed.), *Zero tolerance: Policing a free society* (pp. 29–43). London: Institute of Economic Affairs.

Brooks, L. (1989). Police discretionary behavior: A study of style. In Dunham, R., & Alpert, G. (Eds.), *Critical issues in policing: Contemporary readings* (pp. 121–145). Prospect Heights, IL: Waveland.

Bruns, D.L., & Bruns, J.W. (2015). Assessing the worth of the college degree on self-perceived police performance. *Journal of Criminal Justice Education, 26*(2), 121–146.

Caplan, J. (2003). Police cynicism: Police survival tool? *The Police Journal, 7,* 304–313.

Caro, C.A. (2011). Predicting state police officer performance in the field training officer program: What can we learn from the cadet's performance in the training academy? *American Journal of Criminal Justice, 36,* 357–370.

Cathey, D., & Guerin, P. (2009). *Analyzing calls for service to the Albuquerque police department.* Albuquerque, NM: Institute for Social Research.

Chappell, A. (2009). The philosophical versus actual adoption of community policing: A case study. *Criminal Justice Review, 34,* 5–38.

Chappell, A., & Lanza-Kaduce, L. (2010). Police academy socialization: Understanding the lessons learned in a paramilitary-bureaucratic organization. *Journal of Contemporary Ethnography, 39*(2), 187–214.

Chermak, S., Carter, J., Carter, D., McGarrell, E., & Drew, J. (2013). Law enforcement's information sharing infrastructure: A national assessment. *Police Quarterly, 16*(2), 211–244.

Cordner, G., & Cordner, A. (2011). Stuck on a plateau? Obstacles to recruitment, selection, and retention of women police. *Police Quarterly, 14*(3), 295–310.
Corsaro, N., Frank, J., & Ozer, M. (2015). Perceptions of police practice, cynicism of police performance, and persistent neighborhood violence: An intersecting relationship. *Journal of Criminal Justice, 43*, 1–11.
Critchley, T. (1972). *A history of police in England and Wales* (2nd ed.). Montclair, NJ: Patterson Smith.
Dabney, D. (2010). Observations regarding key operational realities in a CompStat model of policing. *Justice Quarterly, 27*, 28–51.
Das, D. (1987). *Understanding police human relations*. Metuchen, NJ: Scarecrow Press.
Eck, J., & Spelman, W. (1987). Who you gonna call? The police as problem busters. *Crime & Delinquency, 33*(1), 31–52.
Edwards, B., & Pealer, J. (2018). Policing special needs offenders: Implementing training to improve police–citizen encounters. In Dodson, K.D. (Ed.), *Handbook of offenders with special needs*. New York: Routledge.
Ellwanger, S.J. (2017). Learning police ethics. In Braswell, M., McCarthy, B., & McCarthy, B. (Eds.). *Justice, crime, and ethics* (9th ed.). New York: Routledge.
Famega, C. (2005). Variation in officer downtime: A review of the research. *Policing: An International Journal of Police Strategies & Management, 28*(3), 388–414.
Federal Bureau of Investigation (2016). *Crime in the United States, 2015*. Retrieved from: https://ucr.fbi.gov/crime-in-the-u.s/2015/crime-in-the-u.s.-2015/tables/table-74
Fielding, N. (2005a). *The police and social conflict* (2nd ed.). London: Glasshouse Press.
Fielding, N. (2005b). Concepts and theory in community policing. *The Howard Journal, 44*(5), 460–472.
Fridell, L., & Binder, A. (1992). Police officer decision making in potentially violent confrontations. *Journal of Criminal Justice, 20*(5), 385–399.
Fritsch, E., Caeti, T., Tobolowsky, P., & Taylor, R. (2004). Police referrals of crime victims to compensation sources: An empirical analysis of attitudinal and structural impediments. *Police Quarterly, 7*(3), 372–393.
Gachter, M., Savage, D., & Torgler, B. (2011). Gender variations of physiological strain amongst police officers. *Gender Issues, 28*, 66–93.
Gaines, L., & Falkenberg, S. (1998). An evaluation of the written selection test: Effectiveness and alternatives. *Journal of Criminal Justice, 26*(2), 175–183.
Gill, C., Weisburd, D. Telep, C.W., Vitter, Z., & Bennett, T. (2014). Community-oriented policing to reduce crime, disorder and fear and increase satisfaction and legitimacy among citizens: A systematic review. *Journal of Experimental Criminology, 10*, 399–428.
Hale, D., & Wyland, S. (1993). Dragons and dinosaurs: The plight of patrol women. *Police Forum, 3*(2), 1–6.
Harris, C. (2009). Exploring the relationship between experience and problem behaviors: A longitudinal analysis of officers from a large cohort. *Police Quarterly, 12*(2), 192–213.
Hassell, K., & Brandi, S. (2009). An examination of the workplace experiences of police patrol officers: The role of race, sex, and sexual orientation. *Police Quarterly, 12*(4), 408–430.
Henson, B., Reyns, B., Klahm, C., & Frank, J. (2010). Do good recruits make good cops? Problems predicting and measuring academy and street-level success. *Police Quarterly, 13*(1), 5–26.
Hickman, M., & Reaves, B. (2006). *Local police departments, 2003*. Washington, DC: Bureau of Justice Statistics.
Holmes, S. (1997). *The occupational definition of police use of excessive force* (Unpublished doctoral dissertation). Cincinnati, OH: University of Cincinnati Division of Criminal Justice.
Huey, L., & Ricciardelli, R. (2015). This isn't what I signed up for: When police officer role expectations conflict with the realities of general duty police work in remote communities. *International Journal of Police Science & Management, 17*(3), 194–203.
Ingram, J.R., & Lee, S.U. (2015). The effect of first-line supervision on patrol officer job satisfaction. *Police Quarterly, 18*(2), 193–219.
Ingram, J.R., Paoline, E.A., III., & Terrill, W. (2013). A multilevel framework for understanding police culture: The role of the workgroup. *Criminology, 51*(2), 365–397.
Jackson, A., & Wade, J. (2005). Police perceptions of social capital and responsibility: An explanation of proactive policing. *Policing: An International Journal of Police Strategies & Management, 28*(1), 49–68.
Jiao, A. (1998). Community-oriented policing and policing-oriented community. *Journal of Crime and Justice, 20*(1), 135–158.
Johnson, D.R. (1981). *American law enforcement: A history*. St. Louis, MO: Forum Press.
Johnson, I.M. (1999). School violence: The effectiveness of a school resource officer program in a southern city. *Journal of Criminal Justice, 27*(2), 173–192.
Johnson, R. (2012). Police officer job satisfaction: A multidimensional analysis. *Police Quarterly, 15*(2), 157–176.
Johnson, R. & Rhodes, T. (2009). Urban and small town comparison of citizen demand for police services. *International Journal of Police Science and Management, 11*(1), 27–38.
Johnson, S.D. (2017). Crime mapping and spatial analysis. In Wortley, R., & Townsley, M. (Eds.), *Environmental criminology and crime analysis* (pp. 199–223). New York: Routledge.
Jones, M., & Johnstone, P. (2012). *History of criminal justice* (5th ed.). Boston: Elsevier (Anderson Publishing).
Kane, R. (2000). Permanent beat assignments in association with community policing: Assessing the impact on police officers' field activity. *Justice Quarterly, 17*(2), 259–280.
Kane, R., & Cronin, S. (2013). Associations between order maintenance policing and violent crime: Considering the mediating effects of residential context. *Crime & Delinquency, 59*, 910–929.
Kappeler, V. (1996). Making police history in light of modernity: A sign of the times? *Police Forum, 6*(3), 1–6.
King, W. (1999). Time, constancy, and change in American Municipal Police Organizations. *Police Quarterly, 2*(3), 338–364.
King, W. (2003). Bending granite revisited: The command rank structure of American police organizations. *Policing: An International Journal of Police Strategies & Management, 26*(2), 208–230.

King, W. (2005). Toward a better understanding of the hierarchical nature of police organizations: Conception and measurement. *Journal of Criminal Justice, 33*(1), 97–109.

Kraska, P. (1994). The police and the military in the post-cold war era: Streamlining the state's use of force entities in the drug war. *Police Forum, 4*(1), 1–8.

Kurtz, D. (2008). Controlled burn: The gendering of stress and burnout in modern policing. *Feminist Criminology, 3*(3), 216–238.

LaFrance, C., & Day, J. (2013). The role of experience in prioritizing adherence to SOPs in police agencies. *Public Organization Review, 13*, 37–48.

Lee, J. (2010). Policing after 9/11: Community policing in an age of homeland security. *Police Quarterly, 13*(4), 347–366.

Liederbach, J., & Travis, L. (2008). Wilson redux: Another look at varieties of police behavior. *Police Quarterly, 11*(4), 447–467.

Liederbach, J., Fritsch, E., Carter, D., & Bannister, A. (2007). Exploring the limits of collaboration in community policing: A direct comparison of police and citizen views. *Policing: An International Journal of Police Strategies & Management, 31*(2), 271–291.

Lonsway, K. (2003). Tearing down the wall: Problems with consistency, validity, and adverse impact of physical agility testing in police selection. *Police Quarterly, 6*(3), 237–277.

Lundman, R. (1980). *Police and policing: An introduction.* New York: Holt, Rinehart & Winston.

Lundman, R. (2009). Officer gender and traffic ticket decisions: Police blue or women too? *Journal of Criminal Justice, 37*(4), 342–352.

Luo, F., Ren, L. & Zhao, J. (2017). The effect of micro-level disorder incidents on public attitudes toward the police. *Policing: An International Journal, 40*(2), 395–409.

Lynch, C.G., Gainey, R.R., & Chappell, A.T. (2016). The effects of social and educational disadvantage on the roles and functions of school resource officers. *Policing: An International Journal of Police Strategies & Management, 39*(3), 521–535.

Ma, C.C., Andrew, M.E., Fekedulegn, D., Gu, J.K., Hartley, T.A., Charles, L.E., et al. (2015). Shift work and occupational stress in police officers. *Safety and Health at Work, 6*, 25–29.

Magers, J.S. (2004). CompStat: A new paradigm for policing or a repudiation of community policing? *Journal of Contemporary Criminal Justice, 20*, 70–79.

Maguire, E., Shin, Y., Zhao, J., & Hassell, K. (2003). Structural change in large police agencies during the 1990s. *Policing: An International Journal of Police Strategies & Management, 26*(2), 251–275.

Manning, P.K. (1978). The police: Mandate, strategies and appearances. In Manning, P.K., & Van Maanen, J. (Eds.), *Policing: A view from the street* (pp. 7–31). Santa Monica, CA: Goodyear.

Mastrofski, S.D., Ritti, R.R., & Hoffmaster, D. (1987). Organizational determinants of police discretion: The case of drinking-driving. *Journal of Criminal Justice, 15*(5), 387–402.

McCampbell, M.S. (1986). *Field training for police: State of the art.* Washington, DC: National Institute of Justice.

McCarty, W.P., & Skogan, W.G. (2012). Job-related burnout among civilian and sworn police personnel. *Police Quarterly, 16*, 66–84.

McNeeley, S., & Grothoff, G. (2016). A multilevel examination of the relationship between racial tension and attitudes toward the police. *American Journal of Criminal Justice, 41*, 383–401.

Menard, K.S., & Arter, M.L. (2013). Police officer alcohol use and trauma symptoms: Associations with critical incidents, coping, and social stressors. *International Journal of Stress Management, 20*, 37–56.

Metchik, E. (1999). An analysis of the "screening out" model of police officer selection. *Police Quarterly, 2*(1), 79–95.

Monkonnen, E. (1981). *Police in urban America: 1860–1920.* Cambridge: Cambridge University Press.

Moore, R. (1987). *Posse comitatus* revisited: The use of the military in civil law enforcement. *Journal of Criminal Justice, 15*(5), 375–386.

Morabito, M. (2010). Understanding community policing as an innovation: Patterns of adoption. *Crime & Delinquency, 56*(4), 564–587.

Morley, B.S., & Hadley, J.M. (2013). Public safety consolidation: Does it make sense? *FBI Law Enforcement Bulletin.*

Muir, W. (1977). *Police: Streetcorner politicians.* Chicago: University of Chicago Press.

Nowacki, J.S. (2015). Organizational-level police discretion: An application for police use of lethal force. *Crime & Delinquency, 61*(5), 643–668.

O'Connell, P. (2008). The chess master's game: A model for incorporating local police agencies in the fight against global terrorism. *Policing: An International Journal of Police Strategies & Management, 31*(3), 456–465.

Osborne, R.E. (2014). Observations on police cynicism: Some preliminary findings. *North American Journal of Psychology, 16*(3), 607–628.

Paoline, E.A., III. (2003). Taking stock: Toward a richer understanding of police culture. *Journal of Criminal Justice, 31*, 199–214.

Paoline, E.A., III. (2004). Shedding light on police culture: An examination of officers' occupational attitudes. *Police Quarterly, 7*(2), 205–236.

Payne, B.K., Berg, B.L., & Sun, I.Y. (2005). Policing in small town America: Dogs, drunks, disorder, and dysfunction. *Journal of Criminal Justice, 33*, 31–41.

Pelfrey, W. (2007). Local law enforcement terrorism efforts: A state level case study. *Journal of Criminal Justice, 35*(3), 483–518.

Phillips, S., & Varano, S. (2008). Police criminal charging decisions: An examination of post-arrest decision-making. *Journal of Criminal Justice, 36*(4), 307–315.

Police Executive Research Forum (2013). *CompStat: Its origins, evolution, and future in law enforcement agencies.* Washington, DC: Bureau of Justice Assistance.

Poteyeva, M., & Sun, I. (2009). Gender differences in police officers' attitudes: Assessing current empirical evidence. *Journal of Criminal Justice, 37*(5), 512–522.

Potts, L. (1983). Equal employment opportunity and female employment in police agencies. *Journal of Criminal Justice, 11*(6), 505–524.

President's Commission on Law Enforcement and Administration of Justice (1967). *Task Force Report: Police.* Washington, DC: U.S. Government Printing Office.

Price, P. (2009). When is a police officer an officer of the law? The status of police officers in schools. *Journal of Criminal Law & Criminology, 99*, 541–570.

Randol, B.M. (2012). The organizational correlates of terrorism response preparedness in local police departments. *Criminal Justice Policy Review, 23*(3), 304–326.

Ratcliffe, J.H. (2016). *Intelligence-led policing* (2nd ed.). New York: Routledge.

Reaves, B. (2011). *Census of state and local law enforcement agencies, 2008.* Washington, DC: Bureau of Justice Statistics.

Reaves, B. (2012). *Hiring and retention of state and local law enforcement officers, 2008–Statistical tables.* Washington, DC: Bureau of Justice Statistics.

Reaves, B. (2015). *Local police departments, 2013: Personnel, policies, and practices.* Washington, DC: Bureau of Justice Statistics.

Reaves, B. (2016). *State and local law enforcement training academies, 2013.* Washington, DC: Bureau of Justice Statistics.

Reuland, M., Schwarzfeld, M., & Draper, L. (2009). *Law enforcement responses to people with mental illnesses: A guide to research informed policy and practice.* New York: Council of State Governments Justice Center.

Riksheim, E., & Chermak, S. (1993). Causes of police behavior revisited. *Journal of Criminal Justice, 21*(4), 353–382.

Riley, J.K., Treverton, G., Wilson, J., & Davis, L. (2005). *State and local intelligence in the war on terrorism.* Santa Monica, CA: Rand Corporation.

Roberts, A., Roberts, J., & Liedka, R. (2012). Elements of terrorism preparedness in local police agencies, 2003–2007: Impart of vulnerability, organizational characteristics, and contagion in the post-9/11 era. *Crime & Delinquency, 58,* 720–747.

Rose, T., & Unnithan, P. (2015). In or out of the group? Police subcultures and occupational stress. *Policing: An International Journal of Police Strategies & Management, 38*(2), 279–294.

Rossler, M., & Terrill, W. (2012). Police responsiveness to service-related requests. *Police Quarterly, 15,* 3–24.

Rydberg, J., & Terrill, W. (2010). The effect of higher education on police behavior. *Police Quarterly, 13,* 92–120.

Sabol, J.J., Wu, Y., & Sun, I. (2013). Neighborhood context and police vigor: A multilevel analysis. *Crime & Delinquency, 59*(3), 344–368.

Santos, R.B. (2014). The effectiveness of crime analysis for crime reduction: Cure or diagnosis? *Journal of Contemporary Criminal Justice, 30*(2), 147–168.

Schafer, J., Burruss, G., & Giblin, M. (2009). Measuring homeland security innovation in small municipal agencies: Policing in a post-9/11 world. *Police Quarterly, 12*(3), 263–288.

Schaible, L.M., & Sheffield, J. (2012). Intelligence-led policing and change in state law enforcement agencies. *Policing: An International Journal of Police Strategies & Management, 35*(4), 761–784.

Schlosser, M.D. (2014). Multiple roles and potential role conflict of a school resource officer: A case study of the Midwest police department's school resource officer program in the United States. *International Journal of Criminal Justice Sciences, 9,* 131–142.

Schuck, A.M. (2014a). Female representation in law enforcement: The influence of screening, unions, incentives, community policing, CALEA, and size. *Police Quarterly, 17,* 54–78.

Schuck, A.M. (2014b). Gender differences in policing: Testing hypotheses from the performance and disruption perspectives. *Feminist Criminology, 9*(2), 160–185.

Stein, R.E., & Griffith, C. (2017). Resident and police perceptions of the neighborhood: Implications for community policing. *Criminal Justice Policy Review, 28*(2), 139–154.

Stewart-Brown, R. (1936). *The Serjeants of the peace in medieval England and Wales.* Manchester, UK: Manchester University Press.

Sun, I., & Triplett, R. (2008). Differential perceptions of neighborhood problems by police and residents: The impact of neighborhood-level characteristics. *Policing: An International Journal of Police Strategies & Management, 31*(3), 435–455.

Surette, R. (2015). *Media, crime, and criminal justice: Images, realities, and policies* (5th ed.). Stamford, CT: Cengage.

Terrill, W., & Ingram, J.R. (2016). Citizen complaints against the police: An eight city examination. *Police Quarterly, 19*(2), 150–179.

Toch, H. (1997). The democratization of policing in the United States: 1895–1973. *Police Forum, 7*(2), 1–8.

Travis, L., & Langworthy, R. (2008). *Policing in America: A balance of forces* (4th ed.). Englewood Cliffs, NJ: Prentice Hall.

Varano, S., Schafer, J., Cancino, J., & Swatt, M. (2009). Constructing crime: Neighborhood characteristics and police recording behavior. *Journal of Criminal Justice, 37*(6), 533–563.

Vila, B., & Kenney, D. (2002). Tired cops: The prevalence and potential consequences of police fatigue. *National Institute of Justice Journal, 248,* 16–221.

Vogel, R., & Adams, R. (1983). Police professionalism: A longitudinal cohort study. *Journal of Police Science and Administration, 11*(4), 474–484.

Walker, S. (1977). *A critical history of police reform: The emergence of professionalism.* Lexington, MA: Lexington Books.

Walker, S. (2015). *Sense and nonsense about crime, drugs, and communities* (8th ed.). Stamford, CT: Cengage.

Walsh, W.F., & Vito, G.F. (2004). The meaning of CompStat: Analysis and response. *Journal of Contemporary Criminal Justice, 20,* 51–69.

Weisburd, D., Greenspan, R., Mastrofski, S., & Willis, J.J. (2008). *CompStat and organizational change: A national assessment.* Washington, DC: U.S. Department of Justice.

Willis, J.J., Mastrofski, S.D., & Weisburd, D. (2004). CompStat and bureaucracy: A case study of challenges and opportunities for change. *Justice Quarterly, 21*(3), 463–496.

Wilson, J.M., & Grammich, C.A. (2015). Deconsolidation of public-safety agencies providing police and fire services. *International Criminal Justice Review, 25*(4), 361–378.

Wilson, J.M., Weiss, A., & Grammich, C. (2016). *Public safety consolidation: A multiple case study assessment of implementation and outcome.* Washington, DC: Office of Community Oriented Policing Services.

Wilson, J.Q. (1968). *Varieties of police behavior.* Cambridge, MA: Harvard University Press.

Wood, J.D., Watson, A.C., & Fulambarker, A.J. (2017). The "gray zone" of police work during mental health encounters: Findings from an observational study in Chicago. *Police Quarterly, 20,* 81–105.

Zhao, J., Ren, L., & Lovrich, N. (2010). Police organizational structures during the 1990s: An application of contingency theory. *Police Quarterly, 13*(2), 209–232.

Discussion Questions

1. What are your thoughts on the zero-tolerance policy?
2. Do you believe that broken windows theory is accurate?
3. What are some issues within policing that you have noticed?

CHAPTER 3

Court of Law

The Courts

Mia R. Ortiz

Mia R. Ortiz, "The Courts," *Introduction to Criminal Justice: Structure, Process, Principles and Morality*, ed. Carolyn Petrosino, pp. 82–106.

Brief Outline

1. Introduction
2. Development and Evolution of the Courts
3. Due Process Rights of the Accused
4. A Profile of Criminal Defendants
5. Problem-Solving Courts
6. Courtroom Professionals
7. The Trajectory of the Accused into the Criminal Justice System
8. Summary and Analysis of the American Court System

Key Terms

Bail
Beyond a Reasonable Doubt
Exclusionary Rule
Felony
Grand Jury
Miranda Warnings
Misdemeanor
Plea Bargaining
Trial
Voir Dire

> Equal justice under law is not merely a caption on the facade of the Supreme Court building; it is perhaps the most inspiring ideal of our society. It is one of the ends for which our entire legal system exists ... it is fundamental that justice should be the same, in substance and availability, without regard to economic status.
>
> Lewis Powell Jr., U.S. Supreme Court justice

A. Introduction

The judicial branch of American government is responsible for interpreting laws as they pertain to the Constitution, state, or local laws. The U.S. court system is a multilayered, multi-tiered institution governed and directed by the Constitution, rules of evidence, and the local jurisdiction. Its foundation is based on reviewing and evaluating evidence based on a mandate of justice and fairness. Thus, the decisions made by courts have a direct impact on the accused, the victims, and the community at large. This [reading] provides an overview of the court system, which includes the development and organization of the federal and state court systems, a discussion on the constitutional rights of the accused, a description of the courtroom work group, as well as detail of the trajectory of how criminal cases are processed. Woven into these sections are historical and contemporary court cases as well as discussion on the impact that the U.S. court system has on matters of social justice and ethical concerns among disenfranchised communities.

B. Development and Evolution of the Courts

The initial development of the U.S. court system emerged from the Constitution, specifically through the first acts of Congress under the Judiciary Act of 1789 as part of maintaining checks and balances with the legislative and executive branches of government. Court system began on the principle of federalism, which is the idea of having a central or federal government. Over time, with the emergence of states (and state government), federalism evolved to include the recognition of autonomous state governments and therefore dual court systems: the federal courts and the state courts. Although these systems have for the most part distinct jurisdictions, the court of last resort for both is the Supreme Court of the United States. The description of the federal court system is discussed in the next section.

Federal Court System

District Courts

The structure of the federal court system consists of district courts, appellate courts, and the Supreme Court. The federal district courts consist of 94 judicial districts and the U.S. bankruptcy courts. There is at least one district court in each state as well as in the U.S. territories of American Samoa, Guam, Northern Mariana Islands, Panama, U.S. Virgin Islands, and Puerto Rico. An important question to ask is what cases do the federal courts have jurisdiction over (what types of cases are heard)? The federal court system has jurisdiction over matters that include "the constitutionality of the law, cases involving U.S. laws and treaties, disputes between two or more states, maritime law, and bankruptcy cases" (United States Courts, 2015, nd).

One of the most recent high-profile cases in the federal court system was the matter of the *United States v. Dzhokhar Tsarnaev, 2013*. Tsarnaev was arrested, indicted, and convicted for manufacturing and detonating two pressure cooker bombs near the finish line of the Boston Marathon in 2013, which resulted in the deaths of four people (an act that he did with his deceased brother, Tamerlan Tsarnaev). Additionally, he was convicted of carjacking and killing a university police officer during a shootout. Among many charges, Tsarnaev was charged in the federal system because the bombs were considered a weapon of mass destruction (U.S.C. § 2332a) and the bombing occurred in a place of public use (U.S.C. § 2332), which resulted in malicious destruction of property (U.S.C. § 844).

An important question to raise is why was Tsarnaev charged in federal court instead of the Massachusetts state court? The prosecution can charge a defendant on the federal level if it can be determined that the crime committed impacted interstate commerce. In Tsarnaev's case, the charges of mass destruction and malicious destruction of property had a direct impact on the role of commerce on marathon Monday. Each year, the Boston Marathon attracts millions of runners, and spectators from around the world who rely on the hotels, restaurants, and other businesses that offer special services for marathon participants. The prosecution argued that the bombing significantly interrupted interstate commerce in Boston.

In addition to these offenses, Tsarnaev was also charged with conspiracy (the planning and commission of the bombings). On April 8, 2015, he was found guilty of 30 counts of federal crimes, and on May 15, 2015, the jury recommended death by lethal injection. Tsarnaev's conviction or death sentence will likely be sent to the U.S. Court of Appeals for the First Circuit—the same court where the trial took place—on grounds that he did not have a fair trial (the defendant's request to have the trial outside of Boston for purposes of having a fair jury and trial was denied during pretrial motions). The First Circuit includes the districts of Maine, Massachusetts, New Hampshire, Puerto Rico, and Rhode Island.

U.S. Courts of Appeals

When cases heard in district courts are appealed, they proceed through one of 12 appellate courts. In 2013 there were nearly 60,000 appeals filed on the appellate level (United States Court of Appeals, 2014). The majority of the cases involve petitions from prisoners to seek sentence reductions or appeals of trial convictions. In criminal cases, the losing party of the initial court matter, known on the appellate level as the appellant, will either present written legal grounds (known as a brief) or engage in oral argument against the appellee (the side arguing to uphold the initial court decision). The briefs or arguments are heard by a panel of appellate judges, and their ruling is final. At the appellate level, it is usually the defendant who challenges the conviction (the prosecution may never appeal an acquittal but may contest the sentence) (Administrative Office of the U.S. Courts, 2015). If one of the litigants is unsatisfied with the judgement of the appellate court or the highest state court, he or she may file a petition to the U.S. Supreme Court for review (known as a writ of certiorari).

One federal court case that proceeded to the appellate court involved Boston attorney Simon Glik, who was arrested in 2007 for videotaping an arrest by police officers in Boston Commons. The police charged Glik with illegal wiretapping, aiding the escape of the prisoner, and disturbing the peace. Although all criminal charges were eventually dropped, Glik sued the city of Boston and the police officers in district court for violating his civil rights. Glik was awarded $170,000 for damages and legal fees. The appellants (the city and the police officers) contested the settlement because the police officers argued that they had *qualified immunity*, in that by their public office status, they could not be held responsible. However, the decision by appellate court judge Kermit Lipez upheld Glik's civil rights; here is an excerpt of his opinion:

> The filming of government officials engaged in their duties in a public place, including police officers performing their responsibilities, fits comfortably within these principles. Gathering information about government officials in a form that can readily be disseminated to others serves a cardinal First Amendment interest in protecting and promoting "the free discussion of governmental affairs" (655 F.3d 78).

The Supreme Court

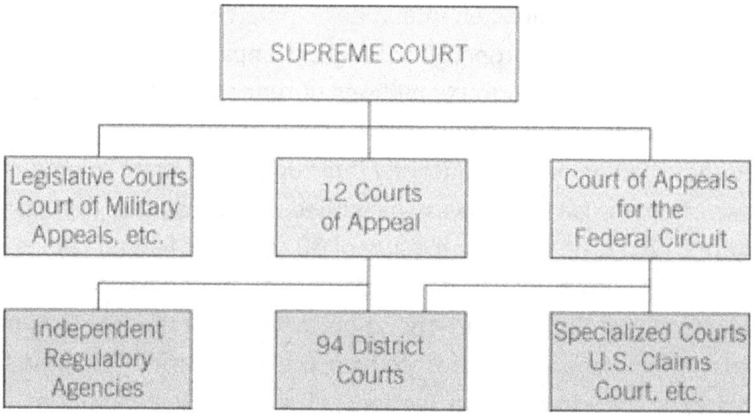

FIGURE 3.1

The Supreme Court was created through a provision under Article III of the Constitution. In addition to executing its responsibility of maintaining checks and balances as the head [of] the judiciary branch of government of the United States, the role of the Supreme Court is to operate as the final court for both state and federal jurisdictions and to review cases over concerns of constitutionality. The decisions of all of these matters not only provide a sense of justice in the immediate case, but also provide a precedent (a rule) for decisions in future court cases.

Supreme Court Justices

Currently there are nine Supreme Court justices. Justices are nominated by the president, and then vetted through extensive congressional hearings. Once confirmed by Congress, justices are appointed for life. Although the Supreme Court operates as an independent branch like the executive and legislative branches, presidents typically nominate potential justices with political ideologies that are similar to their own, which may affect court decisions on criminal or civil proceedings in the future. Over the years, the composition of the Supreme Court has changed from solely White men to the inclusion of female and minority justices. In 1967 Thurgood Marshall, an accomplished lawyer who successfully challenged racial segregation in public schools in *Brown v. Board of Education of Topeka* (1954), was appointed as the first African American justice of the Supreme Court. Fourteen years later, Sandra Day O'Connor was the first female justice appointed to the high court. Currently on the bench are three female and one African American justice. With the exception of Justice Ruth Bader Ginsburg (who attended Columbia University's Law School), current justices have graduated from either Harvard or Yale Law Schools.

The State Court System

In most states, the state court system is typically divided into three levels: trial courts, appellate courts, and the court of last resort (typically called supreme courts). It is within the state court system that most of the criminal and civil court cases are processed.

Trial Courts

Trial courts are typically the court where most criminal and civil matters enter after arrest. Depending on the state, trial courts may be further divided into courts of limited or special jurisdiction, where the court only hears certain cases (such as **misdemeanor**, family court, community courts, or other specialized court). Courts of general jurisdiction oversee a variety of criminal and civil matters.

The organization of state court structure varies from state to state. In New York State, the highest court in the state is the Court of Appeals, followed by the Appellate Terms of the Supreme Court, which is followed by Supreme Courts, District Courts, and then City Courts. In the state of North Dakota, the Supreme Court is the highest court, followed by the Temporary Court of Appeals, the District Court, and Municipal Courts. Every state court system is designed to fit the needs of its state jurisdiction.

Court of Appeals

The purpose of the court of appeals is to challenge the ruling of the lower trial court. The court of appeals does not hear new cases, but rather makes rulings as to whether to affirm the lower court's rulings (that is, agree), remand (return to the lower court for retrial), or overturn (reverse the court's decision). Some of the reasons that cases are brought to the state appellate court include the inclusion of inadmissible evidence or testimony (which should have been excluded) or incorrect jury instructions by the judge. The majority of appeals brought by the defendant are rarely successful. In California, only 6 percent of criminal appeals are considered for further appellate action (Judicial Council of California, 2013).

Wrongful Convictions

The greatest miscarriage of justice occurs when a defendant has been wrongfully incarcerated or worse, put to death. In the United States, there have been a number of defendants who have been wrongfully convicted based on misidentification, unreliable testimony, or racial bias. The Innocence Project, an organization that has used DNA evidence to challenge wrongful convictions since the early 1990s, has been pivotal in addressing these injustices. To date, the organization has been successful in exonerating more than 300 wrongfully convicted persons.

State Supreme Court

In the majority of state case matters, the state Supreme Court is the court of last resort. The Supreme Court on the state level, as on the federal level, is composed of the justices who decide the merits of the decisions from the lower and appellate court. Unlike the U.S. Supreme Court, which does hear new cases, the state Supreme Court does not oversee trials. The state Supreme Court will consider cases that were not settled on the appellate level to determine if judicial or other court error in the original court of jurisdiction occurred. There are many notable cases that have been settled on the state Supreme Court level. In California, under *Jones v. Chappell*, the state justices found that chemical elements used in lethal injections were found to be cruel and unusual; this was the impetus toward establishing a moratorium on capital punishment in the state in 2014. In 1783 in the *Commonwealth of Massachusetts v. Nathaniel Jennison*, the court found that slave masters could be held criminally responsible for assaulting runaway slaves in free states.

C. Due Process Rights of the Accused

In the United States defendants are afforded certain rights outlined by the Constitution to ensure that they are treated fairly during the judicial process. Specifically, certain rights (known as due process rights) are outlined within the 4th, 5th, 6th, and 14th Amendments of the Bill of Rights in the Constitution. Due process is the foundation for justice and fairness and is afforded to every defendant who comes before the courts (even for the most egregious of alleged acts or the most notorious of offenders). Moreover, there have been a series of landmark Supreme Court cases that have reaffirmed the significance of these amendments.

Fourth Amendment

Under the Constitution, the Fourth Amendment states the following:

> The right of the people to be secure in their persons, houses, papers, and effects, against unreasonable searches and seizures, shall not be violated, and no warrants shall issue, but upon probable cause, supported by oath or affirmation, and particularly describing the place to be searched, and the persons or things to be seized.

Mapp v. Ohio

The right against unlawful search and seizure is invoked prior to arrest and subsequent court involvement and requires law enforcement (in most cases, footnote exceptions) to obtain warrants prior to searching or seizing a defendant's property. However, since such obtained evidence entered into court can affect the liberty of the defendant, it is essential that the evidence be obtained justly as required by the law. One landmark case that tested the constitutionality of search and seizure was *Mapp v. Ohio* (367 U.S. 643). In this case, Cleveland police entered the home of Dollree Mapp without a warrant on a tip that a bomb suspect was in her home. After handcuffing Mapp, the police obtained a gun, communist propaganda, and obscene material in her basement. Mapp was subsequently charged with possession of obscene material. In 1961, in a 6–3 ruling in the Supreme Court, despite the illegal contents that were in the home, the court decided that Mapp's arrest was unlawful because the police failed to enter her home on a valid warrant. This is defined as the *exclusionary rule*, in which evidence that was unlawfully obtained by the police cannot be admitted into evidence against the defendant.

Fifth Amendment

Several important components of the Fifth Amendment are relevant to the criminal justice system. These include the right against self-incrimination and double jeopardy, as well as protection against disclosing privileged communication. In many respects, the Fifth Amendment protections serve as a safeguard against coercive practices that have occurred during police interrogations in which confessions were obtained.

The Right Against Self-Incrimination

The most well-known constitutional right involves what the police are required to say to suspects and detainees at the time of arrest and questioning. These statements, called the ***Miranda warnings***, generally consist of the following:

> You have the right to remain silent. Anything you say can and will be used against you in a court of law. You have the right to speak to an attorney, and to have an attorney present during any questioning. If you cannot afford a lawyer, one will be provided for you at no cost to you.

The Miranda warnings stem from the landmark Supreme Court case *Miranda v. Arizona* (384 U.S. 436, 1966). In this case, Ernesto Miranda was charged, convicted, and sentenced for rape and kidnapping after confessing to the crime during interrogation, in which he had no attorney, nor was he advised that he could remain silent during questioning. In 1966 the Warren court ruled that the police had violated Fifth Amendment rights due to their neglect of Miranda's rights, and accordingly the conviction was reversed. Additionally, illegally obtained confessions or evidence that has been entered into court can be stricken from consideration in future court actions. The right against self-incrimination extends from any onset of any police involvement. Additionally, Fifth Amendment protects the accused from being required to testify against themselves in court. Should a defendant voluntarily testify, the defendant may invoke his or her Fifth Amendment rights at any time to avoid self-incrimination (that is, "I plead the fifth").

In addition to the Fifth Amendment's protections against self-incrimination, there are also other persons with a direct relationship to the accused who may not be compelled to testify in the effort to incriminate the accused. These persons include spouses, doctors, psychiatrists, the accused's attorney, and clergy.

While *Miranda* has far-reaching implications in the criminal justice system, there are many examples that reflect illegal police practices imposed on suspects. In *Brown v. Mississippi*, police officers whipped and hung defendants in order to obtain a confession to murder. In the case of the Scottsboro Boys, eight young Black men who were accused of raping two White girls were not allowed to consult with an attorney (despite being charged with a capital crime that would lead to a death sentence) and were denied the ability to waive their right to a speedy trial. In fact, the court wanted to try the entire case [in one] and a half days. The trial (and subsequent trials) were heard by all-White juries since Alabama had highly discriminatory practices, which prevented African Americans from serving. (For more information on this compelling case, see Carter, 1979.)

The Right Against Double Jeopardy

Another component of the Fifth Amendment is the right against being tried for the same crime twice (also known as double jeopardy). Essentially, a defendant may not be punished for the same conviction twice and may not be retried after an acquittal. Double jeopardy violations do not include grand jury deliberations or mistrial. Additionally, double jeopardy violations do not include criminal cases that are tried at the state and federal level. Because the state and federal courts, in many respects, are separate entities, a defendant may be tried in both courts for the same offense. For example, a person could send child pornography through the mail and be charged with a state offense of possession of child pornography and a federal offense of sending child pornography through the U.S. mail. In addition, double jeopardy has not been violated if the defendant is held to answer in criminal court and is sued in civil court for the same offense. For instance, former football star O. J. Simpson was acquitted of the murder of his ex-wife, Nicole Brown Simpson, and her friend Ronald Goldman but was sued (and was held responsible) in civil court for wrongful death.

Sixth Amendment

Rights of the accused under the Sixth Amendment involve several important matters within court proceedings specifically as it relates to trial. Within the Constitution, the Sixth Amendment states the following:

> In all criminal prosecutions, the accused shall enjoy the right to a speedy and public trial, by an impartial jury of the State and district wherein the crime shall have been committed, which district shall have been previously ascertained by law, and to be informed of the nature and cause of the accusation; to be confronted with the witnesses against him; to have compulsory process for obtaining witnesses in his favor, and to have the Assistance of Counsel for his defence.

There are several fundamental rights that defendants have. First, the defendant has a right to be informed of the criminal charges placed on him or her. This must occur upon arrest and at arraignment when formal charges are filed by the prosecution. Additionally, defendants have the right to view and/or challenge any evidence or testimony against them in court.

Right to an Attorney

The Sixth Amendment affirms that defendants have the right to have an attorney represent them in criminal proceedings regardless of their ability to pay. In *Gideon v. Wainright* (1963), the Supreme Court held that the state of Florida had violated Clarence Gideon's constitutional rights because it had denied Gideon's request to have an attorney represent him in court. As such, the high court overturned Gideon's state conviction (since he was forced to represent himself).

In today's courts the public defender is responsible for providing representation for defendants who are unable to secure their own defense due to their inability to pay. Indigent defense is the most commonly used defense for defendants. According to the Bureau of Justice Statistics, nearly $3 billion were spent for indigent defense in 2012 (Herberman & Kyckelhahn, 2014). Moreover, only 1 in 4 county public defender offices have enough lawyers to properly manage the caseload as set by the National Advisory Commission on Criminal Justice System Standards and Goals (Farole, 2010). In other words, the majority of the country's indigent defense systems are tremendously overwhelmed by growing caseloads

Right to a Jury Trial

Another constitutional right afforded through the Sixth Amendment is the right to a jury trial. Although this is a constitutional right, it is rarely used (only 10 percent of criminal cases go to trial). The majority of defendants will have their matters resolved during a stage within the criminal court process, typically through a practice called **plea bargaining**. Plea bargaining occurs when the prosecution and the defense come to an agreement on the case that will result in the defendant pleading guilty to the agreed upon charges. For attorneys and the courts, there are benefits to this practice: It reduces the volume of cases that go to trial (which can be extremely costly and time consuming); it can also guarantee conviction rates (for district attorneys) and can be a benefit to defense attorneys (particularly indigent defense attorneys with large caseloads). Although there are direct benefits for the court work group, it has been criticized over several concerns. One concern is that defendants may be under pressure to plea bargain, especially if they are currently in custody, with the agreement that they will be able to be released immediately. In some cases, the pains of pretrial detention may be significant enough that defendants may plead guilty to crimes they may not have committed, thus leading to legal, social, and financial consequences that may affect them for the rest of their lives.

Another criticism of plea bargaining relates to the issue of whether the practice circumvents the intentions of the due process rights of the defendants—specifically their right to a jury trial. Though defendants are informed prior to pleading guilty that they are waiving their constitutional rights to a trial and to the right to appeal, the reality is that plea bargaining was never the intention of (nor explicitly stated by) the framers of the Constitution. Due process rights as stated in the Constitution affirm that defendants who are accused of a crime have the right to trial, the right to testify (if they so choose), as well as the right to challenge the evidence and the witnesses against them. Many critics suggest that plea bargaining bypasses this very important legal process (Lynch, 2003, p. 27).

Eighth Amendment

The Eighth Amendment relates to the rights against cruel and unusual punishment and the rights against excessive bail. The Constitution requires that punishment be proportional to the crime for which the defendant was convicted. For example, an individual convicted for a petty, low-level crime should not have the same punishment as someone convicted of murder. A landmark Supreme Court case that tested the cruel and unusual punishment provision included *Furman v. Georgia* (408 U.S. 238), in which a man was sentenced to death for attempted burglary. The Supreme Court struck down this sentence because of the violation to the defendant's constitutional rights.

A Discussion on Bail

While there is no constitutional right to bail, clauses within the Eighth Amendment of the Constitution affirm that when bail is assigned, it must not be excessive. In determining bail, the judge takes the following into consideration as stated in the Eighth Amendment:

> The court takes into consideration several factors: (1) the seriousness of the offense; (2) the Weight of Evidence against the accused; (3) the nature and extent of any ties, such as family or employment, that the accused has to the community where he or she will be prosecuted; (4) the accused's ability to pay a given amount; and (5) the likelihood that the accused will flee the jurisdiction if released.

Absent of capital offenses (such as capital murder) and certain criminal violations (for example, violation of parole, probation, or bench and arrest warrants for failing to appear in court), most defendants will be assigned bail, and in fact, two thirds of defendants will be released on bail prior to trial. Bail refers to the financial or nonfinancial condition of being released from custody. Most courts yield to a bail schedule that has a bail amount assigned for each charge for which the defendant is arrested or arraigned. Bail is divided into two categories: those with financial conditions and those with nonfinancial conditions. Financial conditions include surety bail (defendants pay 10% of the total bail plus secure their release with property collateral); deposit bail (defendants pay 10% of the total bail with the amount refunded at the conclusion of the case); full cash bond (defendants pay the full amount of the bail to the court with the total amount refunded at the conclusion of the case); and property bond (property, usually a home or business, is put up as collateral).

In the 1960s critics argued that financial conditions of bail created significant disparities between affluent and disadvantaged defendants in that those who could not afford bail had to remain detained at pretrial. Further, it was argued that bail bond agents (a for-profit entity) were largely becoming the decision makers in determining release conditions—solely on the basis that the defendant could pay for the bond and thus circumvent the justice system. In 1961 Vera Institute of Justice conducted the Manhattan Bail Project, a research project designed to test whether defendants who were released without paying a financial bail are likely to skip their court appearances (Kohler, 1962). The results showed that fewer than 2% of defendants released without paying a financial condition of bail failed to appear to future court dates. The results of this research proved to be a watershed moment for the bail reform movement and helped inform courts across the country on ways to implement nonfinancial conditions to bail.

In addition to the noted social class disparities that are present in pretrial release decisions, research has also studied the impact that the race of the defendant has on the conditions of bail. Findings show that Black defendants were least likely to be released from the least restrictive pretrial conditions as compared to White defendants (Demuth, 2003; Schlesinger, 2007).

Fourteenth Amendment

The 14th Amendment affords each defendant equal protection the law. This is of particular importance, since there has been an extensive history of the denial of equal justice among defendants from underrepresented communities within the court of law. Specifically, [the] 14th Amendment to the Constitution affirms the following:

> All persons born or naturalized in the United States and subject to the jurisdiction thereof are citizens of the United States and of the State wherein they reside. No State shall make or enforce any law which shall abridge the privileges or immunities of citizens of the United States; nor shall any State deprive any person of life, liberty, or property, without due process of law; nor deny to any person within its jurisdiction the equal protection of the laws.

Loving v. Virginia

In *Loving v. Virginia* (1967), the Supreme Court ruled that laws which banned interracial marriage violated the equal protection clause of the Constitution. The case was brought forward by Richard and Mildred Loving (a White man and a Black woman), who were sentenced to jail for getting married; under Virginia's Racial Integrity Act of 1924, such marriages were deemed illegal. Similarly, in *Brown v. Board of Education* (1954), the Supreme Court determined that school segregation was in fact unequal and therefore violated the equal protection under the law clause of the 14th Amendment.

Consequences of Convictions

Recently, there has been greater discussion about the impact that misdemeanor and violations have on the defendant, the courts, and the community. These convictions bring many consequences for those convicted of lower level crimes. Certain misdemeanor convictions can lead to deportation, denial to hold certain professional licenses, loss of employment, eviction, and required registry into state sex registries. Moreover, police practices such as "broken windows" (where police are required to arrest or issue summons for minor infractions) increase the volume of misdemeanor cases in the court system as well as the cost to prosecute and defend each of these cases.

D. A Profile of Criminal Defendants

Although there is a high volume of cases that are going through the nation's courts, the reality is that the majority of the defendants come from disenfranchised communities. More than a third of the cases that enter the courts are drug related (that is, possession or intent to sell/trafficking). Violent crimes (murder, robbery, and sexual assaults) make up approximately one quarter of the cases, and the remaining cases involve property offenses (that is, burglary, larceny, and auto theft) (Reaves, 2013). Over the course of 2 decades, Black males represent the bulk (45%) of defendants entering the **felony** criminal courts. White defendants reflect a third of the population, and Hispanic defendants represent a fourth. Black males under age 18 represent more than half (55%) of the juvenile population (Reaves, 2013).

Female defendants are less than a quarter of those who enter the court system; this has remained consistent over the past 20 years. Most crimes that female offenders are charged with tend to be lower level offenses or incidents in which they are accessories to violent crimes (such as robbery) [(Cohen & Reaves,

2007)]. The average age at arrest is currently 32, as compared to 20 years ago, when it was 28. In fact, 1 in 4 defendants are 40 years old or older. This may reflect the revolving door of the criminal justice system in that once a person has been identified through conviction and incarceration, it may be difficult to earn legitimate employment, access to quality housing, and relocating to productive and safer communities; thus, many will return to criminal involvement. Because of the limitations that criminal convictions can have on opportunities for desisting from future criminal behavior, policy stakeholders in the court system have begun to rethink the role of courts and to consider innovative ways in which to address social ills that lead to crime through the use of problem-solving courts.

E. Problem-Solving Courts

Specialized courts are designed to address the defendant's specific criminal, social, or mental health needs more effectively than the traditional criminal court, with the goal of reducing future criminal involvement. Toward the end of the 20th century, there was an emergence of several specialized courts across the country to address specific criminal behaviors and quality of life matters that affect many defendants who come before the court.

Drug Courts

In the past 30 years, the increase in the volume of court cases has largely been attributed to drug-related offenses (for example, possession and distribution). In 1989 the first drug court was enacted in Miami–Dade County, Florida, as a response to the number of drug-related cases that were clogging the criminal courts (National Association of Drug Court Professionals, 2014). Nearly 30 years later, there are close to 3,000 drug courts across the country, with at least one court situated in each state. The purpose of the drug court is to divert defendants away from the traditional criminal court processing so that they may participate in rehabilitation related to their substance abuse. The commitment to the drug court is typically 18 months and requires defendants to attend regularly scheduled meetings where they submit to regular drug testing. Defendants who continually test positive for illicit substances or are charged with new crimes during their drug court involvement may be returned to the regular criminal court processing, where they could be subject to harsher penalties. Participants who successfully complete drug court will have their conviction sealed or the charges dropped entirely. Results from several major studies have concluded that not only are defendants who participate in the drug courts (compared to defendants charged with similar drug charges) more likely to desist from future drug use, they are also less likely to engage in future criminal behavior (Rempel, Green, & Kraelstein, 2012).

Domestic Violence Courts

For nearly a decade, domestic violence has accounted for nearly a fifth of all violent crime in the United States (Truman & Morgan, 2014). Domestic violence cases make up a significant portion of criminal court processing. Domestic violence courts have emerged as another problem-solving [courts] to address this issue. In 2009 there were more than 200 domestic violence courts implemented within the United States and 150 that had been developed internationally (Labriola, Bradley, O'Sullivan, Rempel, & Moore, 2009). Although there is variation, domestic violence court revolve around two goals: (a) to provide greater safeguards in securing the victims' safety, which can include access to victims advocate programs internal and external to the courts; and (b) to ensure offenders' accountability in the alleged crime (Labriola et al., 2009). Additionally, there are integrated domestic violence courts that also incorporate family court matters, which include child custody and child protective service matters (Labriola et al., 2009). Leading experts of domestic violence courts are quick to admit that the success of these courts is not tethered to the rates of recidivism, since there have been no results that show that this particular problem-solving court reduces this crime as compared to domestic violence defendants in traditional court setting (Mazur & Aldrich, 2003). However, the major distinction between the two courts is that there are greater supports for victims in the domestic violence court.

Mental Health Courts

According to the National Alliance on Mental Illness, there are 2 million people arrested every year with a serious mental illness with an additional half a [million being] treated while incarcerated. The purpose of mental health courts is to engage defendants in participating in treatment. Similar to drug courts, defendants are assigned a case manager, who conducts a psychosocial assessment, and must participate in periodic case meetings in court during their treatment.

Assessment of Problem-Solving Courts

These specialized courts provide many benefits not only to the defendant, but also to the community at large. Such courts provide a new view on the purpose of justice—that is, identifying the quality of life and low-level crimes that can plague a community and a society. In many respects, these courts offer individualized treatment that is distinct from the typical criminal court experience. Moreover, for many the participation in these specialized courts is the first time that defendants have had access to treatment or social services. Although these benefits are significant, critics have argued that there are concerns related to this approach. One concern relates to the fact that in order to receive services (like counseling, rehabilitation, and other social services), a person must be identified in the criminal justice system (arrested, charged, or incarcerated). A second concern is that most defendants have to plead guilty to the offense charged (often through a plea bargaining agreement) in order to be diverted to the specialized court. In addition, such problem-solving courts also call into question the historical purpose of the court system, since judges in these particular courts have dual roles as social worker and dispenser of justice (Neyfakh, 2014).

F. Courtroom Professionals

Though the professionals in the courtroom have very distinct roles, they operate as a well-functioning work group with the ultimate goal of carrying out justice to defendants, victims, and society at large. Each of these professionals must deal with the tension between administering justice and the ethical concerns they are confronted with on a daily basis. The following section discusses each professional's responsibility.

Judge

The judge is the sole authority of the courtroom and is responsible for overseeing cases, informing defendants of charges, and determining what evidence or testimony is allowed to be considered during trial. Specifically, as a neutral party, the judge is ultimately an essential arbiter in the administration of justice. Judges are also responsible for overseeing the jury selection process and instructing juries on the law prior to deliberating. Finally, they are also responsible for sentencing convicted defendants. There is a variety of ways in which judges are selected to the bench. On the state level, judges are generally appointed by the governor; however, in subsequent elections, appointed judges will have to be reelected to remain on the bench. Their terms of service can vary depending on the state. For instance, in California the term for judges to serve on the superior court level is 6 years; in Massachusetts judges—regardless of the level at which they serve—are appointed by the governor for life (National Center for State Courts, 2014).

Although judges lead the court's processes, they are not without ethical dilemmas. One ethical issue is in the selection of judges. Judges are generally appointed by governors (or presidents, at the federal level) or are elected by the local constituency. Although judges are charged with neutrality, they are typically elected or appointed by those who assume similar political leanings, which may impact the manner in which justice is administered.

District Attorney

The district attorney (DA) is the chief criminal prosecutor of the jurisdiction (generally situated on a county or city level). The DA is generally an elected official and is typically responsible for personally trying the jurisdiction's most high-profile criminal cases and providing consultation to local mayors and police departments. In their day-to-day responsibilities, DAs are charged with managing the deputy and assistant districts attorneys who are responsible for prosecuting defendants in courts. Cities such as Los Angeles and New York employ thousands of assistant district attorneys.

There are key ethical considerations that DAs face. In many jurisdictions, promotions in the DA's office are based on the conviction rate (the rate of convictions that each DA has prosecuted). Accordingly, plea bargaining becomes a convenient way to ensure conviction; however, DAs are required to uphold ethical standards (in the interest of justice) to ensure that there is sufficient evidence to charge a defendant with a crime before the defendant pleads guilty, because the consequences of conviction can be extreme.

Another ethical dilemma involves the DA's relationship with the police. Similar to what you have seen on television shows, the police are responsible for investigating crimes, and the district attorney is responsible for prosecuting the defendants in court. An important question to consider is what happens when it is the police who are being charged with criminal offenses? Recently six Baltimore police officers were indicted on second-degree murder charges of Freddie Gray for failing to secure him in a lockup van after arrest and then driving recklessly to cause his death. As with any other defendant, it is the responsibility (as well as ethical obligation) of the DA's office to prosecute any defendant (regardless of relationship with the office) to the full extent of the law if there is evidence to support it.

Defense Attorneys

The defense attorney is responsible for representing the defendant and ensuring that his or her due process rights are being upheld from arrest to sentencing. The Sixth Amendment guarantees the right of the defendant to be represented by counsel. There are several types of defense attorneys.

Private Defense Attorneys

Private attorneys generally have smaller caseloads, which provide the opportunity for greater attention to the client. However, they are significantly more expensive. Since such attorneys are at a premium, this prevents many indigent defendants access to this resource; such people are likely to be represented by public defenders, who may not provide the same amount of attention for each client.

Court Appointed Attorneys

In certain situations where the defendant is ineligible to receive the services of the public defender's office or where there may be a conflict of interest (where there are codefendants in the case that are being represented by the public defender's office), a private attorney is appointed by the court as defense attorney.

One of the most discussed ethical issues pertains to criminal defense attorneys representing defendants where it was clear that the defendants are guilty of the crime charged. Recall from the discussion of due process rights that every defendant is entitled to representation under the Fifth and Sixth Amendments, regardless of guilt or innocence. It is also important to remember that the burden is on the prosecution to prove that the defendant is guilty of the crime charged. Finally, it is the responsibility of the defense attorney to show that the prosecution failed to prove its case, regardless of whether the defendant actually committed the crime.

G. The Trajectory of the Accused into the Criminal Justice System

Immediately upon arrest, the accused begins the path into the court system. The American court system is a series of many routes that lead to several final outcomes, including acquittal, dismissal, diversion, conviction, and sentencing.

After arrest, the police will send the arrest report to the county district attorney's office for consideration of filing formal charges. The district attorney will dismiss either some or all of the charges. Those charges that will be filed require the defendant to proceed through the next court phase. In some states defendants who have been arrested on felony charges or are involved in high-profile cases will be subject to a **grand jury**. A grand jury is responsible for considering the evidence and/or witnesses to determine if there is sufficient evidence to formally charge (or indict) the defendant.

Arraignment

The next step in the court process after charges have been filed is **arraignment**. Arraignment is the court hearing where the judge informs defendant of the charges as well as his or her constitutional rights to due process. This is also the stage of the process where the defendant enters a plea (guilty or not guilty) to the charges. The court will set the **bail** (either a monetary or nonmonetary guarantee to return for future court dates) and impose protective orders (those that require the defendant to stay away from the victim or location) or other conditions (for example, a curfew or being required to stay away from codefendants who are also charged in this case) on the defendant while the case is being considered in court.

Preliminary Hearings

At the preliminary hearing the district attorney, the defense attorney, and the judge have the opportunity to assess the status of the case to determine if there is a sufficient basis to proceed with a trial. There is no set number of hearings. In the criminal courts, the burden is on the prosecution to bring forth evidence and witnesses against the defendant to establish that there is probable cause (which is a lower standard than beyond a reasonable doubt at trial) that the defendant committed the crimes alleged. In these hearings, the defense attorney is responsible for ensuring that the defendant's rights are being upheld, specifically in relation to concerns of violations of the Fourth Amendment (unlawfully obtained evidence by the police) and/or Fifth Amendment rights (failure to read rights or unlawful confessions). Reliant on the rules of evidence, the judge's responsibility is to determine what evidence is sufficient to proceed with trial.

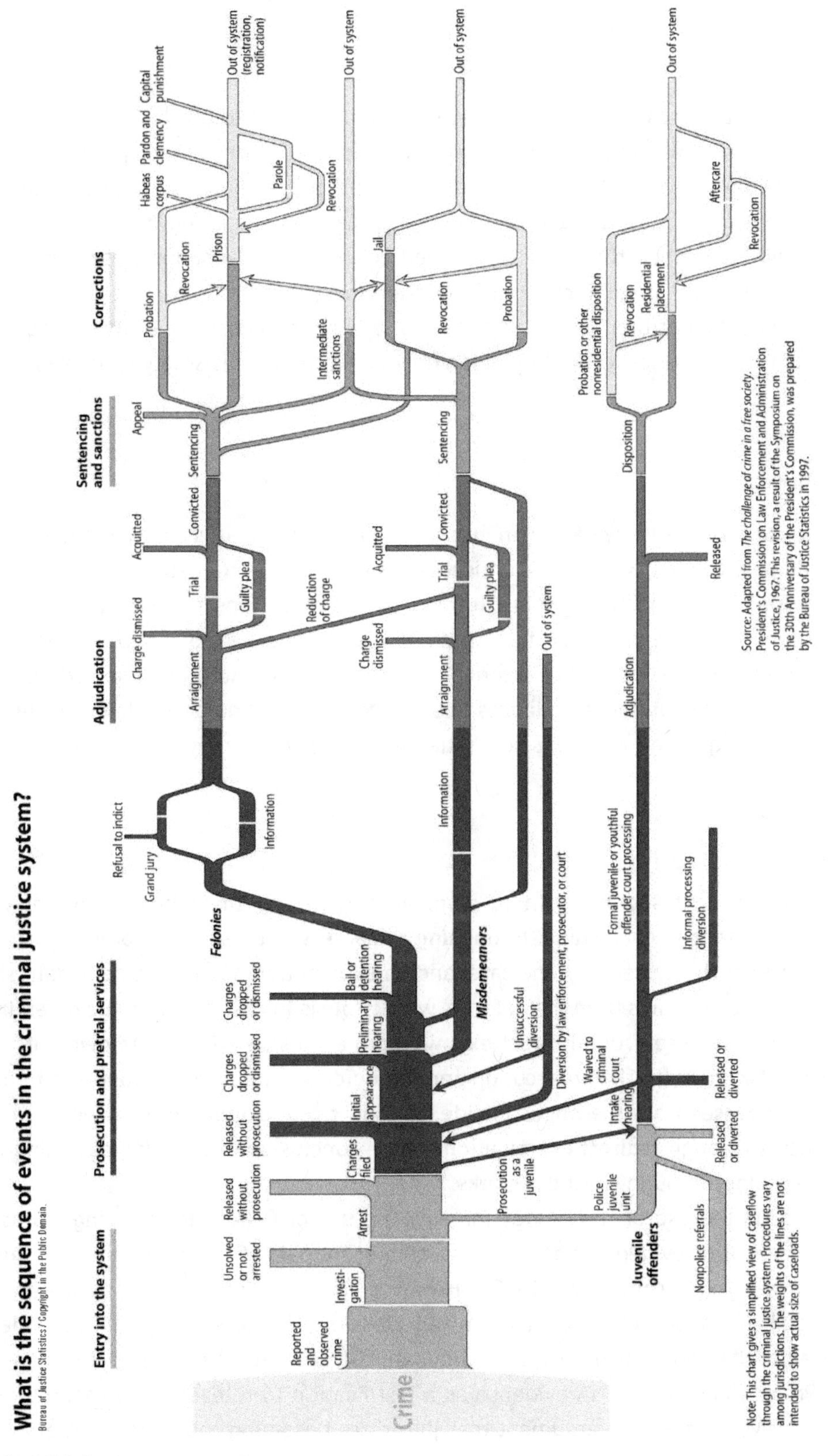
What is the sequence of events in the criminal justice system?
Bureau of Justice Statistics / Copyright in the Public Domain.
Entry into the system
Prosecution and pretrial services
Adjudication
Sentencing and sanctions
Corrections
Crime
Reported and observed crime
Investi-gation
Unsolved or not arrested
Arrest
Released without prosecution
Charges filed
Released without prosecution
Initial appearance
Charges dropped or dismissed
Preliminary hearing
Charges dropped or dismissed
Bail or detention hearing
Felonies
Grand jury
Refusal to indict
Information
Arraignment
Charge dismissed
Trial
Guilty plea
Acquitted
Convicted
Sentencing
Appeal
Probation
Revocation
Prison
Habeas corpus
Pardon and clemency
Capital punishment
Parole
Revocation
Out of system (registration, notification)
Reduction of charge
Intermediate sanctions
Out of system
Misdemeanors
Unsuccessful diversion
Information
Arraignment
Charge dismissed
Trial
Guilty plea
Acquitted
Convicted
Sentencing
Revocation
Probation
Jail
Out of system
Out of system
Diversion by law enforcement, prosecutor, or court
Prosecution as a juvenile
Police juvenile unit
Juvenile offenders
Nonpolice referrals
Released or diverted
Intake hearing
Waived to criminal court
Released or diverted
Informal processing diversion
Formal juvenile or youthful offender court processing
Adjudication
Released
Disposition
Probation or other nonresidential disposition
Revocation
Residential placement
Aftercare
Revocation
Out of system
Note: This chart gives a simplified view of caseflow through the criminal justice system. Procedures vary among jurisdictions. The weights of the lines are not intended to show actual size of caseloads.
Source: Adapted from The challenge of crime in a free society. President's Commission on Law Enforcement and Administration of Justice, 1967. This revision, a result of the Symposium on the 30th Anniversary of the President's Commission, was prepared by the Bureau of Justice Statistics in 1997.

FIGURE 3.2

Trial

In the instances where the prosecution and the defense cannot agree to resolve the case, the matter will be held for trial. A **trial** is a legal event in which the prosecution is responsible for proving that the defendant was responsible for committing the crime charged. In criminal proceedings, the burden is on the prosecution to prove the case **beyond a reasonable doubt** (a level of certainty that the defendant did in fact commit the crime). In a civil trial, when the case that is tried is about legal responsibility, the legal standard for responsibility is based on the **preponderance of the evidence** (which assumes that more likely than not, the defendant was legally responsible). Trials can consist of two approaches: jury trials (a group of citizens who will determine guilt or innocence) or trial by judge (in which the judge is solely responsible for determining the outcome).

Jury Selection

Although jury service is typically viewed as an inconvenient obligation, it is a civic responsibility (absconders can face fines and possible jail time) and a critical component to the trial stage as well as a constitutional right for the accused. Selecting the jury has tremendous ramifications for both the prosecution and the defense. During jury selection, large pools of potential jurors are vetted based on their background (by completed juror questionnaires as well as attorney oral questions at the time of selection), attitudes on the criminal justice system, and possible allegiances to either the prosecution or the defense. This process (called **voir dire**) allows for judges and attorneys to challenge potential jurors in the effort of having a fair and impartial jury.

Stages Within the Trial

In most trials a typical format is followed. In the criminal court setting, since the burden is on the prosecution, it is always first to present in each stage. In **opening remarks**, the prosecution provides an introduction to the case, an overview of the evidence in the case, and an explanation of why the defendant should be found guilty. This is followed by remarks from the defense, whose role is to cast doubt on the defendant's culpability to commit the alleged offense. During **direct examination**, each side will ask its own witnesses questions related to the case. Additionally, the prosecution and the defense will have the opportunity to challenge the testimony of the witnesses from the opposite side through **cross-examination**, as well as opportunities to recall past witnesses through **redirect examination**. At the conclusion of the trial, each side will surmise its position to the juror pool through **closing remarks**.

In today's courts the use of technology (namely the use of DNA, fingerprinting, ballistics, and other forms of physical, scientific evidence) has become a significant part of trials and has been further bolstered by popular culture television shows such as *CSI*. However, the inclusion of such physical evidence in terms of determining guilt or innocence serves as a mixed blessing. In one sense, physical evidence can either place the accused at the scene of the crime or eliminate the accused as the suspect (organizations such as the Innocence Project have used DNA evidence as a justification to release the wrongfully convicted from incarceration). However, there is an argument that jurors are becoming too dependent on such evidence to convict. In other words, there is a growing interest among jurors to have scientific certainty rather relying on beyond a reasonable doubt. Such a dependency on certainty may result in acquittals and arguably an injustice.

At each stage of the proceedings, the judge is charged with ruling over objections from the attorneys. During these objections, the judge may either **sustain** the objection (that is, there was an error committed either in the phrasing of a question or in the answer of a witness) or **overrule** the objection (that is, no error has been made and the trial may continue). The judge is also responsible for instructing the jury on the law as well as giving deliberating instructions prior to deliberation.

Verdict

After the jury deliberates, the jury foreperson will deliver the verdict form to the court clerk, who will then read the verdict aloud in court. If the defendant is found not guilty, the defendant's involvement in the criminal portion of the case is over. If the defendant is found guilty, in most cases he or she will be immediately **remanded** (detained) to county jail until sentencing.

H. Summary and Analysis of the American Court System

The American judicial system is, without question, one of the best court systems in the world. Its system and processes have withstood the shifting political identities of presidencies and members of Congress for more than 2 centuries. The institution has been the executor of social change and equality. Beyond that, it subscribes to an essential mandate in which all accused persons who enter the legal process are entitled to due process and equal treatment under the law. Although this institution serves as a model to other countries around the world, it is certainly not without criticism or limitations.

A criticism to consider is the role of the victim in criminal court proceedings. Typically, the main parties in a criminal case involve the jurisdiction (represented by the prosecution) and the defendant (represented by a defense attorney). Until the past 20 years, victims (with exception to eyewitnesses or subpoenaed testimony) were rarely integral to this process. Victims' rights movements and funds for victims' assistance from the federal government have provided financial assistance for victims. Restorative justice (a system of criminal justice that focuses on the rehabilitation of offenders through reconciliation with victims and the community at large) has been implemented in many courts, but many crime victims still remain disconnected from the court process and feel a sense that their victimization is not taken into account during sentencing. This is a particular concern for survivors of violent crime and survivors of murder victims.

It is also important to recognize that the American judicial system has largely contributed to the largest prison population in the world as a result of draconian and publicly charged sentencing policies such as mandatory minimums, truth in sentencing, three-strikes laws, and harsh sentencing policies for those convicted of drug possession. Not only do these policies increase the state and federal prison rate, they remove the right of the sentencing judge to use discretion in determining a custom punishment.

Connected to the rate of high incarceration is the overrepresentation of minority and economically disenfranchised offenders who proceed through the nation's court system. Although such involvement begins prior to the court process (that is, at arrest), the reality is that poor defendants and defendants of color are more likely to suffer stricter pretrial and bail conditions, remain incarcerated while their case is being processed, and suffer the "pains of incarceration" (that is, employment and family interruption) than their White and/or affluent counterparts. As mentioned earlier in this [reading], the pressure to plea bargain their case remains very high for such defendants, who desire to end the court process quickly regardless of their guilt or innocence. Finally, it is important to consider that the American court system (as with other institutions within the criminal justice system) continues to magnify the growing root problems that exist within our society today, particularly in relation to the lack of access to educational and employment opportunities (especially to those with criminal records), family involvement and reunification, and financial investment in struggling communities. As mentioned in an earlier section, problem-solving courts focus on addressing these root cause issues; however, services are provided to those who are identified in the criminal justice system.

Discussion Questions

a. In your opinion, what group of defendants is most impacted in the criminal justice system—African Americans, women, or economically disenfranchised people?
b. How can victims be better served throughout the court process?
c. What consequences may be associated with the popular culture portrayal of courtroom proceedings?

References

655 F.3d 78

(2014). U.S. Courts of Appeals-Judicial Business 2014. United States Courts. Accessed at: http://www.uscourts.gov/statistics-reports/us-courts-appeals-judicial-business-201

(2015). Administrative Office of the Court of Appeals. United States Courts. Accessed at: http://www.uscourts.gov/about-federal-courts/types-cases/appeals

(2015). United States Courts. *Court Role and Structure.* Accessed at: http://www.uscourts.gov/about-federal-courts/court-role-and-structure

(2014). History, Justice Professionals pursue a vision. National Association of Drug Court Professionals. Accessed at: http://www.nadcp.org/learn/what-are-drug-courts/drug-court-history

(2014). National Center for State Courts. Judicial Selection in the States.

Carter, D. T. (1979). *Scottsboro: A tragedy of the American South* (rev. ed.). Baton Rouge: Louisiana State University Press.

Cohen, T. D. & Reaves, B. A. (2007). Pretrial release of felony defendants in state courts (NCJ 214994). Bureau of Justice Statistics. U.S. Department of Justice. Retrieved from: http://www.bjs.gov/content/pub/pdf/prfdsc.pdf

Demuth, S. (2003) Racial and ethnic differences in pretrial release decision and outcomes: a comparison of Latino, Black, and White felony arrestees. Criminology, 41: 873–907.

Farole, D. (2010). A national assessment of public defender office caseloads. Bureau of Justice Statistics. Presented at Justice Research and Statistics Association Annual Meeting. Retrieved from http://www.jrsa.org/events/conference/presentations-10/Donald_Farole.pdf

Herberman, E., & Kyckelhahn, T. (2014). State government indigent defense expenditures, FY 2008–2012. Bureau of Justice Statistics. Retrieved from http://www.bjs.gov/content/pub/pdf/sgide0812.pdf

Judicial Council of California. (2013). Court statistics report: Statewide trends 2002–2003 through 2011–2012. Retrieved from http://www.courts.ca.gov/documents/2013-Court-Statistics-Report.pdf

Kohler, S. (1962). Case 29: Vera Institute of Justice: Manhattan Bail Project. Ford Foundation. Retrieved from https://cspcs.sanford.duke.edu/sites/default/files/descriptive/manhattan_bail_project.pdf

Labriola, M., Bradley, S., O'Sullivan, C. S., Rempel, M., & Moore, S. (2009). *A national portrait of domestic violence courts.* New York: Center for Court Innovation.

Lynch, T. (2003). The case against plea bargaining. Regulation. Cato Institute. Retrieved from http://www.cato.org/sites/cato.org/files/serials/files/regulation/2003/10/v26n3-7.pdf

Mazur, R., & Aldrich, L. (2003). What makes a domestic violence court work? Lessons from New York. *Judges' Journal*, American Bar Association. Retrieved from http://www.courtinnovation.org/pdf/what_makes_dvcourt_work.pdf

Neyfakh, L. (2014, March 23). The custom justice of "problem-solving courts": A new kind of court is reshaping the American legal system—with little oversight. *Boston Globe*. Retrieved from https://www.bostonglobe.com/ideas/2014/03/22/the-custom-justice-problem-solving-courts/PQJLC758Sgw7qQhiefT6MM/story.html

Reaves, B. (2013). Felony defendants in large urban counties, 2009–Statistical Tables. State Court Processing Statistics, Bureau of Justice Statistics. Retrieved from http://www.bjs.gov/index.cfm?ty=pbdetail&iid=4845

Rempel, M., Green, M., & Kralstein, D. (2012). The impact of adult drug courts on crime and incarceration: Findings from a multi-site quasi-experimental design. *Journal of Experimental Criminology*, *8*(2), 165–192.

Schlesinger, T. (2005). Racial and ethnic disparity in pretrial criminal processing. *JQ: Justice Quarterly*, 22(2), 170–192.

Truman, J. L., & Morgan, R. E. (2014). Nonfatal domestic violence, 2003–2012 (NCJ 244697). Bureau of Justice Statistics. Retrieved from http://www.bjs.gov/content/pub/pdf/ndv0312.pdf

United States v. Dzhokhar Tsarnaev, 2013 (13-cr-10200)

US Const. amend. IV

US Const. amend. VI

US Const. amend. VIII

US Const. amend. XIV

U.S.C. § 844

U.S.C. § 2332

U.S.C. § 2332a

Discussion Questions

1. What issues do you think come from trying to be an ethical judge, prosecutor, or juror?
2. Do you think that the way courts protect the rights of the defendant is sufficient?
3. What are your thoughts on the problem-solving courts? Do they do the job that they need to or is there a better solution?
4. Do you believe that televised court programs glamorize the court system, or do they do a good job of showing how the court system works?

CHAPTER 4

Corrections

A History of Incarceration in the United States

Marilyn D. McShane

Marilyn D. McShane, "A History of Incarceration in the United States," *Prisons in America*, pp. 19–37. Copyright © 2008 by LFB Scholarly Publishing. Reprinted with permission.

The Rise of Incarceration

The use of prisons and the popularity of an incarcerative model are tied to a broader movement in our society where the state is increasingly called upon to address community problems like crime, unemployment and disease. Local officials felt unqualified and financially unable to meet the demands of the care and treatment of the many special populations the scientific community was identifying—the mentally ill, the criminal and the handicapped. Workhouses and penitentiaries, asylums and almshouses were all developed to help the young nation deal with poverty, sickness, and sin.

The penitentiary as a model for punishing criminals was part of an international movement that dealt with the concerns of the nineteenth-century. Distaste for the violent and very public nature of sanctions such as branding, banishment, stocks and executions gave rise to a series of institutions that would better serve any evolving enlightened country. Increased scholarly understanding of the nature and behavior of man led to a new emphasis on the offender (not the system) as the deviant or guilty actor. A criminal lifestyle seemed to indicate that family and religious control or influence had broken down. A disciplined regime within the prison could restore some of the character deficiencies of the prisoner.

In his well-known book, *The State of Prisons in England and Wales*, John Howard suggested prisoners be classified according to their offenses and they be employed in useful labor. He went on to say the prisons should be tended by honest and humane gaolers (jailers), chaplains, and medical officers. Howard proposed that liquor sales to prisoners, who had the means to buy drink, be terminated. He advocated the separation of prisoners at night into small rooms or cabins and the removal of women and young offenders from the ranks of the hardened criminal (Hibbert, 1963).

The Histories of Prison Systems in America

There are two very basic assessments that can be made about the development of prison systems throughout America. The first is that most states developed in a similar fashion with the same types of financial, political, and management problems. They all suffered from incidents of scandal and corruption, they all were vulnerable to public and media censor and they all experienced doubts about the mission and goals of prisons that have led to crises in programming, operations and administration. The executive, legislative and judicial branches of government have all been overzealous regulators of the prison. Grabbing on various appendages of the corrections corpus they have tugged and torn it into a seemingly useless mass of civil service.

The second assessment is that the problems that plague prisons today are the same as they were in the very first prisons. Crowding, under funding, mismanagement, escape, violence, sexual assault, understaffing, inmate idleness, and recidivism are now, and always have been, fixtures in the institution regardless of whether it is run by the state, the federal government or private contractors. For example, in a report to the Colorado legislature in 1899, Warden C. P. Hoyt complained that there were 582 inmates in a prison built for 400 (Chapman, 1992). Keeping these ideas in mind, we can see the patterns and trends in the history of incarceration that lead us to wonder if there can be a solution to the problem that is the American prison.

The Purpose of Prison: The Pennsylvania and Auburn Systems

While there did not appear to be much debate about the need for penitentiaries in the late 1700s, the focus seemed to be on the search for the most efficient and effective method of incarceration. This resulted in the development of two contrasting styles of prison design and management. Differences between the two approaches addressed both the structure and the function of the penitentiary. The first was called the Pennsylvania (or solitary) system. Influenced by the Quakers, officials blended heavy stone architecture with a philosophy of solitary confinement. Inmates spent their entire incarceration without ever seeing another inmate. They entered and left with a head covering to insure that there was no contact between prisoners. Inmates ate, slept, and worked on individual piece production labor in their fortress-like cells. The items were basically handcrafted materials, and the quantity and quality of the goods produced were difficult to control. What officials were proudest of, however, was the routine that insured that no corruptive influence would be rendered by other inmates in this solitary rehabilitative process. "Efforts had to be made to conceal all pipes, and walls had to be a certain thickness to prevent any communication, spoken or in code, between prisoners" (Walker, 1988, p. 6). Even food was passed anonymously through a slot. By meditating on one's sins, repenting, and reading the Bible, the prisoner—reformers believed—could be saved and returned to a productive life in the community.

One of the first Pennsylvania designs was the **Eastern Penitentiary** at Cherry Hill designed by the famous architect **John Haviland**, whose work was influenced by prisons in England, Rome and Russia. Opened in 1829, the radial design of the building–with the foreboding and gloomy facade and the high, vaulted ceilings of the cells—became world famous (Miller, 1974). Haviland also built these extravagantly expensive prisons in New Jersey, Rhode Island, New York City (The Tombs), and Missouri.

The philosophy of the second type of prison system, initiated at **Auburn** prison in New York in 1819, was similar. Like in the **Pennsylvania** system, officials were deeply committed to keeping inmates from associating with one another and contaminating each other with negative ideas. The primary difference between the two, however, was that under the Auburn system inmates would work together during the day in a common area. This allowed goods to be mass-produced in an assembly-line fashion, although inmates were forbidden from communicating with each other. For this reason, this arrangement was referred to as the silent system (because they didn't talk) or the congregate system (since they worked together). After work, the inmates would return to solitary cells for the night. The cells at Auburn were eight feet long, seven feet high and three and half feet wide. Although there were over 1330 inmates in the institution, there was only contract work for 878. The contractors paid 40 to 50 cents per worker per day making shoes, collars, machinery and porcelain hollow ware (Steuben, 1879). One of the most famous Auburn-style prisons was opened in 1825 at **Ossining**, New York, and was referred to as Sing Sing. Of her visit there, reformer **Dorothy Dix** (1845) wrote,

> The officers at Sing Sing certainly deserve high praise for their efforts during the past year, at establishing and maintaining a mild form of discipline. Difficulties and serious obstacles present themselves continually ... since the internal construction and arrangements of the prison prevent separation.

Though Dix clearly favored the Pennsylvania model and opposed business or profit-making motives in prison, the Auburn system boasted better work performance and lower construction as well as operating costs. This cultivated the politicians, and more facilities were built along the Auburn model. Reports also seemed to indicate that the solitary isolation in prisons, like the Eastern, drove many men mad. The debate between the Auburn and Pennsylvania systems was indeed one of the great correctional controversies of all times. Rothman (1971) relates that dignitaries from many foreign countries were drawn into the arguments, and scholars wrote editorials and rebuttals over the advantages and disadvantages of each. Today, penologists still debate some of the basic philosophical questions of reform, work, and the negative influences of other inmates.

By the late 1800s, both sides were coming to the realization that both approaches might be ineffective in reducing criminal tendencies. The desire to give different types of treatment to different categories of offenders, such as juveniles and nonviolent criminals, led to a search for more progressive designs.

The Reformatory—Elmira

A new model of incarceration built on the theme of rehabilitation, with an emphasis on the young offender, was the reformatory. The first reformatory, Elmira in New York, was opened in 1876 under the creative supervision of Zebulon Brockway. "Elmira's inmates were exposed to academic and vocational education, as well as programs of labor designed to teach skills and instill the Protestant work ethic. A carefully planned mark and classification system allowed inmates to earn their own release and promoted internal order" (Pisciotta, 1989). As Rothman (1980) explains, there were three classifications. "The inmate entered at grade two and if he behaved himself well (fulfilling work and school assignments and committing no disciplinary infractions), he could earn up to nine marks a month, thus, six months or fifty four marks later, he could win promotion to grade one—the only grade from which he could be released." Under this system, inmates were, for the first time in the United States, released on parole. There were also three ways the inmate could be demoted: crookedness, quarreling, and disregarding the rules (Rothman, 1980).

The tenure of Zebulon Brockway was not without its alleged abuses. On several occasions, Brockway and his staff were formally questioned over incidents of beatings, sexual improprieties and torture-like punishments dealt to the young men in his care. Details of these events are chronicled by Pisciotta (1994) in his work, *Benevolent Repression* which recounts not only the achievements of this period but the potential problems with overzealous disciplinarians that have haunted the correctional system.

Despite the controversies over Brockway's performance, over the next 25 years, a dozen other reformatories, based on this new penology, were opened. They included facilities in Michigan (1877), Massachusetts (1884), Pennsylvania (1889), Minnesota (1889), Colorado (1890), Illinois (1891), Kansas (1895), Ohio (1896), and Indiana (1897) (Pisciotta, 1989). As Miller (1974, p. 108) explains, the reformatory "served to siphon off the under-thirty prison population, and was an important regulating force in prison population growth." According to Reid (1981), the reformatory movement began to decline in 1910 primarily because funds were not appropriated for the necessary trained professionals to perform the original mission.

Progressive Designs in Old Institutions

The reformatory was not the only attempt to make prisons more rehabilitative and humane. Progressives of the early twentieth century sought to modernize prisons by abolishing the lockstep and striped uniforms, liberalizing correspondence and visitation policies, and burying once and for all the rules of silence (Rothman, 1980). One of the most important figures in this struggle was **Thomas Mott Osborne**, a prison warden who anonymously spent a week as an inmate in the Auburn prison to gain insight into his problems. Certain that such a repressive environment caused deviance and brutality; he sought to create an environment where the inmate could be responsible for his own conduct (Rothman, 1980). Progressives such as Osborne and later Howard Gill sought to redesign the prison by creating communities with outdoor recreation, fund-raising events, and psychiatric services.

The Westward Expansion of Prisons

Unlike the controversy of siting prisons today, where no one seems to want a prison located "in their neighborhood," a state prison was a fiercely competitive undertaking in states and territories throughout the 1800s. The award of construction funds was sought by ambitious developers and political aspirations were tied to the belief that the location of a state prison would insure that a city would eventually become the new state's capital. In Missouri and California, for example, those bidding for the contract to build the first state prison were hoping that additional projects would come with the decision to place the state capital in the same location.

In Arizona, legislators even stooped to trickery to obtain the prison contract. In 1868 the legislature had approved prison construction in Phoenix but had failed to appropriate funds. When the issue came up again seven years later, "Jose Maria Redondo and R. B. Kelly, representatives from Yuma County, amended the bill by inserting the name Yuma where Phoenix had been. Quietly, the bill was brought before the legislature, and was signed by Governor Anson P. K. Safford" while the legislator from Phoenix, who had originally introduced the bill was outmaneuvered (Trafzer & George, 1978).

In the early 1830s, Missouri Governor John Miller proposed a site in Jefferson City for the state's first penitentiary that would strengthen the city's bid to be the state capitol (Schroeger, 1984). Designed by John Haviland, the castle-like structure operated under the Pennsylvania "solitary" system. The development of the state correctional system in Missouri was typical of many other states in that officials hoped the facility would be able to generate profits from industry and be self-supporting. The prison opened in 1836 with a forty-bed capacity and in two years was overcrowded with two inmates in each cell. The first guards employed in the system received no training. They worked 48 hours per week and were on call 24 hours a day, 7 days a week. There was no overtime, insurance, benefits or sick leave. The guards were paid $130 per year, and each person had to purchase their own whistle, club and blue serge suit. Uniforms were not adopted until 1955 (Schroeger, 1984).

The California Prison System

For the first five years of the American occupation of California, there were no fixed laws or prisons (Wilkins, 1918). There were six jails (San Francisco, San Jose, Los Angeles, Monterrey, San Diego and Santa Barbara) at the time California became a state. At the first legislative session in 1850 an extensive penal code was adopted and jails were declared to be state prisons until such time as a state prison could be built. Sheriffs were directed to work convicts on public accounts and if no work was available, they were to be transferred to a county where services were needed. However, jails at this time were flimsy and easy to escape from and serious offenders were thrown together with petty criminals. A variety of scandals ensued.

In 1851 the legislature decided to put an end to the debate over building a prison and ordered the state to lease out the convicts. Prisoners were leased to General Vallejo and General Estill after they posted a $100,000 bond supporting their promise to provide food, clothing, and shelter for their charges. The lessees would build a temporary shelter for housing and provide the tools and chains as well as the expense of the guards, wardens, etc. The Governor appointed Prison Inspectors, volunteers, who would make prison rules and enforce standards of care (Wilkins, 1918).

Women prisoners could not be employed with the men but they could work separately as they lived and ate separately. There were only three women incarcerated in the early 1850s; Scotch Mary, Dolores and Russian Kate) and all had children by high ranking guards in the system which caused a scandal. All three were discharged by 1854.

At this time, sheriffs received $1 per mile for transporting the convicted to prison and overestimating mileage was a well-known form of corruption. If prisoners escaped, the lessees would have to post the reward (up to $2500) for their safe return. Escapes were not uncommon as much of the work the prisoners performed was outside the prison, even outside the county. Once, four to five convicts were sent with a guard to prospect for a gold mine in Mariposa County. The guard returned alone. In addition, in 1851, all 25 prisoners escaped and General Vallejo used the opportunity to convert an old hulk into a prison boat to house the offenders. This was consistent with his plan to develop the north end of the bay where the Army Headquarters at Benicia and a port for Pacific Mail Steamships would be. He hoped that the town of Vallejo would be named the state capitol, and he would receive the contract to construct state buildings using inmate labor, but the legislature rejected this idea. Disappointed, General Vallejo withdrew from the deal and left Estill with the lease (Wilkins, 1918).

The framers of the 1851 Act never anticipated over 50 inmates at any one time. The lessees expected free labor from a small, compact body of men who would be easily guarded, cheaply fed and confined at night on a prison ship.

The legislature directed the prison inspectors and the commissioner of public buildings to spend $10,000 on a 20 acre prison site at Quentin Point. Named after an Indian Chief, historians believe the "San" was later added as Americans attached "San" or "Santa" to everything they believed was Spanish. On July 14, 1852, the hulk with 40–50 convicts was moored at San Quentin as the prisoners built temporary quarters and offices for staff and dug wells. Within one year, 100 inmates were crammed on the ship which grew to 150 as four men were placed in an 8 foot x 8 foot cell. Estill established a brick factory to build the prison with, but the state did not want to reimburse this expense and construction stalled (Wilkins, 1918).

Meanwhile disease was rampant on the ship. Reports criticized conditions, long overlooked, and the state tried to terminate the lease on the offenders. Estill, who was now a state senator, fought back and all that seemed to change was that the Prison Inspectors were no longer allowed their $500 personal expenses. Estill moved the most trustworthy prisoners to temporary sleeping quarters on land.

There were 83 escapes in 1854, some alone, some in groups. The largest group of escaping inmates was 22. Some took boats from the nearby area, others escaped into the brush and woods of Marin County. Upset residents gave chase but the heavy fog in the area and the tendency for the moisture to clog muskets made pursuit difficult and dangerous. Often guards and inmates were killed in escapes and escape attempts. Concerned over lowered property values surrounding the prison, Governor Bigler called on the Prison Inspectors and Legislature to do a special investigative report. The findings were that the principle cause of escape was the trusty system where inmates were unsupervised, sometimes roaming around the county on errands or gone for days at a time. Rumors persisted about "bars" operating in prison areas and that guards were undisciplined, lazy and often drunk on duty. Investigators believed the number of escapes and deaths were actually higher than reported and called for the law to be modified to insure that inmates would only work on prison property (Wilkins, 1918).

At this same time, construction had begun on San Quentin which was now set to hold 300 inmates, far more than anyone ever imagined. Officers' quarters and administration offices were on the first floor with tiers of cells on the second, third and fourth floors. One of the oldest facilities still in use today, San Quentin has undergone significant renovations, but remains rich in historical presence.

Mining, Territories and Prisons for the Lawless

Unlike the rapidly developing trade and industry states, territories like Utah, Arizona, Colorado, Montana and Alaska were just being settled when the need for prisons arose. Federal interests in having peaceful, orderly areas for families to ranch and mine, establish homes and contribute toward the young nation's powerful image had the government carefully monitoring the territories. Gold rushes and land fights, the vast wealth that changed hands daily, the flood of bars, brothels, and gun fights emphasized the dangerous lawlessness that pervaded the area. Officials feared that news accounts of scandals, vigilante justice, and bands of outlaws would curtail the westward migration of decent God-fearing families who would play a vital role in America's economic growth.

To insure order in the territories, weak law enforcers were quickly replaced and requests for territorial jails and prisons were funded expediently. In some instances, territories had prisons before statehood was sought or a state capital. Still, the politics of site selection and control of the prisons was as controversial as everywhere else. In Colorado, an ambitious newcomer, attorney Thomas Macon lobbied for the territory's prison to be at Canon City. As a member of the territorial legislature, he agreed to support his cronies' efforts to make Denver the future state capital in return for their votes for his penitentiary site. In 1867, the U.S. Congress authorized the Colorado Territory to use its entire fiscal revenue from 1866 to construct their penitentiary, which was the sum of $40,000. Although some of the territories' facilities were only small log cabins, the Colorado prison was an imposing two story, 40-cell stone structure (Chapman, 1992).

In 1871 the federal government authorized the building of Montana's territorial prison at Deer Lodge although it reverted to the state in 1889 when it was admitted to the union (Edgerton, 2004). As were the other territorial prisons in Utah, Arizona (Yuma) and Colorado, it was overcrowded soon after it was built. Alaska suffered through long periods of neglect from the government as a civil and judicial district even before it became a territory. An outbreak of smallpox in 1892 meant the makeshift jail would have to be abandoned and the weeks of delay in correspondence with Washington led U. S. Marshals to improvise inmate care including using a moored schooner and a rented house. It wasn't until after the Klondike gold rush that Alaska became a territory in 1912 and funds were set aside to build a jail. Unfortunately, no additional money was allocated to heat the facility and it sat unused for quite some time. The Federal Bureau of Prisons provided oversight of an Alaskan jail system until the territory became a state in 1959 (Keve, 1992).

The 1930s–1940s: Social Problems and Prison Responses

The 1930s and the Great Depression brought many socio-economic problems that changed the structure and function of American prisons. Nationwide, institutions suffered from economic and political neglect. Touring the Texas prisons in 1930, one legislator commented that they were "not fit for a dog" (Martin and Ekland-Olson, 1987). Attempts to make prisons profitable or at least self-sustaining meant that institutions were built on remote farms where crops and livestock were tended by inmates. Growing cities, particularly capitols, no longer wanted unsightly prison facilities within their boundaries.

The Depression also meant years of record high unemployment, and Prohibition meant bootlegging and organized crime. The FBI grew to be a powerful crime-fighting establishment under J. Edgar Hoover, and G-men rounded up "gangsters" considered the most dangerous in the country. Looking for the most secure facility possible, the government adopted a military prison at Alcatraz, California. This island prison off the coast of San Francisco was described by the Attorney General as

> ... the ultimate punishment society could inflict upon men short of killing them, the point of no return for multiple losers, the threat which harassed or malicious wardens could dangle over unruly charges, the one place in the American penal system that made not even a pretense at rehabilitation, whose one avowed aim was to confine and punish—the great garbage can of the San Francisco Bay into which the Feds dumped its most rotten apples.

Indeed, Alcatraz was equipped to be escape proof. It had automatic locking devices, a tear gas release system, and bars over all the sewer outlets. As time went on, however, incarceration without rehabilitation became unpopular, the cost of running Alcatraz became prohibitive, and two very highly publicized escape attempts made the institution less worthwhile; it was finally closed in 1963.

During the 1940s, all of the problems of limited resources, violence, and overcrowding were put on the back burner while the production of clothing for the war effort took priority. According to the Bureau of Justice Statistics, during WWII the country's prison population declined by nearly 50,000 in five years as most of the pool of potential offenders was drafted. By 1946, the incarceration rate had dropped to 99 per 100,000. This trend was seen again during the Vietnam Era when the prison population declined by 30,000 in the years 1961–68. The 1968 incarceration rate dropped to the lowest point since the late 1920s.

The Prison Image Problem

Prisons have historically been plagued by an unprofessional image. According to Carleton (1971), there are several reasons for this. First, the locations of the facilities were, especially across the South and Midwest, remote farms. Employees drawn from these rural sites were undereducated and unsophisticated. The culture conflict that developed between the city inmates and the country guards usually resulted in power struggles and brutality. Another related problem was that there was no systematic officer training taking place. Officers had little of no understanding of the broader goals of penology. The salaries, as shown in the case of Missouri and California, were exceptionally low. Likewise in Louisiana, a guard in 1945 made between $130 and $180 per month. However, one of the most serious problems in rural prisons was that few guards were even employed. At Angola prison in Louisiana in 1942 there were only 14 civilian employees whose duties were "purely custodial" (Carleton, 1971). In most instances, the toughest inmates were selected to supervise the others. Parker (1986) describes the Arkansas system:

> ... in the absence of sufficient free world employees, a hierarchy developed among the inmates. Long-line workers were called rankmen. Inmates who worked without armed supervision were called do-pops. These two groups lived together in the wooden barracks. The inmates in authority were called trustees, and lived apart from other inmates. Along with authority went special privileges, including being able to run money making enterprises. The long-line rider sold food and drinks in the field. The floorwalker sold beds and mattresses.

In evaluating the problems historically faced by prison officials in Louisiana, Carleton (1971) touches on factors common in most states during the period from 1900 to 1950. First, public opinion, the ultimate arbiter of policy formation, was not interested in the prison system. The public abandoned it, ignored it, and gave it no support. When this happens, the void represented by the citizens' lack of interest is filled by political control. Time and time again, efforts by a few dedicated reformers were subverted by the insurmountable costs accompanying improvements and the disfavor this incurred with politicians. Thirdly, the more contemporary penological goal of rehabilitation, perhaps because of its associated expenses, has been unable to overcome the farm-for-profit image that many officials and perhaps some of the public still maintain.

Finally, one of the most damaging policies in prison operations was the use of management positions as gifts of political patronage. In many states, jobs running prisons were given as rewards to political supporters or to family members and friends. Jacobs (1977, p. 20) describes circumstances in Illinois:

> Elmer Greene, for example, former sheriff of Lank County became the Stateville/Joliet warden in 1926. As Sheriff he had earned the indebtedness of Governor Len Small by helping the latter sway public opinion in Waukegan, where Small had been tried (and found innocent) of converting public funds to his own use. ... As warden, Greene considered it a matter of course to require employees to contribute to the governor's political party and to the payment of the $650,000 judgment that had been entered against Small in a related civil suit.

One of the chief consequences of political ties is that wardens or prison superintendents have traditionally held office for very short periods of time. When the reformist warden of Sing, Thomas Mott Osborne, resigned in 1916 after less than two years, he was the eighth man to leave that office in twelve years (Takagi, 1975). Theoretically, a short tenure disrupts prison operations, destabilizes other employees, and impedes the progress of planned reforms.

A study by Lunden (1957) examined 612 wardens who had held office in 43 states over a period of 50 years. He found that 37 percent of the officials served 2 years or less, 24 percent held office from 3 to 4 years and another 26 percent served between 5 and 9 years. This means that 87 percent were in office less than 10 years. The author explained that "In the 50 years from 1906 to 1955, the annual rate of turnover in wardenships varied from the lowest of 3.4 in 1930 to the highest of 35.6 percent in 1935" (p. 15). In Missouri, no warden served over four years in the period from 1880 to 1920 as they changed with each governor (Schroeger, 1984). The same happened in Arizona where the warden of the Yuma State Prison changed almost every two years. Another interesting phenomenon that Lunden (1957, p. 15) refers to is the in-and-out of power career. "Twenty-seven wardens were in and out of office twice, 5 three times, and 1 four times." He relates that "No facts are available to explain this revolving-door procedure, but in all probability political patronage played an important part in the changes."

The Civil Rights Revolution and Experiments in Treatment

The 1960s presented this country with human rights challenges that were met with reform legislation, innovative programs and court cases that changed the policies and practices of prisons nationwide. In 1963, Attorney General Robert Kennedy closed the Alcatraz prison, perhaps as a reflection of his combative relationship with FBI Director J. Edgar Hoover but most likely because of the awareness that image no longer trumped practical expenditures. The labeling perspective presented by criminologists created an awareness of the need to explore deinstitutionalization, due process, diversion and decriminalization. Experiments with shock probation placed many offenders in prison for only short periods of time and the *Prisoner Rehabilitation Act* and the *Narcotic Addict Rehabilitation Act* provided prison treatment initiatives. In 1964, the Supreme Court's decision in *Cooper v. Pate*, meant that prisoners could sue for violations of their constitutional rights, which mirrored the growing civil rights movement around the U.S.

The decade between the Attica riot of 1971 and the New Mexico riot of 1980 was one of political turmoil and a rapidly changing correction's landscape. Protests on the outside were *Furman v. Georgia* (1972) struck down the death penalty, converting death row offender's terms to life in prison. The *Vocational Rehabilitation Act* was passed at about the same time that most states were maximizing work release programs. Prison industries were revived under the *Prison Industry Enhancement Act* and *Dothard v. Rawlinson* cleared the way for more females to be hired as correctional officers. Despite many promising treatment initiatives, the optimism of a program friendly experimental movement was derailed by Robert Martinson's "Nothing Works" article published in 1974.

The dramatic increases in prison populations throughout the 1980s led many jurisdictions to search for meaningful alternative punishments. In 1982 Georgia began Intensive Supervision Probation which was soon copied by most other states. The first boot camps opened soon afterward as did electronic monitoring. Policymakers wanted to appear conservative and tough on crime, despite the need to save money in the face of ballooning correctional expenses. Private prisons were contracted as another way to potentially reduce costs while still appearing "tough on crime." Legislators believed, despite some evidence to the contrary that their constituents were dissatisfied with rehabilitation efforts, punitive and willing to spend whatever it would take to lock up offenders for ever-increasing periods of time.

Incarceration From the Jacksonian Era to the Drug War Era

Historians often label the early development of prisons as the Jacksonian Era 1825–1850. This period is dominated by the large fortress like institutions. Support for solitary confinement was eventually offset by the need to establish factory enterprises that would help make the prisons self-sustaining. In the south, large plantations produced crops and livestock for consumption as well as sale. Critics of the large scale warehousing and oppressive conditions were able to make piecemeal reforms toward more humane conditions and the implementation of some programs aimed at improving the future for inmates. The Progressive Era, 1850 to 1900 was characterized by a medical model of corrections that led to experiments with treatment facilities, inmate self-government and parole. Despite attempts to make prisons impressive fortresses that protected society and reformed the individual, problems of overcrowding, unhealthy conditions, understaffing and mismanagement were common.

The period from 1900 to 1940 is often referred to as a Bureaucratic or Business Era where leasing, farm work and road building crews [...] reflected the states' interest in finding alternative arrangements for funding incarceration. The Modern Era in corrections, from about 1940 to 1980, refers to a period where more emphasis was on efficient operations, the installation of technology to enhance security, and the professionalizing of the officer workforce. Finally, the Drug War Era, beginning in the early 1980s reflects the political emphasis on combating the sale and use of narcotics throughout the country. Waves of prison facility construction and tougher sentencing laws made this period infamous for its get-tough approach to addressing what was perceived to be a major social problem. Still, overcrowding and under funding has meant that there is pressure on officials to find more alternatives and cost-cutting measures to sustain the corrections network. Private prisons and upgraded "self-pay" jails like those in Santa Ana, California (Steinhauer, 2007) where low security inmates can pay anywhere from $75 to 127 per day to have clean, quiet, upscale facilities to serve their sentences in seem likely to continue debates about discrimination and differing levels of justice in this country.

References

Carleton, M. (1971). *Politics and punishment.* Baton Rouge, LA: Louisiana State University Press.

Chapman, J. (Ed.). (1992). *This is the prison: Colorado Penitentiary, Canon City* (3rd ed.) Canon City, CO: Colorado Territorial Prison Museum.

Clauss, F. J. (1981). *Alcatraz: Island of many mistakes.* Menlo Park, CA: Briarcliff Press.

Dix, D. (1845). *Remarks on prisons and prison discipline in the United States.* Montclair, NJ: Patterson Smith (reprinted 1967).

Edgerton, K. (2004). *Montana justice: Power, punishment and the penitentiary.* Spokane: University of Washington Press.

Hibbert, C. (1963). *The roots of evil.* Boston: Little, Brown.

Jacobs, J. (1977). *Stateville: The penitentiary in mass society.* Chicago: University of Chicago Press.

Keve, P. W. (1992, Winter). The BOP's Alaskan adventure. *Federal Prisons Journal,* 43–47, 55.

Lunden, W. A. (1957). The tenure and turnover of state prison wardens. *American Journal of Corrections, 19,* 6, 14.

Martin, S., & Ekland-Olson, S. (1987). *Texas prisons.* Austin, TX: Texas Monthly Press.

Miller, M. (1974). At hard labor: Rediscovering the 19th century prison. *Issues in Criminology, 9,* 1, 91–114.

Parker, M. L. (1986). *Judicial intervention in correctional institutions: The Arkansas odyssey.* Unpublished doctoral dissertation. Huntsville, TX: Sam Houston State University.

Pisciotta, A. (1994). *Benevolent repression: Social control and the American reformatory-prison movement.* NY: New York University Press.

Pisciotta, A. (1989). Eugenics, social control and the state: Progressive penology at the Indiana Reformatory, 1897–1923. Paper presented at the annual meeting of the Academy of Criminal Justice Sciences, Washington, DC.

Reid, S. (1981). *The correctional system.* New York: Holt, Rinehart & Winston.

Rothman, D. (1971). *The discovery of the asylum.* Boston: Little, Brown.

Rothman, D. (1980). *Conscience and convenience.* Boston: Little, Brown.

Schroeger, D. (1983–84). The course of corrections in Missouri, 1833–1983. *Manual of the State of Missouri.* Jefferson City: Office of the Secretary of State.

Steinhauer, J. (2007, April 29). Great deal: clean cell, nice neighbors. *Houston Chronicle,* A3.

Steuben. (1879, May 29). A visit to Auburn Prison. *New York Evangelist, 50,* 22. (APS Online)

Takagi, P. (1975). The Walnut Street Jail: A penal reform to centralize the powers of the state. *Federal Probation, 39,* 4, 18–25.

Trafzer, C., & George, S. (1978). *Prison centennial, 1876–1976.* Yuma, AZ: Rio Colorado Press.

Walker, D. (1988). *Penology for profit.* College Station, TX: Texas A&M University.

Wilkins, J. H. (1918). The evolution of a state prison: Historical narrative of the ten years from 1851 to 1861, during the period when the care and employment of convicts was turned over to lessees. *The Bulletin (San Francisco).* June 13 to July 10.

Online Exercise

Go to the website for corrections history (the URL is below) and find an article called "A Tale of the Tombs" about the New York City Department of Corrections infamous facility built in the late 1830s.

http://www.correctionhistory.org/html/chronicl/nycdoc/html/histry3a.html

Read the short article and make notes about:

1. the problems the facility encountered in its construction
2. the executions that were conducted there
3. the housing arrangements made for children and women
4. How do you think this period in the Tombs history compares to today's correctional approach?

Questions for Thought and Discussion

1. What were some of the reforms of the progressive era in prisons?
2. What themes and similarities seem to characterize the conditions of prisons throughout their development and even today?
3. Compare and contrast the Pennsylvania System and the Auburn systems and give examples of each.
4. Who were some of the contributors to and shapers of the developing prison system and how did they influence the nature of prisons and prison reform?

Books You May Want to Read

Rideau, W., & Wikberg, R. (1992). *Life sentences.* New York: Times Books
Hassine, Victor. (1996). *Life without parole: Living in prison today.* Los Angeles: Roxbury.

Movies You May Want to See

Brubaker
Cool Hand Luke

Discussion Questions

1. Do you think that social issues have changed how we handle punishment?
2. Do you believe that incarceration is most important when punishing offenders?
3. How do you think you would handle working in a prison or being a prisoner?
4. What are your thoughts on the death penalty?

CHAPTER 5

Juvenile Justice

Policing and Juveniles

John T. Whitehead and Steven P. Lab

John T. Whitehead and Steven P. Lab, "Policing and Juveniles," *Juvenile Justice: An Introduction*, pp. 169–202, 449–505.

Key Terms

"broken windows" policing
community policing
deadly force
disproportionate minority contact
gatekeeper role
juvenile curfew laws
mission distortion
police effectiveness
police use of excessive force
problem-oriented policing
professional policing
restorative justice conferences
school resource officers (SROs)
school-to-prison pipeline

WHAT YOU NEED TO KNOW

- In 2015, police arrested 709,333 persons under age 18. The majority of these (59 percent) were referred to juvenile court jurisdiction. The police used their discretion to handle and release 26 percent of these youths.

- A new view of the police role is one of community or problem-solving policing. This view tries to include the community as a partner in defining and solving crime and disorder problems.
- "Broken windows" policing places emphasis on policing disorder such as loitering and vagrants because this model sees disorder as a factor associated with street crime. The theory is that if police can reduce disorder, crime will also decrease.
- Research indicates that some departments using traditional police strategies refer to it as community or problem-solving policing. So not all departments are actually following the directions of innovators.
- African Americans generally hold less positive views of the police than whites. Many youths appear to be either indifferent or less than overwhelming in their support of police.
- Racial issues have been at the center of media and political attention in the last five years. Particular concern has arisen over police shootings and practices such as Stop, Question, and Frisk.
- Disproportionate minority contact refers to the overrepresentation of any racial group in arrest and court statistics compared to the proportion of that group in the population.
- Research indicates that juvenile curfew laws are not effective in reducing crime.

Introduction

Policing brings to mind images of arresting suspects, shooting at criminals, writing traffic tickets, testifying in court, driving on patrol, and interrogating murder suspects in the detective bureau. Police still do these things, but they also engage in activities that many people are not aware of. For instance, today police also lead community meetings to discuss the extent and causes of neighborhood crime and disorder. Together with community members, they are searching for solutions to urban problems. Police go to homes of juveniles who are on probation to assist probation officers in making curfew checks and try to determine what can be done to help juvenile probationers stay out of trouble and adjust. Police also facilitate **restorative justice conferences**, in which, for instance, a burglary victim meets a juvenile burglar and explains precisely how the burglary impacted the victim. Supporters for both sides are present and, with the help of the police officer leader, they work out an agreement on how the youth can make amends for what he or she did.

So policing today means much more than it did 35 years ago. Back then police were wondering how they could adjust car patrol to reduce crime. They were wondering if more cars would reduce crime or if faster response time would reduce crime. Today police are raising questions about the definition of policing. What is policing? What role do the police have in a democratic society? These questions and the solutions raised so far are having important effects on how police interact with juveniles.

In this [reading,] we will look at police and juveniles. We will discuss the changing police role, particularly as it involves contact with youths. We will also look at attitudes and the police, including both citizen attitudes toward the police and police attitudes toward citizens, some recent developments in policing, the effectiveness of policing, and improper use of police force.

Statistics on Police Work With Juveniles

The FBI's Uniform Crime Reporting (UCR) Program presents the basic picture of what police do with juvenile offenders. Other than traffic and neglect cases, in 2015, police arrested 709,333 persons under age 18. (Note: This number is reported in the FBI UCR, Tables 38 and 41. The *OJJDP Statistical Briefing Book* reports an estimate of 921,600 such arrests.) The majority of these (59 percent) were referred to juvenile court jurisdiction. Twenty-six percent were handled within the police department and released. Eight percent were referred to criminal or adult court, and the rest were referred to a welfare agency or to another police agency (FBI, 2017).

Two points are noteworthy. First, the percentage of offenders that police refer to juvenile court (approximately 60 percent) is similar to 1980. Second, the fact that 26 percent of the juveniles taken into custody are simply handled and released shows the discretion that police have with juveniles. Such discretion can have critical consequences for youths. A youth released in this manner does not have to worry that if he or she commits a new delinquent act a year later the first one will be held against him or her and he or she will be treated as someone with a prior record. The juvenile may be treated as someone without any record. If police impose any racial or other biases into their decisions, those racial biases can have serious effects on later decisions by police, prosecutors, and judges. Much of this discretion is hidden and thus difficult to discover.

WEB ACTIVITY

One source of information about juvenile arrest statistics is the *OJJDP Statistical Briefing Book*, available at www.ojjdp.gov/ojstatbb. Arrest statistics can also be found in the FBI's *Uniform Crime Reports*, available at www.fbi.gov. See especially Table 68, Police Disposition: Juvenile Offenders Taken into Custody, 2015.

A highlight of the arrest statistics on juveniles is that in 2015 there were an estimated 605 arrests of juveniles for murder (FBI, 2017). This is a 38 percent decrease compared to 2006. In addition, the 2015 number is down considerably from the peak year of 1993, when there were approximately 3,790 juvenile arrests for murder. In 2015, juvenile arrests for all crimes were down 56 percent from 2006. Property crime arrests were down 48 percent. Drug abuse violations were down 50 percent (OJJDP, 2017a).

The overall crime decline that started in the 1990s has yet to be fully explained. Some credit the crime decrease to changes in policing that involved targeting disorder based on a belief that loitering, panhandling, and other types of disorder cause crime (Braga & Bond, 2008). Some credit the decrease to the increase in imprisonment that has been going on for more than 20 years. Others argue that broader trends seem to be at work. Zimring (2007; 2012), for example, argues that crime also decreased in Canada even though that country did not use the police tactics that New York City used. In the next section we will discuss the police role in general and also devote more attention to the effectiveness of police efforts to reduce disorder as a strategy to reduce crime and delinquency.

Professional Policing and Juveniles

For much of the twentieth century, police tried to be professional crime fighters. This often translated into police driving in one- or two-officer patrol cars until they saw something suspicious or received a radio call to respond to a crime or a call for service. The rationale was that quick response to calls would enable the police to apprehend suspects or deal quickly with problems that citizens reported to central dispatch. Many called this the **professional policing** model. Others have called it "911 policing" because 911 is the emergency phone number used to contact police.

There were several problems with this professional or 911 policing model. One was that increased professionalism did not reduce crime. Studies showed, for example, that simply increasing the extent of patrol in a given sector did not reduce crime. In addition, research showed that quicker response time did not have dramatic effects on crime (Walker, 2011), and that much of a police officer's shift did not even involve crime. Citizens call the police for all types of problems that are not directly crime-related. Some of the actions prompting those calls could escalate into crime, but many of the calls occur because people regard the police as government workers who are available seven days a week, 24 hours a day, and thus should be able to deal with their problems.

Another problem with the professional model is that it built barriers between the police and citizens. When officers sit in one- or two-person cars, they do not have the opportunity to interact with citizens. Interaction can have positive consequences. It can alert police to problems in the neighborhood, or it can produce tips about who might be engaged in either criminal activity or disorder. The old-fashioned foot patrol officer could get to know both neighborhood problems and tips about who might be causing the problems by having opportunities to meet with shopkeepers, pedestrians, and people sitting or standing near corners or other gathering places. Professional policing decreased the number of foot patrol officers and put the police car as a barrier between the officer and citizens.

Custody Rules with Youths

Police action in relation to detaining youths has been an interesting problem since the inception of the juvenile court. Under the *parens patriae* doctrine, the use of arrest tactics typically invoked by police in relation to adult offenders would normally be avoided with youths. Fingerprinting, photographing, and incarcerating youths were all either forbidden or severely restricted. The shift to a more punitive orientation in recent years, including mandatory sentencing and more liberal waiver procedures, has resulted in major changes to police procedure and practice with youths.

Perhaps the clearest rules for police handling of youths involve holding juveniles in secure facilities. When a youth is taken into custody there are clear guidelines that must be followed in terms of the custody facility. Youths must be segregated from adults. This segregation has to be physical, visual, and aural (sound) separation. These requirements pose special problems for many police departments. Those that are very small, especially in rural, isolated areas, typically have very small jails where it is often impossible to separate the youths from adults. The choice facing the police, therefore, is either violating the laws on conditions of holding youths in custody or releasing the youths outright.

The rules governing fingerprinting and taking photographs of youths vary from state to state and have changed a great deal over the past several decades. The traditional prohibition against these practices has been replaced with rules outlining who and under what circumstances photos and fingerprints can be gathered, as well as the use and disposition of those records. The state of Ohio, for example, requires judicial consent before fingerprinting and photographing of juveniles is undertaken (Ohio Revised Code [ORC], §2151.313). The law allows the police to obtain these records without judicial consent if the arrest involves a felony or an act besides a traffic offense or minor misdemeanor. The police must immediately inform the juvenile court that this action has been taken, and provide details on the youths and number of fingerprints and photos taken. Further, these materials are to be destroyed within 30 days unless the youth is adjudicated delinquent for an act that is a violent misdemeanor or felony, at which time the judge will set parameters for the retention and/or destruction of the records (ORC, §2151.313). These rules illustrate an attempt to balance protection of the child with the needs of the juvenile and criminal justice systems.

Other states take a more liberal approach to allowing fingerprinting and photographing of youths. Florida, for example, lists a number of specific crimes for which these actions should be taken (Florida Statutes, §985.11). At the same time, fingerprints and photographs can be taken of any child taken into custody, regardless of the offense, at the sole discretion of the agency. These records are considered confidential but can be shared with other agencies and are part of the youth's permanent record that is accessible by the adult court (Florida Statutes, §985.11).

Most states allow some form of fingerprinting and photographing of youths. These requirements, however, vary from state to state and from what are permissible with adults taken into custody. This is one example of how policing youthful misbehavior raises new and unique challenges for the professional police model.

Interrogation Tactics with Juvenile Suspects

[T]he Supreme Court has held that a juvenile suspect can waive the privilege against self-incrimination and the right to consult with an attorney and go ahead and agree to be interrogated. Then a court will judge the voluntariness of any confession by looking at all the circumstances of the interrogation and confession. However, the Court did note in 2011 that police should consider the age of the child as one of the custody factors. In other words, a youth may feel less free in an interrogation situation, and this factor affects how a judge assesses the voluntariness of any apparent waiver (*J.D.B. v. North Carolina*, 2011).

A study by Barry Feld examined the transcripts of 66 police interrogations of juvenile suspects in Minneapolis, Minnesota. Eighty percent of the juveniles waived their *Miranda* rights and agreed to interrogation. On the positive side, police immediately stopped questioning those youths who invoked their rights. On the negative side, police questioned juvenile suspects in much the same manner as they questioned adults. The police often suggested that talking would be beneficial to the suspect, or they phrased the warnings as if they were just a bureaucratic formality instead of a serious constitutional issue with important consequences for the suspect (Feld, 2006). Feld also concluded that the behavior of 16- and

17-year-olds parallels the behavior of most adult suspects; the adult waiver rate is also about 80 percent. So he thinks that 16- and 17-year-olds are about as psychologically mature as adults and understand their rights to the same extent as adults.

In a second study, Feld (2013a) analyzed the interrogation files (including transcripts) of 307 juvenile suspects in four Minnesota counties. As in his 2006 article, Feld noted that 16- and 17-year-olds are similar to adults but that younger youths "lack ability to understand and competence to exercise rights" (Feld, 2013a:24). So he recommends that youths 15 and younger be required to consult with an attorney prior to waiving constitutionals rights. Based on his research, he also recommends that interrogations not be allowed to take longer than four hours and that all interrogations be recorded.

In a study of 57 recorded interrogation sessions from 17 police agencies, no attorneys were present for any of the interrogations. The author concludes that this total absence of attorneys "suggests the widespread occurrence that juvenile suspects are making interrogation decisions without the knowledge or advice of counsel" (Cleary, 2013).

An important concern is the danger of false confessions. More than one-third of proven false confessions come from suspects under 18 years of age. In a recent study of 193 14- to 17-year-olds incarcerated for serious offenses, Malloy, Shulman, and Cauffman (2014) found that 17 percent of the youths stated they had made a false confession to police, 81 percent reported having been threatened, and 21 percent experienced force. Feld thinks that 16- and 17-year-olds are similar to adults, but that younger suspects do need greater protection. He argues for recording all confessions as a safeguard (Feld, 2006).

An intriguing issue about police interrogation techniques is that although the police think they are very good at detecting deception in suspects, research indicates that they are not. Although interrogation experts claim 85 percent accuracy, research puts police accuracy at about 50 percent. What is particularly disturbing about juvenile suspects, moreover, is that juveniles often exhibit behaviors that the interrogation experts claim are deceptive, such as slouching and not making eye contact with the interrogator. Therefore, when a youth is just "being youthful," an interrogator will interpret that behavior as evidence that the youth is lying. Another problem is suggestibility. The desire to please or the tendency to trust authority figures, for example, can influence youths to confess falsely (Meyer & Reppucci, 2007).

In their study of more than 300 police investigators in Baltimore, Meyer and Reppucci (2007) found that police used the same interrogation techniques with children under age 14, youths ages 14–17, and adults (age 18 and older). Police believed that children and youths outside the context of interrogation do not understand some words used by adults but then stated that they thought that children, youths, and adults all understand their rights in the interrogation session and the purpose of interrogation. The researchers found that 83 percent of their sample used body language as an indicator of deception despite the problem noted previously that youths are likely to slouch and avoid eye contact. Finally, the Baltimore police also reported using coercive and deceptive interrogation techniques with suspects, regardless of age, even though there is greater likelihood of getting inaccurate reports from youthful suspects (Meyer & Reppucci, 2007). In summary, many juveniles waive their rights, and consent to interrogation. Despite age-related problems with interrogating youthful suspects, many police investigators use techniques, including threats and force, that can lead to inaccurate statements and even false confessions from juvenile suspects.

The Police and Juveniles

A long record of research on the role of police in controlling juveniles has described that role as one of "**gatekeeper**" to the juvenile justice system. This means that police officers exercise considerable discretion with juveniles; officers are often the ones who decide whether a juvenile is processed in the juvenile justice system. Police also experience conflicting feelings toward juveniles. Police want to prevent and control crime, but they also feel a duty to prevent harm to the juvenile and prevent delinquency. These conflicts can result in police taking different actions with juveniles than they would with adults (Brown, Novak, & Frank, 2009).

An observational study of 20 nonurban police departments in southwestern Ohio confirmed the gatekeeper role. Field observation resulted in 195 encounters between police and juveniles ages 13–17 years. In cases involving juveniles initially assuming the role of a suspect or a disputant, only 23 (16 percent) of those 138 juveniles were actually arrested. In cases in which a juvenile actually committed a crime, only 42 percent of those cases ended in an arrest. As previous research found:

> the deviant behavior of juveniles will more often than not involve less serious offenses, and nonurban police appear to be just as inclined as urban cops to act as "gatekeepers" by resolving juvenile encounters informally without an arrest (Liederbach, 2007:119).

In traditional terminology, much police work with juveniles involves order maintenance rather than crime fighting, as well as discretion (see, e.g., Hurst, Frank, & Browning, 2000; Walker, 1992).

An interesting side note from this Ohio study is that the most frequent police encounters with juveniles were traffic-related offenses, including speeding, accidents, violations, and others. Part of the reason for this may be that it was a study of suburban police departments and the automobile is a central feature of suburban life. So while older studies involved police on foot making contact with juveniles, many of the police contacts with juveniles now involve traffic-related problems (Liederbach, 2007). The importance of traffic stops is also seen in an analysis of contacts between the police and the public (age 16 and older) in 2005. About 18 million people—41 percent of all contacts that year—reported that their most recent contact with the police was as a driver in a traffic stop, most frequently for speeding (Durose, Smith, & Langan, 2007). Clearly, we are a nation of drivers, and this affects even contacts with police for both juveniles and adults.

Prior research indicated that gender (being male) and demeanor are important correlates of police officers' decisions to take a youth into custody (see, e.g., Morash 1984; Lundman 1994). Most of that research was based on observational study of police. One study took a different approach. Allen (2005) surveyed more than 400 police officers in Cleveland, Ohio, and found that disrespect on the part of a youth, being out late at night, being male, and indicators of suspicious behavior, such as clothing and hair style, were factors influencing the police officers to conclude that the youth should be taken into custody or at least stopped and questioned. Allen (2005) commented that clothing and hairstyle could result in more black youths being stopped or taken into custody but also noted that there are more black police officers today, which should reduce discrimination against black youths.

Brown et al. (2009) conducted systematic social observation of street-level police officers in Cincinnati, Ohio, from 1997 to 1998. They found that police are more likely to arrest juveniles than adults and more likely to arrest juveniles in distressed communities. A number of factors influenced police to arrest both adults and juveniles, namely offense seriousness, quantity of evidence, commission of a crime in the officer's presence, race (white), and intoxication. Interestingly, disrespect on the part of an adult suspect but not a juvenile suspect also influenced officers to make an arrest (Brown et al., 2009).

In summary, the police continue to operate as gatekeepers to the juvenile justice system. They exercise considerable discretion in their encounters with juveniles. It is critical that police have guidelines to ensure that such discretion is not abused.

Police Use of Excessive Force (Brutality)

Police use of excessive force is a sensitive topic and thus it is difficult to gain accurate information about its extent. Like any profession, police will not just open up and reveal professional secrets. They will not readily disclose how frequently and under what circumstances they may use excessive force. So researchers often survey citizens to derive estimates of police use of force.

Based on an observational study of police–citizen encounters over three decades ago, Albert Reiss reported that teens were the most likely targets of the least damaging type of police brutality, namely abusive language and commands to "move on." Such commands were particularly frequent in the summer when youths living in the ghetto were likely to spend more time on the streets. Police told both black youths and white youths to leave or go home (Reiss, 1980). More recent research shows that such problems continue, especially for African-American youths. A 1991 survey of more than 300 Cincinnati youths revealed that almost one-half (46.6 percent) of the black youths reported having been personally hassled by police, compared to only about 10 percent of white youths. In addition, approximately two-thirds of the blacks said that they knew someone who had been hassled (Browning, Cullen, Cao, Kopache, & Stevenson, 1994).

As noted later in the section on attitudes, a study in Hartford, Connecticut, found that the 132 youths interviewed reported approximately 400 negative experiences (Borrero, 2001). Thirty-nine percent involved physical encounters (force, hitting, injury), 24 percent involved verbal harassment, and 34 percent were categorized as "other."

Geller and Toch (1996) argue that the process of stereotyping can be an important factor leading to the use of force against juveniles. A police officer can stereotype a youth as a "typical gang member," and a youth can stereotype a police officer as a "white cop." This stereotyping very easily leads to a process of arrest, resistance, or actions interpreted as resistance, and excessive force or actions so interpreted that a series of self-fulfilling prophecies are set in motion. The problem is to stop the start of such self-fulfilling prophecies.

A hopeful note is that one review concluded that "physical force is infrequently used by the police and that improper force is used even less" (Worden, 1996:46). One problem with this research conclusion is that it may not be in sync with perceptions on the street, especially perceptions in some of the trouble spots of inner-city areas of cities such as New York and Los Angeles. In such locations, contrary perceptions help to trigger the stereotyping process just noted and lead to tragic results. A national survey on this topic, the Police Public Contact Survey, showed that in 1999 about 3 percent of 16–19-year-old respondents reported force or threat of force, compared to 1.4 percent of 20–29-year-old respondents and less than 1 percent of all age categories 30 or older (Langan, Greenfield, Smith, Durose, & Levin, 2001). Most of those who experienced force (76 percent) said the force was excessive. Most persons (85 percent) involved in force incidents said the officer was white. (For a discussion of possible use of force in schools, see Box 5.1.1.)

BOX 5.1.1 BAN ON POLICE USE OF TASERS IN SCHOOLS?

When a student tried to break up a fight in a Texas high school, an officer shot the 17-year-old youth to the floor. His head hit the concrete floor so hard that he suffered a severe brain hemorrhage and spent 52 days in a medically induced coma. His parents are suing. Several groups have urged the Texas Education Agency to end the use of tasers and pepper spray.

Police report that a review of the case showed that the officer followed use of force policy and guidelines. A grand jury declined to indict the officer.

What do you think? Is there a need for such devices in schools? Are they also necessary in elementary schools?

Source: Werner (2014).

Worden (1996) thinks the use of improper force is infrequent, a conclusion supported by the national survey. The hopeful conclusion is that Worden and the national survey are correct. A more pessimistic conclusion is that force is more frequent, especially against minority youths, and that efforts are required to reduce any use of force as much as possible.

An extreme example of the use of excessive force is the use of **deadly force**. In 2015, 995 persons were killed by police, and 963 in 2016 (*The Washington Post*, 2017). Police deadly force is extremely rare, as there are more than 40 million police contacts with citizens each year. A recent study found that "most civilians killed by police were armed with a deadly weapon or were actively attacking officers. Less than 10 percent (N = 93) of civilians shot and killed by police in 2015 were unarmed" (Nix, Campbell, Byers, Alpert, 2017:327–328). Another study found that:

> officers involved in shootings tend to be younger [w]hite males at the rank of officer and possess a high school diploma. Moreover, officers who have experienced one shooting are more likely to become involved in a future shooting (McElvain & Kposowa, 2008:519).

As will be discussed later in this [reading], the issue of race and police shootings has become a critical one in the last few years.

In Philadelphia, however, the race of officer and suspect was not related to contagious fire, that is, multiple officer shootings and multiple shots fired (White & Klinger, 2012). Interestingly, William Geller (1983) describes the typical victim of police shooting as between 17 and 30 years of age. This means that not many juveniles—only the 17-year-olds—are likely to be shot by police officers. All police shootings, however, are not typical; some do involve younger victims. In fact, the primary test case on the use of deadly force involved the shooting of a 15-year-old youth in Memphis, Tennessee. A Memphis police officer shot and killed Edward Garner, a 15-year-old eighth-grade student, under that state's common law "fleeing felon" rule, which authorized police to shoot any fleeing felon—even nondangerous ones. Garner had been prowling inside an empty house and refused to halt in the yard when the police officer warned him to stop. Consequently, the officer shot the youth as he tried to climb a fence to escape. In *Tennessee v. Garner et al.* (1985), the United States Supreme Court ruled that police may not institute a policy to shoot any and all fleeing suspects; rather, they may shoot only those escaping felons who pose a threat to the officer or to others. Box 5.1.2 presents excerpts from the decision.

BOX 5.1.2 THE U.S. SUPREME COURT ON DEADLY FORCE

In *Tennessee v. Garner et al.*, the U.S. Supreme Court set down guidelines for the constitutional use of deadly force by police officers. Here are some excerpts from the majority opinion by Justice White:

> The use of deadly force to prevent the escape of all felony suspects, whatever the circumstances, is constitutionally unreasonable. It is not better that all felony suspects die than that they escape. Where the suspect poses no immediate threat to the officer and no threat to others, the harm resulting from failing to apprehend him does not justify the use of deadly force to do so. It is no doubt unfortunate when a suspect who is in sight escapes, but the fact that the police arrive a little late or are a little slower afoot does not always justify killing the suspect. A police officer may not seize an unarmed, nondangerous suspect by shooting him dead ...
>
> Where the officer has probable cause to believe that the suspect poses a threat of serious physical harm, either to the officer or to others, it is not constitutionally unreasonable to prevent escape by using deadly force. Thus, if the suspect threatens the officer with a weapon or there is probable cause to believe that he has committed a crime involving the infliction or threatened infliction of serious physical harm, deadly force may be used if necessary to prevent escape, and if, where feasible, some warning has been given.

Source: *Tennessee v. Garner et al.*, 1985.

Community or Problem-Solving Policing

One response to the shortcomings of the professional policing model is **community policing**, which is also called problem-solving or **problem-oriented policing**. Community policing does not necessarily mean exactly the same thing to everyone who subscribes to it. Some key features do emerge, however, as critical common elements.

One critical factor is problem solving. As Herman Goldstein (1990) has noted, police can and should be problem solvers in the community. Problem solving involves an effort to deal with conditions or factors that lead to crime or disorder. If the police can solve the problem, then they prevent crime from happening. A simple example with juveniles is police in one community leading the community to transform a vacant lot into a skateboard park. This solved the disorder problem of kids skating in the street and on sidewalks

(Chaiken, 2004). Another critical element of community policing is community building (Novak, Frank, Smith, & Engel, 2002). An important part of community policing is to strengthen the community and its ability to solve problems and prevent and minimize crime, disorder, and other difficulties. In essence, this involves establishing partnerships between the police and the public (Schnebly, 2008).

In **"broken windows" policing**, the police also broaden their concerns and actions, compared to traditional 911 policing. Instead of focusing only on crime, the police pay attention to both crime and disorder. Based on the "broken windows" hypothesis, police consider disorder—for example, rowdy teens hanging out on street corners, "squeegee men" offering to wash car windows for cash "contributions," prostitutes plying their trade, youths or adults trying to jump turnstiles to avoid paying subway fare, "winos" urinating on the street or sleeping in public places like subway stations, and so on—as a serious problem that leads to street crime.

> Disorder demoralizes communities, undermines commerce, leads to the abandonment of public spaces, and undermines public confidence in the ability of government to solve problems; fear drives citizens further from each other and paralyzes their normal, order-sustaining responses, compounding the impact of disorder (Kelling & Coles, 1996:242).

"Broken windows" theory holds that disorder creates fear in citizens, causing them to stay off the streets. The more citizens avoid streets, the more deserted the streets get, and the more citizens avoid them. This affects urban trafficking, both auto and pedestrian, hurts business, and can contribute to crime. Some of the strategies used as part of "broken windows" policing are opportunity reduction, problem solving, and crime prevention through environmental design (Kelling & Coles, 1996). Some cities (e.g., Indianapolis, IN) have focused on the "broken windows" model of community policing, while other cities (e.g., St. Petersburg, FL) have focused more on police–community cooperation and problem solving (Paoline, Myers, & Worden, 2000).

In New York City, police focused broken windows order maintenance activities on stop, question, and frisk actions hoping to catch serious offenders engaging in public marijuana smoking or drinking. Critics see unjustified racial imbalances and constitutional violations that make the strategy "misguided" (Geller & Fagan, 2010). Police argue that proactive police strategies have taken guns off the streets and saved more than 7,000 lives (Kelly, 2013).

Problem solving, community building, and addressing broken windows can directly target youthful problems and concerns. For example, citizens might complain that a particular street corner or bus stop is a center for gang-related activity. After problem identification, police and citizens together explore possible solutions. In Chicago, citizens decided to conduct marches in gang-related areas to discourage gang activity there. Together with police, Chicago citizens also worked with the bus company to relocate a particular bus stop where school children were being harassed. Citizens and police also sought the help of city housing inspectors and housing courts to close down buildings where drug dealers were conducting business.

In another Chicago neighborhood, citizens found that the local juvenile court was so busy that it was ignoring minor offenders. In response to this problem, the community started an alternative-consequence program. This was a program that gave out community service orders for juveniles accused of misdemeanors such as underage drinking, graffiti, vandalism, shoplifting, and bicycle theft. Youthful offenders usually performed between 8 and 100 hours of community service, usually in beautification projects (Skogan & Hartnett, 1997).

In Indianapolis, police act as facilitators at restorative justice conferences. [...] This program is intended for first-time offenders, age 14 and younger, charged with battery, trespass, mischief, conversion, or felony D theft. If the youth is willing to participate, supporters from both sides (offender and victim) meet in a conference. The facilitator tries to get the group to understand what happened. For example, the facilitator asks the youth about the effects of his or her behavior on the victim and asks the victim how the crime affected him or her. After a thorough exploration of the event, the group tries to work out an agreement to repair the harm that was done. Restitution and community service are key elements of agreements. In Indianapolis, police and others (e.g., neighborhood prosecutors, civilian volunteers) have coordinated restorative justice conferences, which have taken place in police stations, schools, libraries, and community centers (McGarrell, Olivares, Crawford, & Kroovand, 2000).

More than 90 percent of victims in conference cases report being satisfied with the way the case was handled. Ninety-eight percent said they would recommend the conference approach. At six months after the initial incident, only 20 percent of the youths who went through restorative justice conferences recidivated, compared to 34 percent in the control group. One year after the initial incident, 31 percent of the restorative justice conference youths had been rearrested, compared to 41 percent of the control group. Both differences were statistically significant (McGarrell et al., 2000).

In Houston, Texas, community police officers provide a "Knock and Talk" service for truants; they visit truants and talk to them about their truancy problems. In Tacoma, Washington, community police officers deliver truants to a community truancy center (Baker, Sigmon, & Nugent, 2001). In Cleveland, Ohio, police converted houses used as crack houses into police substations. In these so-called "RAPP houses" (named for the Residential Area Policing Program) youths could come in and talk to police officers who were there around the clock (Dunworth, 2000). All of these examples are efforts to both solve problems related to crime and disorder and to enhance the ability of the community to participate in policing itself.

Boston police have taken an approach considerably different from the restorative justice approach used in Indianapolis, but it is still considered to be a problem-solving approach. The problem targeted was violence, specifically homicide. In the Boston Gun Project's Operation Ceasefire, police targeted gangs engaged in violent behavior and used a strategy called "pulling levers," which entailed delivering a message to violent gangs that violence will not be tolerated. In Operation Ceasefire, police hold forums with gang members to announce their intent to apply whatever sanctions they can. Police then arrest gang members for trespassing, public drinking, overt drug use, disorder offenses, probation violations, and outstanding warrants. Evaluators report that Operation Ceasefire "was associated with a 63 percent decrease in youth homicides per month, a 32 percent decrease in shots-fired calls for service per month, a 25 percent decrease in gun assaults per month, and a 44 percent decrease in the number of youth gun assaults per month in the highest risk district" (Braga, Kennedy, Piehl, & Waring, 2001:3). It should be noted, however, that other research indicates that youth gun homicides had begun to decline in 1995 and that they declined 75 percent in other Massachusetts cities during this period (Fagan, 2002).

The Office of Juvenile Justice and Delinquency Prevention has supported the development of comprehensive, community-wide approaches to gang prevention. These programs involve both suppression and services. Suppression means that police—and often probation—work together in surveillance and information sharing. Service means efforts to provide academic, economic, and social opportunities for gang members. One program targeted older members (17–24 years old) of two of the most violent gangs in the Little Village neighborhood of Chicago. Results were favorable, including reduced serious gang violence among the targeted gang members, compared to gang members in a comparison group. Specifically, the program resulted in reduced arrests for serious gang crimes (especially aggravated batteries and assaults) among the targeted youths (Howell, 2000).

In summary, community or problem-solving policing tries to solve or prevent problems that contribute to crime and delinquency. Community policing has resulted in a number of innovative strategies in the last 25 years. A recent review of research found that hot spots policing efforts (focusing on high crime locations) with a problem-solving emphasis are effective in crime prevention (Braga, Papachristos, & Hureau, 2014).

Citizen Attitudes Toward Police

Contrary to what many police believe, citizens actually hold rather positive attitudes toward the police. For example, a recent Gallup Poll reported that 58 percent of those polled rated the honesty and ethical standards of police either very high or high (Gallup, 2016). Respondents rated police sixth in the list of professions, only below nurses, pharmacists, doctors, engineers, and dentists (Gallup, 2016).

Citizens vary considerably, however, in their approval of the police. For example, in a recent survey, 64 percent of whites but only 40 percent of nonwhites rated the honesty and ethical standards of police as high or very high. Similarly, 61 percent of whites but only 30 percent of blacks reported a great deal or quite a lot of confidence in the police. Younger respondents (ages 18–34) report lower confidence at 44 percent, compared to older respondents at 63 percent confidence for those 55 and older. Republicans report higher confidence (69 percent) than Democrats (44 percent) (Gallup, 2017). Gallup points out that "[o]n the surface, Americans' confidence in the police appears strong and steady but [a] closer look [examining subgroup differences] reveals a troubling loss of confidence among key groups in U.S. society" (Gallup, 2017). Overall, 17 percent of blacks report having been treated less fairly in the last 30 days (University at Albany, 2014). Similarly, 61 percent of whites but only 43 percent of blacks and 41 percent of Hispanics think that the police treat all races fairly. Less than one-half of young respondents (age 18–24 years) think that the police treat all races fairly, compared to more than 50 percent for all other age groups, including 71 percent of senior citizens (age 65 and up). Only 16 percent of whites but 42 percent of blacks and 39 percent of Hispanics fear that the police may stop and arrest them when they are completely innocent (Maguire & Pastore, 2004). In a survey in New York City, "blacks were three times more likely than non-blacks to perceive that racially biased policing was widespread, that it was unjustified, and that it had been experienced personally" (Rice & Piquero, 2005:111). Thus, citizen attitudes toward the police are not uniform. Some citizens are more positive, while others are more negative.

Of great relevance to the police and juvenile justice is the fact that lower-class youths comprise one group holding negative attitudes toward the police. Anderson (1994) argues that lower-class youths have little faith in the police and subscribe to a street code whereby the "police are most often seen as representing the dominant white society and not caring to protect inner-city residents" (Anderson, 1994:82). As a result of the perception and/or the reality that police do not respond when called, the inner-city youth often relies on self-protection: "taking care of himself" (Anderson, 1994:82) is a critical part of this street code.

Results from a study in St. Louis, Missouri, confirm Anderson's argument. This was a qualitative study that used a purposive sample of 75 African-American youths, a number of whom were highly active in delinquency. High percentages of the youths in St. Louis had been harassed or mistreated by the police. About half of both male and female respondents agreed that the police engage in frequent harassment or mistreatment of people. In summary, young men "described being stopped on a regular basis and treated as suspects. They said officers routinely used disrespectful language, engaged in physically intrusive actions such as strip searches and cavity probes, and assumed young men 'got lucky' rather than were innocent when no evidence of criminal wrongdoing was discovered" (Brunson & Miller, 2006:548). Several of the young men reported that if police lacked enough evidence to arrest them, the officers would drive them to another area, let them out, and make them walk home (Brunson, 2007). Simply being a young black male in a disadvantaged neighborhood put these males at risk of police suspicion of criminal activity (Cobbina, Miller, & Brunson, 2008).

WEB ACTIVITY

Gallup conducts polling on numerous attitudes, including attitudes about criminal justice. Consult the Gallup website (www.gallup.com) for up-to-date polling results.

A slightly older study, however, found the issue to be more complicated. Hurst, Frank, and Browning (2000) surveyed more than 800 students in Cincinnati, Ohio. Like prior research, questions about police effectiveness in general showed less positive attitudes for black teens, but black teens were more positive than white teens when asked to consider police behavior in specific encounters. Then, after control variables were added, "the strongest predictor of less positive attitudes was seeing and hearing about the police misconduct aimed at another person (vicarious conduct)" (Hurst et al., 2000:49).

One study offers a suggestion for getting beyond the issue of race and attitudes toward the police. A study of four dimensions of trust in the police found that youths, whether white, black, or Latino, who had less commitment to school and who had seen police stop other youths and treat those other youths with disrespect had significantly less trust in the police. The lesson for police is that their behavior with the public can affect not only those with whom they are interacting but will also affect any witnesses (Flexion, Lurigio, & Greenleaf, 2009). Even delinquent youths who reported that they felt police treated citizens more fairly rated the police higher on legitimacy (Lee, Steinberg, & Piquero, 2010).

A study of more than 5,000 eighth-grade students found that youths were "indifferent" toward the police—that is, they were neither positive nor negative (Taylor, Turner, Esbensen, & Winfree, 2001). Part of the reason for youths' indifference or negative attitudes toward the police is that youths often have negative experiences with the police. A study in Hartford, Connecticut, for example, found that the 132 youths interviewed reported approximately 400 negative experiences. Thirty-nine percent involved physical encounters (force, hitting, injury), 24 percent involved verbal harassment, and 34 percent were categorized as "other." For example, a 15-year-old Hispanic female reported being thrown against the ground and then against a wall when she was hanging out on the street with friends. A black youth suspected of dealing drugs when he was talking to a friend on the street was grabbed, thrown up against the car, and hit with billy clubs. (He admitted possessing but not dealing drugs.) Another youth was driving and was signaled to pull over. The officer smashed his car window and several officers grabbed, beat, and injured the youth (Borrero, 2001).

A national survey of 1,289 youths in middle and high schools found that youths who had been arrested had significantly less positive attitudes toward the police than youths who had not been arrested or who had other types of contact with police. There were no gender differences in attitudes toward the police, but black youths had less favorable attitudes. Based on these findings, the authors suggest that police officers need to be aware of the troubled history between blacks and the police, and "efforts are made to become more inclusive of [b]lack perspectives" (Brick, Taylor, & Esbensen, 2009:493).

It is interesting to speculate about how changes in the nature of policing might affect attitudes toward the police. Recall that Chicago made a major effort to implement community policing. In four of the five experimental districts, residents reported improved police responsiveness to neighborhood concerns, and African-American residents had improved perceptions about police misconduct (Skogan & Hartnett, 1997). In Boston, where Operation Ceasefire meant a tough, deterrent message and approach to violent gang members, interviews with community members indicated that they felt the deterrence strategy was effective but worried about the long-term effects. They were concerned that simply sending troubled youths to prison was not the complete answer and might just increase youths' hostility and hopelessness (Stoutland, 2001).

These variations in attitudes toward the police help to explain the paradox that police often hold negative or cynical views of citizens while citizen attitudes toward the police are actually rather positive. Part of the explanation for this apparent contradiction is that the police are much more likely to come in contact with citizens with less positive views—minority and younger citizens—than with older citizens who hold more positive views. A second explanation for the paradox is that the police often come into contact with citizens at inopportune times—in instances in which citizens have broken the law (even if only a traffic law), been victimized, or witnessed a crime. At such times, citizens are likely to be under stress. They may react with frustration at receiving a speeding ticket or at hearing an officer say that there is little hope of recovering their stolen property. Citizens may lash out at the available target (i.e., the police officer), much like a frustrated customer reacts to a customer service representative who is not responsible for the problem but has the unpleasant job of trying to rectify it. Repeated contacts with citizens in times of crisis can also lead the police to job burnout (Maslach & Jackson, 1979), cynicism (Niederhoffer, 1967), suspicion (Skolnick, 1966), and/or stress (Crank & Caldero, 1991; Kroes, Margolis, & Hurrell, 1974). In addition, dissatisfaction with a specific police contact leads to lower evaluations of police services in general (Huebner, Schafer, & Bynum, 2004).

One final observation on this matter concerns the fact that any victim of crime views his or her situation as unique, while the police view the same situation as routine. The victim often is a first-time victim who is frightened, stunned, and excited about something that is entirely new to him or her. The officer is simply experiencing the third burglary report that night, the twentieth that week, or the one-thousandth in his or her career. Additionally, the officer's realistic judgment that little or nothing can be done to "solve" the crime leads him or her to rush through the encounter with the citizen in order to write up a report so that the victim can file an insurance claim. Based on television or movie stereotypes, the naive citizen may expect the officer to drop everything, spend as much time as possible on the victim's case, and solve it. Realizing that the officer has a very different definition of the situation, the citizen becomes upset and reacts accordingly—possibly accusing the officer of incompetence or laziness. Such negative encounters reinforce officer perceptions of citizens as being negative toward the police, even while the public opinion poll research shows the contrary.

Implications of the Attitudinal Research

Several conclusions can be drawn from this discussion of police attitudes toward citizens and citizen attitudes toward the police. First, both sides could benefit from clarification. The police might benefit from becoming aware that citizens generally are positive about the police. Citizens, on the other hand, need to know why police may be somewhat cynical toward them. Citizens should be aware that police officers have likely seen their problem before and have had contact with some victims who precipitated the crime or were otherwise tainted. More importantly, citizens must be realistic in their expectations of what the police can do. For example, the police often can do little or nothing to recover a stolen television or car. Second, police need to be careful in their dealings with citizens who hold less positive attitudes—namely, youths and minorities. Because these groups may be less favorable in their attitudes toward the police, the police need to target them for more positive treatment. Otherwise, these groups may interpret police indifference and cynicism as evidence of prejudicial attitudes and discriminatory behavior. Furthermore, police sensitivity to the attitudes of youthful and minority citizens can lead to improved police–community relations.

As noted, there has been recent emphasis on the police as problem solvers. Some police experts think that traditional policing can do little more than take reports for many problems. If policing were restructured, however, perhaps more could be done about many of the concerns that citizens have. If police spent less time running from call to call and more time exploring the causes and solutions of various problems, then the police could be more effective and have greater impact (see, e.g., Trojanowicz, Kappeler, Gaines, & Bucqueroux, 1998).

Recent Issues in Policing Concerning Juveniles

Police work with juveniles has undergone various changes over the past several decades. Among these initiatives are the introduction of police in schools, the problem of racial profiling and disproportionate minority contact, enforcement of curfew laws, participation in intensive supervision of probationers, and policing of underage drinking.

Police in Schools

Since the early 1990s, police presence in schools has grown considerably. By 2013–2014, about two-thirds of both middle schools and high schools had either security guards or police officers on the premises (Musu-Gillette, Zhang, Wang, Zhang, & Oudekerk, 2017). Part of this growth is due to a number of highly publicized shootings in schools such as Columbine, Colorado, and Newtown, Connecticut, which attracted attention and action. Violent crime, drug violations, weapons violations, and bullying have also aroused concern and calls for increased police officer presence in schools (Booth, Van Hasselt, & Vecchi, 2011). One article claimed that both school police and surveillance cameras are in "widespread" use in urban, suburban, and rural schools (Hirschfield & Celinska, 2011). Specifically, 93 percent of schools now control access to school buildings, and 75 percent of schools use security cameras to monitor school buildings (Musu-Gillette et al., 2017).

The presence of **school resource officers** (SROs) has become commonplace. For the 2013–2014 school year, principals in 24 percent of U.S. schools reported having at least one full-time police officer at their school at least once a week. Another 19 percent of schools had only part-time officers. For high schools, the percentages were 64 percent full-time and 15 percent part-time (Musu-Gillette et al., 2017) (see Table 5.1.1). In 2011, 70 percent of students reported that their school had either security guards or assigned police officers (Musu-Gillette et al., 2017).

Table 5.1.1 Percentage of Schools with Full-time or Part-time Security at School at Least Once a Week: Selected Years

Time Period	Full-time (%)	Part-time (%)
2005–2006	27.0	14.6
2007–2008	30.4	15.9
2009–2010	28.7	14.1
2013–2014	24.0	19.0

Source: Robers, Kemp, Rathbun, and Morgan, 2014; Musu-Gillette et al., 2017.

Most police in schools were involved in traditional police functions, including patrolling, making arrests, and providing security (see Table 5.1.2). At the same time, many police officers in schools, particularly those in an SRO capacity, provided counseling, mentoring, and referrals as well as training to teachers and parents; taught programs such as Drug Abuse Resistance Education (D.A.R.E.); and chaperoned school events (Travis & Coon, 2005). [...]

Table 5.1.2 Activities of Law Enforcement in Schools

Law enforcement patrol
Operate metal detectors
Conduct safety inspections
Respond to crime/disorder reports
Make arrests
Write reports
Perform drug sweeps
Advise/mentor staff
Mediate disputes

Advise students
Work with parent–teacher groups
Advise athletic teams
Mentor students
Chaperone events
Present awards
Teach D.A.R.E.
Anti-gang classes
Anti-hate classes
Law-related education
Firearm safety
Crime awareness and prevention
Conflict resolution
Problem solving

Source: Travis and Coon (2005).

The introduction of police to schools has not been without controversy. Some observers argue that SROs try to balance their roles as law enforcers and mentors/instructors/problem solvers. Others contend that the widespread introduction of police into the school setting criminalizes school discipline.

At the same time as police have been introduced to school, there has been an introduction of zero-tolerance policies whereby students are suspended or expelled for certain behaviors such as bringing a weapon to school. Critics contend that the introduction of police resource officers and zero-tolerance policies are signs of criminalization in schools. In other words, instead of seeing discipline problems as requiring solutions by teachers and principals, these practices treat students as quasi-criminals and mandate quasi-criminal justice solutions and thereby label youths as criminals. Critics see this as part of a more general trend to ignore problems of poverty and deindustrialization. For example, "the transfer of disciplinary responsibilities from school professionals to the police also supports this purpose given that police are ill-equipped to recognize and address the psychological and social roots of school misconduct" (Hirschfield & Celinska, 2011:7).

This emphasis on police in schools and zero-tolerance policies are part of what is called the **school-to-prison pipeline** (Kim, Losen, & Hewitt, 2010). This refers to a combination of factors that appear to criminalize much youthful behavior and facilitate the eventual placement of youths in our nation's prisons. Kupchik (2014) argues that educational approaches such as tutoring, improved classroom management techniques, and increasing staff diversity are steps that schools could take to reduce problems.

A dramatic example of the school-to-prison pipeline is the Texas practice of handling truancy cases in adult court: 113,000 such cases in 2012. Part of the reason for this is that fines pay for more than half of the operating costs of truancy courts in Dallas County. Dallas County collected $2.9 million in such fines in 2012 (National School Boards Association, 2013). A complaint has been filed with the U.S. Department of Justice to investigate the practice.

One study found that arrest is related to a 20 percent increase in dropping out of high school and thus "hinders the transition to adulthood" (Kirk & Sampson, 2013:54). As a response to the more general problem, Connecticut probation officers are now reviewing each summons to avoid criminalizing "school incidents that are in keeping with normal adolescent behavior" (Bracey et al., 2013:428). More generally, the Council of State Governments Justice Center has recommended that police should not be involved in routine classroom management and minor offenses at school should not be referred to the courts (Morgan, Salomon, Plotkin, & Cohen, 2014).

Na and Gottfredson (2013) found that increasing the presence of police officers in schools is related to increases in weapon and drug crimes but not other types of crime. So they found no evidence that SROs improve school safety. On the other hand, police presence is not related to changes in the use of harsh discipline. They think that further research is needed on this issue and that in the meantime schools should emphasize proven school-based approaches to maintain order in schools.

As in other areas of juvenile justice, diversion programs have been instituted to offer another way to deal with school problems. One program in Florida had misdemeanor school offenders perform community service instead of being processed in juvenile court. The referred students completed 96 percent of the community service hours that they had been ordered to perform and a preliminary analysis of recidivism was promising (Sullivan, Dollard, Sellers, & Mayo, 2010). These positive findings indicate that there are at least some youths who do not need harsh punishment for school infractions but who will respond positively to programs that use more of a problem-solving approach.

Evaluations of effective school–police partnerships also indicate that more is needed than simply placing police officers in schools. First, many schools have problems such as overcrowding, lower attendance rates, larger minority populations, and lower funding than other schools. Second, evaluations of effective partnerships show the need for both parent cooperation and supplementing law enforcement presence "with intensive monitoring, counseling, and other related services that strengthen cooperation and collaboration with other community-based groups having a vested interest in the social justice needs of students attending schools in the community" (Brady, Balmer, & Phenix, 2007). This is congruent with research on Scared Straight [...]. Simple solutions such as prison confrontation programs and putting police in schools are not cure-alls for complex problems such as delinquency.

Race and Policing

For decades, the issue of race has been a critical concern in any discussion of policing. In the last edition of this text we focused on the specific issue of racial profiling. In the last five years, the focus has turned to police shootings of black citizens. Several shootings in particular, such as the shooting of Michael Brown in Ferguson, Missouri, and the shooting of LaQuan McDonald in Chicago, have raised charges that police have one trigger finger for white suspects and another for minority suspects. Some claim that in response to anger over shootings, police have experienced a so-called "Ferguson effect" in which they have become reluctant to intervene in situations in order to avoid charges of improper behavior, especially improper shootings. Many people have joined the Black Lives Matter movement to protest what they feel are instances of improper police shootings of black citizens. Others have criticized the Black Lives Matter movement for racializing relations between police and citizens.

Citizens have also been concerned about police stop-and-frisk policies. In New York City in 2006, for example, police made more than 500,000 stops of citizens, including 64,166 stops of black males between the ages of 15 and 19 (Geller & Fagan, 2010). In Chicago, in the summer of 2014 alone, there were more than 250,000 stops that did not lead to an arrest. Blacks were the target of 72 percent of police stops in Chicago, although blacks only made up 32 percent of the city's population (ACLU of Illinois, 2015).

Several cautions are in order. First, each shooting incident needs to be examined thoroughly. For example, an investigation of the shooting of Michael Brown in Ferguson, Missouri, concluded that the police officer did not act improperly but that there had been problems in the Ferguson Police Department. Second, official findings, such as the Department of Justice finding in Ferguson, do not automatically calm citizen concerns. Some citizens continue to think that a shooting may have been improper despite the findings of an official investigation. Third, the information we have about police shootings nationwide is incomplete. It appears that most victims of police shootings in 2015 were armed or were actively attacking officers. On the other hand, there is some indication of implicit bias (Nix et al., 2017). Fourth, the issue of shootings must be placed in the broader context. For example, police decisions to engage in a war on drugs and to engage in aggressive stop-and-frisk actions in cities such as New York and Chicago often are interpreted by minority citizens as discriminatory. As a result, many agree with Michelle Alexander that the criminal justice system in general is racist. Specifically, Alexander calls the criminal justice system "the New Jim Crow," which operates on the principle that "black people, especially black men, are criminals" (Alexander, 2012:197). Likewise, the American Civil Liberties Union states that "the war on marijuana has largely been a war on people of color" (ACLU, 2013:9).

A full discussion of such allegations of racism is beyond the scope of this [reading]. Here we simply note that in the last few years police shootings and policies like Stop, Question, and Frisk in New York City [...] in particular, and police–minority relations in general, have once again captured front-page and cable news show attention. Thus, police administrators and police officers alike must be aware that decisions and actions they take will automatically attract attention and scrutiny.

The issues of police shootings and stop and frisk raise the broader question of the effect of race on police decisions to arrest and juvenile court decisions to detain, petition, and sentence. The outcome of differential decision making is often called **disproportionate minority contact** [...]. While black youths made up 15 percent of the U.S. population in 2014, they made up 31 percent of arrests, 36 percent of youths petitioned to juvenile court, and 39 percent of those detained (Hockenberry & Puzzanchera, 2017). A recent report noted that despite few differences in offending, black youths are "2.3 times as likely to be arrested as white youth for all delinquent offenses" (Rovner, 2016b:7). Arrest differences continue throughout the system: Black youths are more likely to get transferred to adult court and 19 percent more likely to be committed to an institution (Rovner, 2016a). This disproportionate contact raises the question of possible unfair police action.

A study by Pope and Snyder addressed this question. Using police data from the National Incident-Based Reporting System (NIBRS), they found that in the 17 jurisdictions analyzed there was "no evidence to support the hypothesis that police are more likely to arrest nonwhite juvenile offenders than white juvenile offenders, once other incident attributes are taken into consideration" (Pope & Snyder, 2003:6). Overall, victims identified 69.2 percent of offenders to be white, and 72.7 percent of juvenile offenders arrested were white. The only indication of bias was indirect: "Nonwhite juveniles ... are more likely to be arrested when the victim is white than when the victim is nonwhite" (Pope & Snyder, 2003:6).

In a report on disproportionate minority contact in Pittsburgh, Rochester, and Seattle, evidence of such contact was found at all three sites. Huizinga et al. (2007) did not find evidence that differences in offending behavior explained the disproportionate contact. In other words, it is not the case that minorities clearly commit more delinquency and that this explains why police arrest more minorities. Risk factors such as type of neighborhood, family economic status, and youth education problems did substantially reduce the disproportionate minority contact. These findings do not necessarily prove police bias but are consistent with bias if bias does in fact exist (Huizinga et al., 2007). See Box 5.1.3.

BOX 5.1.3 DOES THE OFFICER'S RACE MATTER?

In an observational study of Cincinnati, Ohio, police officers, Brown and Frank found that white officers are more likely to arrest suspects in general than black officers. The suspect's race had no effect on white officers' decisions to arrest, but it did have an impact on black officers' decisions. With situational circumstances being equal, the probability that a white officer would arrest a black suspect was 93 percent; the probability that a black officer would arrest a black suspect was 98 percent.

Source: Brown and Frank (2006).

In an analysis of disproportionate minority contact in general, Bishop (2005) noted some of the subtler ways that race can enter into the policing of juveniles. First, police views of neighborhoods as dangerous or having suspicious persons are related to considerations of race and class. Related to this are high crime rates in urban underclass neighborhoods. A result is that police devote more surveillance to such neighborhoods, which leads to more encounters with juveniles and more arrests. Second, race can have an indirect effect via demeanor in police encounters with juveniles. For example, police can interpret a hostile or less cooperative demeanor as a sign of criminal propensity. Complainant preference can also have an effect. Complainants more often press for arrest of African-American suspects. Bishop thus concludes:

> In sum, the literature indicates that, for a number of reasons, minority youths are more likely than whites to be arrested, referred to court, and detained by police ... The overrepresentation of minorities in police arrest data, especially for violent offenses, reinforces racist expectancies (Bishop, 2005:45).

In an attempt to come up with a definitive answer on this question, Kochel, Wilson, and Mastrofski (2011:498) conducted a meta-analysis of 40 research reports and conclude "more definitively than prior nonsystematic reviews that racial minority suspects experience a higher probability of arrest than do Whites." Specifically, a minority suspect's probability of arrest is 30 percent higher than that of a white suspect (Kochel et al., 2011).

The clear lesson is that race is a factor that needs close attention. Police need to be aware of how race can affect decisions to stop and decisions to arrest. They also need to be clear that factors such as a youth's neighborhood and demeanor can bring in race as an indirect influence on those critical decisions. Moreover, police officials need to consider the racial impact of organizational decisions about which crimes to focus on, which neighborhoods to devote attention to, which policies (e.g., stop and frisk, any police war on drugs) to emphasize or de-emphasize, and hiring policies. Police officials need to make sound decisions about such issues as mandating body cameras, hiring minority officers, and providing effective training and oversight. As writers such as Rovner (2016b) stress, police are the gatekeepers of the system. Decisions police make have ripple effects throughout.

Juvenile Curfew Laws

Juvenile curfew laws have been enacted in numerous cities across the country in an effort to reduce victimization of and by juveniles. The curfew law in Charlotte, North Carolina, included such objectives and also strove to "reinforce and promote the role of parents in raising and guiding children" (City of Charlotte Code, cited in Hirschel, Dean, & Dumond, 2001). To accomplish these goals, children under 16 years of age were prohibited from being on the streets from 11:00 P.M. to 6:00 A.M. during the week and from midnight to 6:00 A.M. on Friday and Saturday nights. Other cities with curfews may have different age or time stipulations. Vernon, Connecticut, for example, enacted a curfew for juveniles under 18 and prohibited them being on the streets from 11:00 P.M. to 6:00 A.M. every night of the week (Males, 2000). In one California city, the curfew applied from 11:00 P.M. to 5:00 A.M. on week nights and from 1:00 A.M. to 5:00 A.M. on weekends. Exceptions involved standing in front of their own homes, returning home within one hour of attending certain activities, working, or being in the company of a parent (Sutphen & Ford, 2001).

Research on the effectiveness of curfews indicates that curfew laws do not reduce crime or victimization. For example, after the implementation of the curfew law in Vernon, Connecticut, Part I crimes did decrease, but the decrease "was similar to or less than the crime declines experienced in similar cities and the state as a whole" (Males, 2000:259). A time-series analysis of victimizations in New Orleans showed that the law was "ineffective for reducing victimizations, victimizations of juveniles, and juvenile arrests" (Reynolds, Seydlitz, & Jenkins, 2000:219). A study of a curfew law in Washington, DC, that included a sophisticated replication design showed that it did not reduce juvenile crime (Cole, 2003). In addition, the laws do not appear to reduce subsequent offending by juveniles who are cited for curfew violations. In Charlotte, for example, 40 percent of the youths cited for curfew violations were arrested for an offense following their first curfew violation (Hirschel et al., 2001). A national evaluation of 52 counties showed that curfew laws only affected significant decreases in 3 of 12 crimes (burglaries, larcenies, and simple assaults). The authors concluded that their research "provides, at best extremely weak support for the hypothesis that curfews reduce juvenile crime rates" and that the "results do not encourage the idea that curfews help prevent juvenile crime" (McDowall, Loftin, & Wiersema, 2000:88).

In a review of studies of teen curfews, Adams (2003) identified 10 empirical studies of juvenile curfews. Adams concluded that the weight of the evidence from these 10 studies overall "fails to support the argument that curfews reduce crime and victimization" (Adams, 2003:155). Adams also questions the fairness of curfew law enforcement, arguing that curfew enforcement relies heavily on officer discretion. Adams worries that curfew enforcement will "fall most heavily on low-income and minority areas" (Adams, 2007:666). Two recent reviews failed to find support for curfews. One review found that the limited quality and number of research studies prevents drawing conclusions about the effectiveness of curfew laws (Grossman & Miller, 2015). Likewise, finding problems with the available research, a Campbell Systematic Review noted (not conclusively) that the "evidence suggests that juvenile curfews are ineffective at reducing crime or victimization" (Wilson et al., 2016:8).

One reason for the ineffectiveness of curfews is that the hours covered by the laws may not be times evidencing high victimization. In Vernon, Connecticut, for example, it was found that juvenile crime was much more likely to occur in the afternoon (Males, 2000). Nationally, it appears that violent offenses and gang crimes peak at approximately 3:00 P.M. (Sickmund, Snyder, & Poe-Yamagata, 1997). One response to this issue is to have daytime curfews for those youths who are not under the jurisdiction of truancy laws. One survey found that 10 percent of the responding jurisdictions had daytime curfews. In fact, some were so restrictive that even a youngster cutting class and not being in the place he was supposed to be in was technically in violation of that city's daytime curfew law (Bannister, Carter, & Schafer, 2001).

Another problem is that juveniles do not necessarily comply with curfew laws. In New Orleans during the first year of the law, more than 3,500 youths were taken into custody just for curfew violations (Reynolds et al., 2000). Most importantly, curfew laws do nothing to improve juveniles' relationships with peers, schools, and family, all of which are important correlates of delinquency. [P]arental supervision and attachment to parents are critical factors in preventing delinquency. Curfew laws do nothing to strengthen such supervision or bonding.

It is interesting that police think curfew laws are effective even though they do not have concrete evidence that the curfews are effective in reducing crime (Bannister et al., 2001). Perhaps police enthusiasm for curfews would decrease if they became more familiar with the literature showing that curfews are not effective.

Part of the reality of curfew laws is the panacea phenomenon. [I]n the discussion of Scared Straight programs, we are often guilty of expecting quick and inexpensive fixes for complicated problems such as delinquency. Unrealistically, we hope that a simple measure such as a curfew law will cure the delinquency problem. We pass curfew laws and expect police enforcement of such laws to magically wipe out juvenile crime. For a note on curfews and high school proms, see Box 5.1.4.

BOX 5.1.4 CURFEWS AND PROMS

In 2001, the Georgia legislature enacted a year-round curfew forbidding anyone under 18 from driving after midnight. So, like Cinderella, prom-goers need to be off the road by the stroke of midnight. Breaking this curfew law can mean a penalty of up to one year in jail or a fine of up to $1,000.

Legislators created this law in response to some highly publicized auto deaths of teenagers in the Atlanta area. Unlike the curfew laws discussed in this [reading], this is a safety curfew more than a crime prevention curfew.

In response, schools are planning to end their proms some time before midnight so that students can get home by 12:00 A.M. One school will end its prom at 11:30 P.M. to allow for plenty of time to beat the curfew. Police say that they are not making any exceptions for prom night.

What do you think? Should there be an exception for prom night?

In Hartford, Connecticut, police decided to step up their enforcement of the city's curfew law after a shooting in which one man died and six young people under 18 were wounded. The curfew prohibited anyone under 18 from being on the streets after 9:00 P.M.

Two points are interesting. First, the police did not have the shooter in custody, and there was no indication of his or her age. Second, this shooting took place after an annual parade and occurred at about 6:30 P.M.

It appears that the Hartford police either are not aware of the research on the ineffectiveness of curfews or they choose to ignore that research. What might influence a police chief to enforce a law that has little empirical support? Might other factors be at work?

Sources: Scott (2002); Associated Press (2008).

In England and Wales, curfew orders in community sentences have increased from 1 percent of youth sentences in 2002–2003 to 7.6 percent of youth sentences in 2008–2009. However, two-thirds of youths sentenced to a curfew order in 2009–2010 were reconvicted within a year (Bateman, 2012). A Scottish study found that such curfew orders were not effective unless rehabilitation components were also included (Deuchar, 2011). So just as community curfews have not been effective, so also correctional curfews have not worked in the United Kingdom.

Assistance with Intensive Supervision of Probationers

Another way the police have enhanced their activity with juveniles is through their participation in probation. Anchorage, Alaska, has tried using police officers to enhance probation officer supervision of juvenile offenders. Anchorage used police officers to turn regular supervision into intensive supervision. This means that the juvenile probationers received additional contacts, contacts with their probation officers, and contacts with police officers. Like many previous intensive supervision programs, there was no reduction in criminal recidivism; there was no significant difference in the percentage of offenders under intensive supervision who committed any new offense or the percentage of offenders under regular supervision who committed any new offense. However, about 30 percent of the intensive supervision offenders had a probation violation, compared to 17 percent of the regular offenders. Thus, increased supervision translates into increased monitoring and detection of technical violations.

It is interesting that Anchorage tried an intensive supervision effort using police when so much prior research on intensive supervision has not been promising. What is promising is a program such as Operation Eiger in Baton Rouge, Louisiana. Here police also help probation officers conduct unscheduled evening visits six times per month, but the program involves addressing needs as well as enforcing probation conditions. Services are provided to deal with substance abuse, anger management, academic difficulties, and employment needs (Lizotte & Sheppard, 2001). Hopefully, this combination of intensive supervision and treatment will have greater success than the program in Alaska using intensive supervision alone.

San Bernardino, California, is another example of a police–probation partnership. There, a police officer and a probation officer together make a home visit to all new juvenile probationers. They explain the rules of probation and also search the probationer's residence for weapons and drugs. The program has had some effect in reducing serious crimes in the city, but one concern is **mission distortion** for probation. In other words, probation officers may no longer see themselves as service providers or social workers but may instead over-identify with a law enforcement role (Worrall & Gaines, 2006). [...]

A survey in Texas showed that most police agencies did not have formal partnerships with juvenile probation agencies. However, 71 percent did report a formal or informal information-sharing partnership with juvenile probation (Kim, Matz, Gerber, Beto, & Lambert, 2013a). This suggests that police–probation partnerships are rather limited at this point in time.

Policing Underage Drinking

The National Minimum Drinking Age Act standardized the legal drinking age at 21 in 1984. Police bear responsibility to enforce this act. Studies show that youths under age 21 are able to purchase alcohol despite the law. Studies in the 1990s using either actual underage buyers or decoy buyers (individuals over 21 who looked younger than 21) showed that purchase rates ranged from 45 percent to 88 percent. A study in a large Midwestern area had an overall sales rate to pseudo-underage buyers of 26 percent (Britt, Toomey, Dunsmuir, & Wagenaar, 2006). The authors concluded that there has been progress in reducing such sales over the last decade, and believed that improved training could result in even lower sales.

Police tend to use compliance checks or "Cops in Shops" programs to combat such underage alcohol purchases. Compliance checks are similar to the research just noted: police use underage decoys to try to purchase liquor. Cops in Shops programs put undercover officers in establishments to detect and cite youths who try to purchase alcohol illegally. Police agencies are twice as likely to use compliance checks as Cops in Shops programs (Montgomery, Foley, & Wolfson, 2006). [...]

Police Effectiveness With Juvenile Crime

In examining **police effectiveness**, it is clear that the police are making a variety of efforts to combat juvenile crime. As noted earlier, police are staffing RAPP houses in Cleveland, working in schools in a variety of capacities, facilitating restorative justice conferences in Indianapolis, going to community meetings in Chicago, enforcing curfews all over the country, and participating in demonstration projects such as Operation Ceasefire in Boston.

Overall, how effective are the police in their new efforts against crime and delinquency? For many of these programs, we have already noted specific outcome results. Here a summary is in order.

First, some things simply do not work. Juvenile curfew laws, for example, have been tried in numerous cities. Most evaluations indicate that they are not very effective in the fight against juvenile crime. Related to this, most police encounters with juveniles are for matters such as "hanging out" that are not easily resolved. Even if the police do resolve them, they do not consider that much of an accomplishment. Youths, on the other hand, often see police reprimands as harassment (Watkins & Maume, 2012).

Second, a possible reason that some interventions do not work is that they are simplistic and contrary to what we know. Both the juvenile curfew laws and the Anchorage intensive supervision program, for example, stem from a Scared Straight panacea phenomenon that looks for simple answers: pass a law to keep juveniles off the street or ask a police officer to stop in at a juvenile's house. Human behavior is more complicated than this.

Third, research has indicated what is effective, such as problem-solving approaches, pulling levers strategies, and hot spots policing (Braga et al., 2014; Braga, 2015). For example, a number of studies have shown that a problem-solving/pulling levers strategy reduces youth violence (Corsaro, Brunson, & McGarrell, 2009). Concerning hot spots, a Seattle analysis revealed that 50 percent of juvenile arrests took place in less than 1 percent of street segments. In general, much juvenile crime occurs on pathways to school or in areas where kids "hang out," such as playgrounds and malls. Accordingly, one author suggests that school officials be present on walk routes to school, that business owners keep an eye on nearby vacant lots, and that police and communities work to provide safe areas where youths can socialize (Roth, 2013).

Fourth, it is critical to avoid unrealistic expectations. In their study of community policing in Chicago, for example, Skogan and Hartnett (1997) found that some neighborhood conditions improved. Every neighborhood had at least one improvement. Victimization declined in two areas, street crime dropped in two others, drug and gang problems declined in two, and graffiti declined in another. Overall, compared to comparison areas, there were positive changes in 27 of the 51 outcomes that the evaluation measured, an overall success rate of 53 percent (Skogan & Hartnett, 1997:244). Skogan and Hartnett emphasize that communities should have realistic expectations from community policing. A success rate of 50 percent appears to be realistic. Expectations of 95 percent or even 75 percent success rates are fanciful.

Fifth, the police are only part of the picture. Eck and Maguire (2000), for example, contend that the decrease in crime in the last 10 years is the result of communities and the nation mobilizing to fight crime. Such mobilization involves police initiatives such as community policing, increased use of prison, demographic trends (the aging of the population and the decrease in the proportion of young males), and the decline of retail drug markets. A realistic perspective on the police impact on crime can be summarized as follows:

> There is one thing that is a myth: The police have a substantial, broad, and independent impact on the nation's crime rate. Rather than think of the police as an isolated institution that has a distinctive impact on crime, perhaps we should think of the police as part of a network of institutions, some of them formal (e.g., courts and schools) and some of them informal (e.g., families and churches), that respond to crime ... When considered in isolation, the effectiveness of any one element of this diverse array of people and organizations may be slight. But collectively, the response might be more dramatic (Eck & Maguire, 2000:247–248).

Summary

It is an intriguing time for policing. Both police themselves and outsiders are debating the meaning of policing. Some, like former New York City police commissioner William Bratton, argue that police should take a tough approach (zero tolerance) and arrest even "squeegee men" who harass motorists by foisting unwanted window washing on them. In Boston, this tough approach, called "pulling levers," takes the form of arresting suspected violent gang members for disorder offenses, criminal acts, and outstanding warrants. It appears that SROs are becoming a fixture of the contemporary school. Some critics see SROs and school policies as detracting from traditional approaches to student problems, and some research indicates that arrest can increase high school dropout rates and decrease a student's chances of going to college. The introduction of SROs and zero-tolerance policies are also seen as contributing to the school-to-prison pipeline.

Other developments in policing, however, take a completely different approach. In Indianapolis, for example, police are coordinating restorative justice conferences in which youths, victims, and supporters on both sides sit down and try to repair the harm done by victimizations. Here offenders learn how they harmed their victims and what they can do to repair that harm.

In other places, such as Chicago, police are attending neighborhood meetings and trying to learn what the community considers to be problems and how those problems should be solved. Problems vary from crack houses operating in residential neighborhoods to gangs harassing youths at bus stops after school.

Whatever specific approaches police are taking, many are also following the lead of CompStat (a strategy developed in New York City that directed police resources based on statistical analysis of criminal activity) in attempting to specify their mission and objectives more explicitly and trying to measure how closely they are actually achieving their goals. Accountability is a current emphasis in both business and government.

Many cities continue to use juvenile curfew laws in an attempt to reduce juvenile crime. The goal is to reduce both offending and victimization. Apparently these curfew laws and their enforcement continue despite a lack of supporting research evidence.

Perhaps the answer is to combine both approaches. Perhaps violent gang members need the tough (pulling levers) approach while first offenders charged with certain offenses can benefit from a restorative justice conferencing approach. What is clear, however, is that policing is changing and will continue to change. Many police officers undoubtedly continue to drive patrol cars and respond to 911 calls. In many communities, however, more innovative efforts are underway. Hopefully, such innovation will continue to change our ideas and expectations of what the police can and should do to prevent and control delinquency, disorder, and crime.

Unfortunately, in the last few years attention has focused on several highly publicized incidents of police shootings. As noted above, there have been charges of racial bias and also concerns that police might refrain from responding to crime situations out of fear of being called racist. In order to prevent problems, police are taking some specific steps, such as mandating body cameras. An important concern for juveniles is the issue of disproportionate minority contact—that is, the concern that black youths are unfairly targeted compared to white youths.

An important point to remember in any consideration of the police is that policing is only part of the effort to prevent, reduce, or control crime. When crime increases, much of society reacts, and many institutions and actors try to mobilize against crime. It is erroneous to think that the police alone can reduce crime. It is erroneous to think that SROs and zero-tolerance policies will be a magical solution to problems in schools. So instead of focusing only on the police, we should think of them as part of an interrelated network of responders.

> When violent crime grows into a serious social concern, it is not just the police that focus more attention on the problem. Schools, community groups, businesses, health officials, and many other organizations and individuals also respond to crime ... In summary, as the police mobilize to address crime more effectively, so do many other institutions (Eck & Maguire, 2000:249–250).

So we will repeat our citation of Eck and Maguire at the end of the section on police effectiveness: It is a myth that the "police have a substantial, broad, and independent impact on the nation's crime rate" (Eck & Maguire, 2000:247), but a realistic review of the research shows evidence "for focused policing strategies contributing to the drop in violent crime" (Eck & Maguire, 2000:245). It is also important to note that "[s]ome of the policing strategies that have received the most attention (for example, CompStat and zero-tolerance policing in New York City) are the least plausible candidates for contributing to the reduction in violent crime" (Eck & Maguire, 2000:245).

We need to be realistic in our expectations of the police. Surely the police play a role in combating delinquency, but to expect the police to be the only factor—or even the most important factor—is unrealistic. Many factors contribute to delinquency and crime. All the institutions of society must play a part in addressing the problem.

Discussion Questions

1. Community policing is based on the assumption that the job of the police is to solve the problems that lead to crime. Do you agree or disagree with this assumption? To what extent can society hold the police responsible for the problems that cause crime?
2. Police are trying new types of policing such as community or problem-solving policing, "broken windows" policing, and CompStat. Which approach do you favor? Discuss. Note any possible problems with the various approaches.
3. What do we know about police attitudes toward citizens? About citizen attitudes toward the

police? What can be done to improve attitudes on both sides?

4. What do curfew laws seek to accomplish? Are they effective?
5. What do we know about police use of force with juveniles? What can be done to minimize any improper use of force by police?
6. Schools are adopting school resource officers and zero-tolerance policies. Some argue that schools should devote more attention to improving classroom teaching and management. The most drastic issue in this area is the so-called school-to-prison pipeline. What can be done to minimize the criminalization of school misbehavior and avoid referring troublesome youths to court?
7. What can be done to improve policing in response to race-related issues such as police shootings, the war on drugs, and disproportionate minority contact?
8. Policing is changing. Would you want to be a police officer in light of all the change that is taking place in policing?

Bibliography

Adams, K. (2003). The effectiveness of juvenile curfews at crime prevention. *Annals of the American Academy of Political and Social Science, 587*, 136–159.

Adams, K. (2007). Abolish juvenile curfews. *Criminology & Public Policy, 6*, 663–670.

Alexander, M. (2012). *The New Jim Crow: Mass incarceration in the age of colorblindness* (Revised ed.). New York: The New Press.

Allen, T. T. (2005). Taking a juvenile into custody: Situational factors that influence police officers' decisions. *Journal of Sociology and Social Welfare, 32*, 121–129.

American Civil Liberties Union (ACLU) (2013). *The war on marijuana in black and white.* New York: ACLU.

American Civil Liberties Union of Illinois (ACLU of Illinois) (2015). *Stop and frisk in Chicago.* Chicago: ACLU of Illinois.

Anderson, E. (1994). The code of the streets. *Atlantic Monthly, 273*(5), 81–94.

Associated Press (2008, August 12). Hartford police to beef up teen curfew after shooting. *Johnson City Press*, 6A.

Baker, M. L., Sigmon, J. N., & Nugent, M. E. (2001). *Truancy reduction: Keeping students in school.* Washington, DC: Office of Juvenile Justice and Delinquency Prevention.

Bannister, A. J., Carter, D. L., & Schafer, J. (2001). A national police survey on juvenile curfews. *Journal of Criminal Justice, 29*, 233–240.

Bateman, T. (2012). Concern that courts in England and Wales may impose curfews in "inappropriate situations." *Youth Justice, 12*, 258–268.

Bishop, D. M. (2005). The role of race and ethnicity in juvenile justice processing. In D. F. Hawkins & K. Kempf-Leonard (Eds.), *Our children, their children: Confronting racial and ethnic differences in American juvenile justice* (pp. 23–82). Chicago: University of Chicago Press.

Booth, B., Van Hasselt, V. B., & Vecchi, G. M. (2011). Addressing school violence. *FBI Law Enforcement Bulletin, 80*(5), 1–9.

Borrero, M. (2001). The widening mistrust between youth and police. *Families in Society: The Journal of Contemporary Human Services, 82*, 399.

Bracey, J. R., Geib, C. F., Plant, R., O'Leary, J. R., Anderson, A., Herscovitch, L., ... & Vanderploeg, J. J. (2013). Connecticut's comprehensive approach to reducing in-school arrests: Changes in statewide policy, systems coordination and school practices. *Family Court Review, 51*, 427–434.

Brady, K. P., Balmer, S., & Phenix, D. (2007). School–police partnership effectiveness in urban schools: An analysis of New York City's impact schools initiative. *Education and Urban Society, 39*, 455–478.

Braga, A. A. (2015). *New perspectives in policing: Crime and policing revisited.* Washington, DC: National Institute of Justice.

Braga, A. A., & Bond, B. J. (2008). Policing crime and disorder hot spots: A randomized controlled trial. *Criminology, 46*, 577–607.

Braga, A. A., Kennedy, D. M., Piehl, A. M., & Waring, E. J. (2001). *The Boston gun project: Impact evaluation findings.* Washington, DC: National Institute of Justice.

Braga, A. A., Papachristos, A. V., & Hureau, D. M. (2014). The effects of hot spots policing on crime: An updated systematic review and meta-analysis. *Justice Quarterly, 31*, 633–663.

Brick, B. T., Taylor, T. J., & Esbensen, F. (2009). Juvenile attitudes towards the police: The importance of sub-cultural involvement and community ties. *Journal of Criminal Justice, 37*, 488–495.

Britt, H., Toomey, T. L., Dunsmuir, W., & Wagenaar, A. C. (2006). Propensity for and correlates of alcohol sales to underage youth. *Journal of Alcohol and Drug Education, 50*(2), 25–42.

Brown, R. A., & Frank, J. (2006). Race and officer decision making: Examining differences in arrest outcomes between black and white officers. *Justice Quarterly, 23*, 96–126.

Brown, R. A., Novak, K. J., & Frank, J. (2009). Identifying variation in police officer behavior between juveniles and adults. *Journal of Criminal Justice, 37*, 200–208.

Browning, S. L., Cullen, F. T., Cao, L., Kopache, R., & Stevenson, T. J. (1994). Race and getting hassled by the police: A research note. *Police Studies, 17*(1), 1–11.
Brunson, R. K. (2007). 'Police don't like black people': African-American young men's accumulated police experiences. *Criminology & Public Policy, 6*, 71–102.
Brunson, R. K., & Miller, J. (2006). Gender, race, and urban policing: The experience of African American youths. *Gender and Society, 20*, 531–552.
Chaiken, J. M., & Chaiken, M. R. (1982). *Varieties of criminal behavior.* Santa Monica, CA: RAND.
Cleary, H. M. D. (2013). Police interviewing and interrogation of juvenile suspects: A descriptive examination of actual cases. *Law and Human Behavior, 38*, 272–282.
Cobbina, J. E., Miller, J., & Brunson, R. K. (2008). Gender, neighborhood danger, and risk-avoidance strategies among urban African-American youths. *Criminology, 46*, 673–707.
Cole, D. (2003). The effect of a curfew law on juvenile crime in Washington, DC. *American Journal of Criminal Justice, 27*, 217–232.
Corsaro, N., Brunson, R. K., & McGarrell, E. F. (2009). Problem-oriented policing and open-air drug markets: Examining the Rockford pulling levers deterrence strategy. *Crime & Delinquency, 59*, 1085–1107.
Crank, J. P., & Caldero, M. (1991). The production of occupational stress in medium-sized police agencies: A survey of line officers in eight municipal departments. *Journal of Criminal Justice, 19*, 339–349.
Deuchar, R. (2011). The impact of curfews and electronic monitoring on the social strains, support and capital experienced by youth gang members in the west of Scotland. *Criminology & Criminal Justice, 12*, 113–128.
Dunworth, T. (2000). *National evaluation of the youth firearms initiative.* Washington, DC: U.S. Department of Justice.
Durose, M. R., Smith, E. L., & Langan, P. A. (2007). *Contacts between police and the public, 2005: Bureau of Justice Statistics Special Report.* Washington, DC: U.S. Department of Justice.
Eck, J., & Maguire, J. (2000). Have changes in policing reduced violent crime? An assessment of the evidence. In A. Blumstein & J. Wallman (Eds.), *The crime drop in America* (pp. 207–265). Cambridge, England: Cambridge University Press.
Fagan, J. (2002). Policing guns and youth violence. *Children, Youth and Gun Violence, 12*, 133–151.
Federal Bureau of Investigation (FBI) (2017). *Crime in the United States, 2015.* Retrieved from https://ucr.fbi.gov/crime-in-the-u.s/2015/crime-in-the-u.s.-2015
Feld, B. C. (2006). Juveniles' competence to exercise Miranda rights: An empirical study of policy and practice. *Minnesota Law Review, 91*, 26–100.
Feld, B. C. (2013a). Real interrogation: What actually happens when cops question kids. *Law & Society Review, 47*, 1–35.
Flexon, J. L., Lurigio, A. J., & Greenleaf, R. G. (2009). Exploring the dimensions of trust in the police among Chicago juveniles. *Journal of Criminal Justice, 37*, 180–189.
Gallup (2016, December 7–11). Americans rate healthcare providers high on honesty, ethics. Retrieved from www.gallup.com.
Gallup (2017, July 10). Confidence in police back at historical average. Retrieved from www.gallup.com.
Geller, A., & Fagan, J. (2010). Pot as pretext: Marijuana, race, and the new disorder in New York City street policing. *Journal of Empirical Legal Studies, 7*, 591–633.
Geller, W. A. (1983). Deadly force: What we know. In C. B. Klockars (Ed.), *Thinking about police: Contemporary readings* (pp. 313–331). New York: McGraw-Hill.
Geller, W. A., & Toch, H. (1996). Understanding and controlling police abuse of force. In W. A. Geller & H. Toch (Eds.), *Police violence: Understanding and controlling police abuse of force* (pp. 292–328). New Haven, CT: Yale University Press.
Goldstein, H. (1990). *Problem-oriented policing.* New York: McGraw-Hill.
Grossman, E. R., & Miller, N. A. (2015). A systematic review of the impact of juvenile curfew laws on public health and justice outcomes. *American Journal of Preventive Medicine, 49*(6), 945–951.
Hirschel, J. D., Dean, C. W., & Dumond, D. (2001). Juvenile curfews and race: A cautionary note. *Criminal Justice Policy Review, 12*, 197–214.
Hirschfield, P. J., & Celinska, K. (2011). Beyond fear: Sociological perspectives on the criminalization of school discipline. *Sociology Compass, 5*, 1–12.
Hockenberry, S., & Puzzanchera, C. (2017). *Juvenile court statistics 2014.* Pittsburgh: National Center for Juvenile Justice.
Howell, J. C. (2000). *Youth gang programs and strategies: Summary.* Washington, DC: Office of Juvenile Justice and Delinquency Prevention.
Huebner, B. M., Schafer, J. A., & Bynum, T. S. (2004). African American and white perceptions of police service: Within- and between-group variation. *Journal of Criminal Justice, 32*, 123–135.
Huizinga, D., Thornberry, T. P., Knight, K. E., Lovegrove, P. J., Loeber, R., Hill, K., & Farrington, D. P. (2007). Disproportionate minority contact in the juvenile justice system: A study of differential minority arrest/referral to court in three cities. An unpublished report submitted to the Office of Juvenile Justice and Delinquency Prevention. Available from the National Criminal Justice Reference Service.
Hurst, Y. G., Frank, J., & Browning, S. L. (2000). The attitudes of juveniles toward the police: A comparison of black and white youth. *Policing: An International Journal of Police Strategies & Management, 23*, 37–53.
Kelling, G. L., & Coles, C. M. (1996). *Fixing broken windows: Restoring order and reducing crime in our communities.* New York: Touchstone.
Kelly, R. (2013, July 22). The NYPD: Guilty of saving 7,383 lives. *Wall Street Journal.* Retrieved from http://online.wsj.com/news/articles/SB10001424127887324448104578616333588719320
Kim, B., Matz, A. K., Gerber, J., Beto, D. R., & Lambert, E. (2013). Facilitating police–probation/parole partnerships: An examination of police chiefs' and sheriffs' perceptions. *Policing: An International Journal of Police Strategies & Management, 36*, 752–767.
Kim, C. Y., Losen, D. J., & Hewitt, D. T. (2010). *The school-to-prison pipeline: Structuring legal reform.* New York: NYU Press.
Kirk, D. S., & Sampson, R. J. (2013). Juvenile arrest and collateral educational damage in the transition to adulthood. *Sociology of Education, 86*, 36–62.

Kochel, T. R., Wilson, D. B., & Mastrofski, S. D. (2011). Effect of suspect race on officers' arrest decisions. *Criminology, 49*, 473–512.
Kroes, W. H., Margolis, B. L., & Hurrell, J. J. (1974). Job stress in policemen. *Journal of Police Science and Administration, 2*, 145–155.
Kupchik, A. (2014). The school-to-prison pipeline: Rhetoric and reality. In F. E. Zimring & D. S. Tanenhaus (Eds.), *Choosing the future for American juvenile justice* (pp. 94–119). New York: New York University Press.
Langan, P. A., Greenfield, L. A., Smith, S. K., Durose, M. R., & Levin, J. J. (2001). *Contacts between police and the public: Findings from the 1999 national survey*. Washington, DC: U.S. Department of Justice.
Lee, J. M., Steinberg, L., & Piquero, A. R. (2010). Ethnic identity and attitudes toward the police among African American juvenile offenders. *Journal of Criminal Justice, 38*, 781–789.
Liederbach, J. (2007). Controlling suburban and small-town hoods: An examination of police encounters with juveniles. *Youth Violence and Juvenile Justice, 5*, 107–124.
Lizotte, A., & Sheppard, D. (2001). Gun use by male juveniles: Research and prevention. *Juvenile Justice Bulletin*. Washington, DC: U.S. Department of Justice.
Lundman, R. J. (1994). Demeanor or crime? The Midwest City Police–Citizen Encounters Study. *Criminology, 32*, 631–656.
Maguire, K., & Pastore, A. L. (2004). *Sourcebook of criminal justice statistics*, 2003. Washington, DC: Bureau of Justice Statistics. Retrieved from www.albany.edu/sourcebook/
Males, M. A. (2000). Vernon, Connecticut's juvenile curfew: The circumstances of youths cited and effects on crime. *Criminal Justice Policy Review, 11*, 254–267.
Malloy, L. C., Shulman, E. P., & Cauffman, E. (2014). Interrogations, confessions, and guilty pleas among serious adolescent offenders. *Law and Human Behavior, 36*, 181–193.
Maslach, C., & Jackson, S. E. (1979). Burned-out cops and their families. *Psychology Today, 12*(12), 59–62.
McDowall, D., Loftin, C., & Wiersema, B. (2000). The impact of youth curfew laws on juvenile crime rates. *Crime & Delinquency, 46*, 76–91.
McElvain, J. P., & Kposowa, A. J. (2008). Police officer characteristics and the likelihood of using deadly force. *Criminal Justice and Behavior, 35*, 505–521.
McGarrell, E. F., Olivares, K., Crawford, K., & Kroovand, N. (2000). *Returning justice to the community: The Indianapolis juvenile restorative justice experiment*. Indianapolis: Hudson Institute.
Meyer, J. R., & Reppucci, N. D. (2007). Police practices and perceptions regarding juvenile interrogation and interrogative suggestibility. *Behavioral Sciences and the Law, 25*, 757–780.
Montgomery, J. M., Foley, K. L., & Wolfson, M. (2006). Enforcing the minimum drinking age: State, local and agency characteristics associated with compliance checks and Cops in Shops programs. *Addiction, 101*, 223–231.
Morash, M. (1984). The establishment of a juvenile police record: The influence of individual and peer group characteristics. *Criminology, 22*, 97–112.
Morgan, E., Salomon, N., Plotkin, M., & Cohen, R. (2014). *The school discipline consensus report: Strategies from the field to keep students engaged in school and out of the juvenile justice system*. New York: The Council of State Governments Justice Center.
Musu-Gillette, L., Zhang, A., Wang, K., Zhang, J., & Oudekerk, B. A. (2017). *Indicators of School Crime and Safety: 2016* (NCES 2017-064/ NCJ 250650). Washington, DC: U.S. Department of Education and U.S. Department of Justice. Retrieved June 30, 2017 from https://nces.ed.gov/pubs2017/2017064.pdf.
Na, C., & Gottfredson, D. C. (2013). Police officers in schools: Effects on school crime and the processing of offending behaviors. *Justice Quarterly, 30*, 619–650.
National School Boards Association (2013, June 12). Advocacy groups file DOJ complaint claiming truancy enforcement at Dallas area districts violates civil rights of disabled and LEP students. *San Francisco Chronicle*. Retrieved from http://legalclips.nsba.org/2013/06/20/advocacy-groups-file-doj-complaint-claiming-truancy-enforcement-at-dallas-area-districts-violates-civil-rights-of-disabled-and-lep-students
Niederhoffer, A. (1967). *Behind the shield: The police in urban society*. Garden City, NY: Anchor Books.
Nix, J., Campbell, B. A., Byers, E. H., & Alpert, G. P. (2017). A bird's eye view of civilians killed by police in 2015. *Criminology & Public Policy, 16*, 309–340.
Novak, K. J., Frank, J., Smith, B. W., & Engel, R. S. (2002). Revisiting the decision to arrest: Comparing beat and community officers. *Crime & Delinquency, 48*, 70–98.
Office of Juvenile Justice and Delinquency Prevention (OJJDP) (2017a). *OJJDP statistical briefing book*. Retrieved from www.ojjdp.gov/ojstatbb.
Ohio Revised Code (2017). Retrieved from http://codes.ohio.gov/orc.
Paoline, E. A., Myers, S. M., & Worden, R. E. (2000). Police culture, individualism, and community policing: Evidence from two departments. *Justice Quarterly, 17*, 575–605.
Pope, C. E., & Snyder, H. N. (2003). *Race as a factor in juvenile arrests*. Washington, DC: U.S. Department of Justice.
Reiss, A. J., Jr. (1980). Police brutality. In R. J. Lundman (Ed.), *Police behavior: A sociological perspective* (pp. 274–296). New York: Oxford University Press.
Reynolds, K. M., Seydlitz, R., & Jenkins, P. (2000). Do juvenile curfew laws work? A time-series analysis of the New Orleans law. *Justice Quarterly, 17*, 205–230.
Rice, S. K., & Piquero, A. R. (2005). Perceptions of discrimination and justice in New York City. *Policing, 28*, 98–117.
Robers, S., Kemp, J., Rathbun, A., & Morgan, R. (2014). Indicators of school crime and safety: 2013. Washington, DC: National Center for Education Statistics, U.S. Department of Education, and Bureau of Justice Statistics, Office of Justice Programs, U.S. Department of Justice. Retrieved from http://nces.ed.gov/pubsearch/pubsinfo.asp?pubid=2014042
Roth, J. J. (2013). Commentary: Place-based delinquency prevention—Issues and recommendations. *OJJDP Journal of Juvenile Justice, 3*, 110–119.

Rovner, J. (2016a). *How tough on crime became tough on kids: Prosecuting teenage drug charges in adult court.* Washington, DC: The Sentencing Project.
Rovner, J. (2016b). *Racial disparities in youth commitments and arrests.* Washington, DC: The Sentencing Project.
Schnebly, S. M. (2008). The influence of community-oriented policing on crime-reporting behavior. *Justice Quarterly, 25,* 223–251.
Scott, M. (2002, May 1). Georgia prom-goers to face curfew thanks to recent legislation. *Johnson City Press,* 6.
Skogan, W. G., & Hartnett, S. M. (1997). *Community policing, Chicago style.* New York: Oxford University Press.
Skolnick, J. (1966). *Justice without trial.* New York: John Wiley and Sons.
Stoutland, S. E. (2001). The multiple dimensions of trust in resident/police relations. *Journal of Research in Crime and Delinquency, 38,* 226–253.
Sullivan, C. J., Dollard, N., Sellers, B., & Mayo, J. (2010). Rebalancing response to school-based offenses: A civil citation program. *Youth Violence and Juvenile Justice, 8,* 279–294.
Sutphen, R. D., & Ford, J. (2001). The effectiveness and enforcement of a teen curfew law. *Journal of Sociology and Social Welfare, 28,* 55–78.
Taylor, T. J., Turner, K. B., Esbensen, F., & Winfree, T. (2001). Coppin' an attitude: Attitudinal differences among juveniles toward police. *Journal of Criminal Justice, 29,* 295–305.
The Washington Post (2017). Fatal force. Retrieved December 3, 2017 from www.washingtonpost.com/graphics/national/police-shootings-2016.
Travis, L. F., & Coon, J. K. (2005). *The role of law enforcement in public school safety: A national survey.* Washington, DC: National Institute of Justice.
Trojanowicz, R., Kappeler, V. E., Gaines, L. K., & Bucqueroux, B. (1998). *Community policing: A contemporary perspective* (2nd ed.). Cincinnati: Anderson.
University at Albany (2014). *Sourcebook of criminal justice statistics.* Albany, NY: Hindelang Criminal Justice Research Center. Retrieved from www.albany.edu/sourcebook.
Walker, S. (1992). *The police in America: An introduction.* New York: McGraw-Hill.
Walker, S. (2011). *Sense and nonsense about crime, drugs, and communities* (7th ed.). Stamford, CT: Cengage Learning.
Watkins, A. M., & Maume, M. O. (2012). Rethinking the study of juveniles' attitudes toward the police. *Criminal Justice Studies, 25,* 279–300.
Werner, A. (2014, April 16). Don't TASE students at school, activists say. CBS News. Retrieved from www.cbsnews.com/news/tasers-plus-teenagers-equal-a-dangerous-mix-activists-say.
White, M. D., & Klinger, D. (2012). Contagious fire? An empirical assessment of the problem of multi-shooter, multi-shot deadly force incidents in police work. *Crime & Delinquency, 58,* 196–221.
Wilson, D. B., Gill, C., Olaghere, A., & McClure, D. (2016). Juvenile curfew effects on criminal behavior and victimization: A systematic review. *Campbell Systematic Reviews,* 2016, 3. DOI: 10.4073/csr.2016.3.
Worden, R. E. (1996). The causes of police brutality: Theory and evidence on police use of force. In W. A. Geller & H. Toch (Eds.), *Police violence: Understanding and controlling police abuse of force* (pp. 23–51). New Haven, CT: Yale University Press.
Worrall, J. L., & Gaines, L. K. (2006). The effect of police–probation partnerships on juvenile arrests. *Journal of Criminal Justice, 34,* 579–589.
Zimring, F. E. (2007). *The great American crime decline.* New York: Oxford University Press.
Zimring, F. E. (2012). *The city that became safe: New York's lessons for urban crime and its control.* New York: Oxford University Press.

Court Cases

J.D.B. v. North Carolina, 564 U.S. 261 (2011).
Tennessee v. Garner et al., 83 U.S. 1035 (1985).

Discussion Questions

1. In what instances do you believe that juveniles should be treated as adults in our justice system?
2. Do you believe there is a better way of handling our young offenders than our current justice system? What is a better way?

CHAPTER 6

Current Issues in Criminal Justice

Societal Justice

Virginia Murphy-Berman

Virginia Murphy-Berman, "Societal Justice," *Justice in Life and Society: How We Decide What is Fair*, pp. 87–106.

Definition of Societal Justice

[...]

In this [reading] we will examine another type of justice that conceptualizes fairness a bit differently. We are going to call this "societal justice." Societal justice is concerned with broad ideas about human rights, and with the relationships that exist between the individual and the larger state or nation. To start thinking about this topic we might consider a number of issues. First, we can reflect on what type of rights, if any, we think individuals should possess simply by virtue of being human. Second, we can ask ourselves whether we believe human rights are universal, or if they are better thought of as being particular to different situational contexts and cultural circumstances. Third, we can ponder what kind of state we think would exist if the human rights of all citizens were fully protected, and if such a state is even possible. And finally, and perhaps most importantly, we can ask who should get to decide who and what should be protected under the rubric of human rights.

Human Rights and the Universal Declaration

The nature of human rights, of course, has been debated by scholars, philosophers, and religious leaders throughout history. Here we are going to examine a specific way of thinking about these rights that emerged during the French Enlightenment period in the 18th century. This view sees human rights resting mainly on secular, not religious, contracts between the people and their leaders (Hayden 2001). An example of this Enlightenment outlook on rights can be found in an important human rights document called the *Universal Declaration of Human Rights* (UDHR) (Hayden 2001). The structure presented in that document will serve as the main framework that we will use for thinking about human rights in this [reading]. The conceptualization of rights presented in this declaration is particularly important because it is one of the first documents of its type to be signed by representatives from multiple nations of the world, and it is one of the few declarations in which the human rights were not just abstractly described, but rather were spelled out in very specific, practical terms.

The UDHR document was written just after hostilities in World War II had ended. As a result of this war, millions and millions of people had been killed or wounded, and much of Europe and parts of Asia and African had been destroyed. The scope of the holocaust had been uncovered. The question on the minds of many was how to form a new kind of world order so that this type of large-scale destruction would be less apt to occur again. In part because of this concern, the United Nations was founded in 1945; it brought 48 countries of the world together in a multinational forum. A Human Rights Commission consisting of 18 individuals from different countries was then created within this new UN structure, and commission members were given the task of defining what types of basic rights all human beings should possess in fair and just societies (Humphrey 1979). Commission members worked tediously for 2 years to craft the specific language that resulted in the UDHR document. Since this declaration was written, other documents have been produced that further codify the social, cultural, economic, and political rights outlined in the UDHR (The United Nations 1966a; 1966b) and that guarantee human rights to particular groups such as women and children (The United Nations 1979; 1989). However, our main attention here will be on the original UDHR framework. Our goal is not to critique or evaluate this document, or even to review its provisions in any detail. Rather, we will use it as a conceptual guide to start thinking about what we mean when we say all humans deserve a certain measure of human rights. What types of rights are we talking about? Is it reasonable, as the writers of the declaration attempted to do, to assert that these rights should exist for all human beings, regardless of culture or context? Are economic and social rights as basic to human beings as broader civic and political rights? Can we define human rights at all, or is the whole attempt to do so just a futile philosophical exercise with no real world consequences? Let's take a look at some of these questions.

The Nature of Human Rights: What Kind of Rights Are We Talking About?

The Key Idea of Dignity

The rights outlined in the UDHR and other UN rights documents rest on the central idea of the inherent dignity of all human life (Howard 1992). It is from this key premise that all of the rights contained in them flow. But what is this illusive concept of dignity? What does it mean to have it or not have it? And can a state provide it? The writers of these documents, in fact, felt that by the promotion of certain practices and policies, the state or nation could enhance the nature of the human experience. The various documents present templates on how to structure environments that promote human flourishing. The rights that are addressed emphasize the necessity of non discrimination for all people, and the importance of freedom and personal autonomy of action. The focus is on the worth of the individual actor, and his or her ability to construct a life of meaning and self-fulfillment (Bietz 2001).

What Is the State Morally Obligated to Do and Not to Do?

In the original UDHR framework, 30 different articles were included that addressed different types of universal human rights. Many of the rights defined are negative, but a few positive rights are enumerated as well. Positive rights are probably the type of rights that first come to mind when we think of human rights. These are rights *to* something. They oblige state action (Centre for Constitutional Studies 2013). We might think, for example, that a civilized state has a moral obligation to provide all its citizens with a certain minimum standard of living in terms of such things as sufficient food for survival or decent shelter for housing. Positive rights can also be defined in terms of certain guarantees for certain types of processes such as access to public hearings for those accused of crimes. These types of positive rights represent notions of what the state should be morally bound to provide for all of its citizens, not as a favor or because of particular merit on the part of the citizens, but simply because all humans deserve these rights. This way of conceptualizing deservingness, it might be noted, is more democratic and nondifferentiating among individuals than [other] models of deservingness [...].

To help us think about this a bit more we can consider an example of an individual named Jennifer who enjoys the right to a free basic education in some country of the world. The framers of these human rights documents would say that Jennifer should be guaranteed this right not because she did anything to earn this, but simply because it is her birthright. Establishing something as a right equalizes power between the rights' giver and the rights' receiver. Jennifer should not feel indebted in any way to the giver of the right (the state in this case) because what was provided was simply her due. The state, in turn, also should not use the allocation of these types of rights to reward some and punish others since they should be granted to everyone without exception. This is quite a radical notion! Of course, it is easier to assert general agreement with these types of abstract ideas than to put them into place in actual practice.

Human rights as exemplified in these types of UN documents can additionally be conceptualized in a negative manner. These types of rights are rights *from* something happening to an individual, and they specify things the state should have a moral obligation *not* to do in a civilized society (Centre for Constitutionalist Studies 2013). For instance, we might believe that everyone should have a right not to be subject to arbitrary arrest or to torture by the state, or not to be impeded from freely practicing the religion of their choice. These rights should be guaranteed to all without exceptions. For instance, I should refrain from torturing you not because you are a particularly nice or a worthy person, but because all individuals deserve some level of humane treatment from others.

Again, we can see that guaranteeing these types of negative rights may be easier to state abstractly than to put in place at a more concrete, specific level. One problem is how to operationalize terms like torture. Is it torture, for instance, to waterboard someone to extract information from them? Should there be any exceptions to this rule of never using torture? Is a definition of torture in one culture apt to be the same as the definition in another culture? These are some of the complicating considerations that can make straightforward implementation of these types of negative guarantees practically difficult.

Thinking About Food versus Freedom

In addition to affirming both positive and negative human rights, the writers of these universal rights documents also made distinctions between rights based more on process factors versus those focused more on outcomes (Patman 2000). Rights of access to certain processes tend to be in the political, civic, spiritual, or cultural domain. An example of a process right would be the right to freedom of assembly.

Outcome rights, on the other hand, guarantee access to more concrete types of benefits. These tend to be more social or economic in nature. Examples of these rights would be things like rights to decent pay for work, or to sufficient food and affordable shelter.

Although the framers of these documents equally valued both outcome and process rights, in some areas of the world more or less emphasis is placed on one or the other of these. For instance, in many Western cultures basic human rights tend to be defined more in terms of civic and political freedoms than economic and social rights. The idea here is not that social and economic benefits are unimportant, but rather that they can best be promoted if these civic and political rights are first protected. Thus, individuals might be granted the right to pursue wealth and an adequate standard of living, but the outcome of this pursuit might not be guaranteed. This is the language, for instance, that is used in the American Declaration of Independence.

In some other areas of the world, human rights are construed more in terms of tangible resources that the state should provide its citizens. Here we would say that individuals do not merely have the right to *pursue* a certain level of health care or an adequate standard of living, but rather, that the state has a moral obligation to provide these benefits to its citizens as their due. These social and economic rights are seen as being fundamental and basic to a just society, and they are considered preconditions to any other types of rights.

Of course, in most cultures some mix of both of these civic/political/spiritual and economic/social types of rights are represented. The issue is often just where the degree of emphasis is placed. Also, how we think about all of this tends to be deeply culturally embedded. We might imagine, for instance, a young man who has grown up in a society called Society Y where civic and political freedoms are strongly emphasized. Perhaps this young man visits a culture called Society X where these freedoms are very restricted. For instance, in Society X people are not allowed free access to information, they are not allowed to express their ideas about the state openly and honestly, and they are not allowed to gather in public places to protest any aspects of their condition. This all might seem horrible and intolerable to the young man from Society Y. Interestingly, however, perhaps many of the citizens in Society X tell this young man that in their society they are treated very justly. The state, they assert, guarantees everyone such things a right to free health care, education, child care, maternity leave, and adequate food and shelter. When they hear about the young man's culture, they are somewhat appalled by what they hear. They point out the tremendous discrepancies between wealth and poverty that exist there, the number of people living on the streets without shelter, the high crime and divorce rates, and the number of children that who do not have adequate child care. Who is right here? This can be difficult to judge.

Rights versus Duties and Religious Obligations

We have seen how the way basic human rights are conceptualized can vary in different cultural and political situations. Also, people in different cultures can differ on whether or not individual rights are even seen as important to the creation of a just society. The "rights centric" view is very in line with values endorsed in the United States and other Western cultures where the focus tends to be on removing restraints that may stand in the way of a personal pursuit of happiness. Here the assumption is that people do best when they are given maximum opportunity to make their own choices and act on their own desires (Pollis and Schwab 1980). In this framework, duty and obligations to others, even to family, are seen as being fairly discretionary and not morally imperative. For example, it is good to be nice to your parents in their old age, but it is not required. Often, in fact, there may be a slight inherent tension between balancing duty and achieving maximal self or individual fulfillment. For instance, if I spend too much time caring for my family, how can my ability to fulfill my own potential be maximized?

In other societies the situation may be very, very different. An alternative viewpoint to the individualism that we have described above is that people exist not to fulfill themselves, but rather to serve the greater good, which is defined by one's family or clan or society as a whole (Jacobson and Bruun 2000; Meijer 2001). In some places of the world, in fact, a word for the notion of individual human "rights" does not even exist as we understand the term in the West (de Benoist 2011). Rather, we would speak more of human obligations defined as the ability to fulfill competently one's duties and roles in society. These duties and roles consist of moral obligations to others, especially the extended family, and they are not discretionary. For instance, in these societies I would not choose to help my aging father because I may want to be a nice person or because I may feel sorry for his suffering. Rather, I would do this because it is a requirement of my role as a good daughter. Interestingly, in the 30 articles of the original UDHR framework only 1 article enumerated the types of duties and obligations that should be required of individuals in a just state. Some see this as an example of Western bias in the document itself.

A second alternative viewpoint to the Western individualistic, secular model is to assert that all human rights should flow from religious prescriptions. These prescriptions should be seen as nonnegotiable and binding, and as a central core of any rights discussion. Religious belief here is not seen as a right to be chosen or not chosen, but rather as a necessary foundational structure that underlies all justice thinking (Baderin 2003; Mayer 2007).

These represent very different worldviews and give rise to very different understandings of human rights and justice. Dissatisfaction with what some people saw as the cultural limits of the original UDHR documents, in fact, led to the creation of several other declarations that the writers thought better reflected regional cultural concerns. One of these was the Bangkok Declaration that was written to represent more Asian views of human rights (UN Regional Asia Pacific World Conference on Human Rights 1993). And, in 2000, several Islamic countries came together to write what was called the "Cairo Declaration of Human Rights" in which it was declared that people should have certain kinds of rights guaranteed only if these rights are found to be in accordance with Shari'ah law (Organisation of the Islamic Cooperation 1990).

Thus, deep cultural disagreements can and do exist over the way that a just life is defined, and over conceptions of the appropriate role of society in promoting such a life. What basic rights may seem obvious to one cultural group may seem peripheral or even unsuitable to another.

Focus on Me versus Focus on My Group

We have seen that when we talk about a just society, the focus can be on the individual standing alone or the individual embedded within the group. Let's talk more about this notion of group rights and how it may differ from conceptualizations of individuals' rights (Jones 1999; Triggs 1988).

To think about this, we might imagine a young girl who is a member of some hypothetical tribe in a certain part of the world. This young girl has been raised according to the traditions of her village. Part of these traditions demand that she becomes a bride at the age of 12 or 13 years old to an older man of her parents' choosing. If she does not marry at this age the chances are high that she will never be deemed a suitable bride for anyone. As you consider this, further imagine that a human rights health worker from some Western country visits this village and talks to the villagers about the health risks that young girls face when they marry so early. She discusses the higher rate of complications from pregnancy when one is so young, and the higher numbers of childbirth deaths that may occur. In order to try to start somewhere to change the villagers' marriage practices, this rights worker then talks to the parents of a young girl who is scheduled to be married the next week. The human rights worker urges this girl's parents to stop the wedding. When they refuse, the worker laments the backward state of their thinking and their selfish inability to focus on their daughter's needs and rights.

We can look at the above as an illustration of a clash between the individual rights of the daughter and the group rights of this tribe. Which rights should be privileged? Should the young girl's individual well-being outweigh decades of tradition in this tribe? What if this tribe existed as a sort of minority group in the midst of a state that had different ideas about raising children and marriage? Would it be just for this majority state to dictate how this tribe should handle their marriage arrangements, or should the tribe's beliefs and practices be protected?

As we think about this we have to consider what we are trying to do when we honor different types of rights (Melton 2008). It is easy to think about why we place so much importance on individual rights. We cherish these rights because we want to enhance a person's human dignity and ability to live unrestricted and self-directed lives. But what do we enhance when we protect group rights? Are not group affiliations and traditions, moral codes and rituals also an important part of individual identity? Wouldn't the young girl in the case discussed above lose an essential connection to her tribe, and her sense of worth and security that flows from that if she individually defied the tribe's marriage traditions? These are not easy questions to answer, and we will come back to them later in this [reading]. For now, suffice it to say that sometimes individual and group rights clash, and favoring one can sometimes have deleterious effects on the other.

Are Any Rights Universal?

A key question underlying all of the previous discussion is whether *any* types of rights are truly universal and apply equally in all cultures and contexts, or whether all rights are culturally relative in nature. This can be complicated to determine. Perhaps, for instance, someone suggests that certainly some rights such as the right to not have physical pain inflicted unjustly on us are so basic that they should be protected for people everywhere. This seems to be a fairly straightforward proposition that would be difficult to argue against. The problem comes, however, when we try to define what we mean by unjust infliction of pain. We might imagine a culture which had a tradition of foot binding for women, as China did in the past. Or maybe in some society various types of body piercing and physical scarring are deemed to be necessary for achievement of cultural standards of beauty. Would these practices, if culturally promoted and, in fact, deemed necessary, involve a violation of an individual's rights to health and bodily integrity, or should we see them simply as cultural practices that we ought to protect? This is the gist of the cultural universalism versus cultural relativism dilemma. Let's think about this some more by arguing for both sides of these ideas.

It Is All in the Eye of the Beholder

Those who argue for a culturally relativist perspective would say that all types of cultural practices, even those we personally find to be repugnant, should be interpreted in light of the prevailing cultural traditions in place within the societies in which they occur. Furthermore, cultural relativists would add that we cannot competently judge practices in other cultures because, as outsiders, we can never achieve full understanding of the context in which they take place (Ignatieff 2001; Renteln 1985).

Consider again the old Chinese custom of foot binding. This custom had a long and complex evolution and, when it was practiced in China, it was embedded within many other types of norms and role obligations for women. Although it may have seemed abhorrent to some Western eyes, it was defined quite differently at the time that it took place in China. So the question becomes who are we to judge? Is it fair to judge anything at all if we risk doing so ignorantly and without full understanding? Would we think it appropriate to have others judge us? For instance, we might ask how outsiders might view some of our own culturally promoted practices to improve appearance such as tattooing, ear or lip piercing, or use of plastic surgery. What about implementation of the death penalty as a form of punishment for some crimes? Can others morally evaluate these types of practices if they do not completely comprehend the cultural environment in which these practices take place? Those who ascribe to the morally relativist viewpoint would say they cannot.

Some Practices Are Just Bad Everywhere

Of course, there is another side to this argument. Some would suggest that cultural relativism should have some limits, and that some practices of the world, even if they are sanctioned by cultural traditions, are so objectionable that we should define them being unjust in any context (Mahoney 2007). If foot binding, for instance, was found to cause great pain and disfigurement, it should be seen as wrong and a violation of human rights in any culture. If one concluded that capital punishment produces intolerable suffering in individuals, it should be considered inhumanly cruel regardless of any cultural beliefs that might exist that support its use. This type of cultural absolutism position, thus, asserts that we can objectively analyze the characteristics of practices outside of their situational circumstances. The "rub," though, is how to determine the exact standards we should use to do this. What is intolerable pain? What type of caused suffering should we protect against? Does the infliction of pain on another always consist of a type of rights denial, or can it ever be justified? When, for that matter, does cultural context matter and when does it not matter?

Rights and Power

We have examined how human rights can be viewed from multiple perspectives by both individuals from within and from outside different types of cultural environments. But how might the way that power is distributed among people in societies affect how we think about what should and should not be considered a rights violation (Binion 1995; Qureshi 2012)? What if, for example, we found that some cultural norms and traditions that we protect were mainly put in place by one group within a culture at the expense of others? We might imagine, for instance, that certain female dress codes and travel restrictions that we observed in a particular culture were put in place not by the women who were directly affected by them, but rather by men in the society to guard their own status and power. Should this matter to us as we think about how and if these women's rights had been abused? Should we be especially sensitive to customs that seem to privilege some groups and not others? These types of issues can make our ability to render morally sound judgments of the cultural traditions of others even more complicated.

Looking Again at Rights Documents

We started this discussion of human rights by talking about certain documents on human rights that were written after the end of World War II. The framers of these documents wrote them with the intention of positively impacting the lives of people throughout the world. The rights they laid out were declared to be universal and nonnegotiable. In a just society, the framers asserted that these rights should be promoted and protected. But how much impact have these types of documents actually had? There is a debate about this. Some suggest that the impact has been minimal, in part, because the documents themselves were nonbinding, and the nations that signed them were not required to agree to any standard way to monitor compliance. Without this enforcement ability, it can be argued that these documents become merely words on paper. Others, however, say that even without strict enforcement capability, these types of rights documents are important. They are important because they can help set a stage for dialogue about the nature of human rights. They provide a framework from which international law can draw. More importantly they set a tone and provide a vision of what a just and humane society might look like (Donnelly 2013). This last point takes us back to the question of whether there can be any one vision of societal justice that fits all. Are the "universal" rights talked about in documents like the UDHR truly universal? Can rights be defined outside of the religious, cultural, and moral context in which they are embedded? These questions are not likely to be resolved soon, if ever.

Applications: Putting This Together to Debate Some Bigger Policy Issues

We have reviewed some of the ideas about how to consider the nature of human rights. Now, [...] you will be given the chance to use the information presented in this [reading] to critically analyze some policy issues pertinent to human rights concerns. There are many such concerns. For example, how should we deal with practices in other cultures that we personally find to be degrading and disgusting and violating of individuals' basic human rights? Can we condemn them without inappropriately imposing on others our own values and sense of right and wrong? How do we decide what is a right in society and what is a privilege? Should economic benefits and social services be considered rights? If so, what kinds of services and benefits, and what standard do we use to decide? And finally, how do we remain sensitive to the importance of group cultural customs and traditions while still supporting freedom of individual choice and initiative? Is this particularly a concern when the groups in question are minority groups who have historically struggled to retain their cultural identity as a people? These are some of the issues we will deal with in this last section of the [reading].

[I]deas and proposals pertaining to some of these issues will be presented, followed by a series of questions. These questions have no clear right or wrong answers. Rather they are included to help you think more critically about these types of human rights dilemmas, and to enable you to view arguments about them from multiple perspectives.

Major Human Rights Dilemma #1: The Case of Female Circumcision

In some countries of the world, young girls are required to have a circumcision procedure (cutting off of the clitoris of the female genitals) take place before they are considered to be eligible for marriage. This is viewed as a sort of rite of passage for girls, and it is often carried out by some of the older women in the community. One purpose of this is to control a woman's sexuality by making sex less pleasurable. Complications from the procedure can be fairly common, especially if it is done without the use of sterile and sanitized instruments. There has been considerable debate from individuals about the moral efficacy of this practice, particularly among those who advocate for human rights for women. Some suggest that because circumcision subjects young girls to great pain and potential long-term suffering, it should be outlawed wherever it takes place around the world. In this view, female circumcision rituals represent a violation of young girls' basic human rights. This is particularly so since in most cases where it is used, young girls often have no choice about whether to have or not have the procedure. It is simply imposed on them.

Others would say that we must be careful about condemning procedures like female circumcision because we may not fully understand the context in which they may take place or the reasons that these practices were initiated in the first place. People also point to inconsistencies in individuals' outrage. For example, are we as concerned about circumcision rituals carried out on young boy babies, as take place in many regions of the world, including the United States? What if other rites of passage rituals that may exist such as body piercing or scarring or burning that may be required practices in some cultural groups? What defines something which should be seen as "wrong" and universally condemned versus something that may be tolerated in the name of cultural diversity? That is the key question.

Construct arguments in support of both sides of this issue. What position seems most fair to you in an ideal world? Why?

1. Should the degree of suffering that the young girls undergo when they have this procedure be the main factor that should be taken into account when deciding if the practice should be universally condemned? Would it be okay if it was carried out under sedation in controlled conditions in modern medical facilities?
2. Does the fact that the girls who undergo this procedure usually have no choice in the matter make a difference to you as you evaluate whether its use represents a violation of the young girls rights? What if girls could opt to have or not have this done? Would that somehow make the practice more acceptable?
3. Would knowledge that these customs often originated from the dictates of male leaders about the types of young girls who should be eligible for marriage affect how you view this practice? Would

you think differently if you thought that it evolved in societies in which women, not men, held most positions of power?

4. Can you think of any circumstances in which this type of practice should be allowed without reservation? What would be the nature of these circumstances?

Major Human Rights Dilemma #2: Human Rights in "Prego"

Imagine a debate taking place about a hypothetical country named "Prego." In this country a revolution just occurred, and the previous democratic leader was replaced by a military dictator. During the earlier regime, people were guaranteed rights to vote, to practice the religion of their choice, to freely express themselves, and to openly gather in public places. Now these rights have been taken away. Access to information is restricted and people are allowed to have no voice in government processes. Freedom of religion is also not tolerated, and individuals now have no rights of free assembly. However, the people now have greater access to a range of government services and resources. Before the revolution, the people of Prego were very poor. Many individuals were homeless and starving in the streets. Medical care was available only for the very rich, and most children were uneducated. Under the new dictatorship all of this has changed. "Pregans" now are provided free housing and medical care. Children can go to public schools where nutritional meals are given to them. All individuals are encouraged to work, and free child care is provided when parents are away from the home.

Your task as a human rights worker is to analyze the human rights situation as it exists now in Prego. Is Prego a better place since the revolution? Are the people's lives "improved?" Are there more or less human rights violations taking place since the revolutionaries took over?

Construct arguments in support of both sides of this issue. What position seems most fair to you in an ideal world? Why?

1. Would it make a difference if you knew that statistics in Prego show that infant mortality and malnutrition rates have significantly decreased since the revolution, and that literacy rates have significantly increased? Why or why not?
2. What if opinion polls showed that the people of Prego are actually happier now post revolution than they were before the revolution? Should that matter in your assessment of the human right situation there?
3. What if you were told that people have been murdered by the government in Prego for trying to speak out about their lack of freedom? Would this impact your thinking about the human rights situation there? What if the murdered people represented only a very small number of the people who live in Prego?
4. Would you think differently about this if you used a long-term versus a short-term perspective to consider what type of state you wanted to permanently promote for the Pregan people?

Major Allocation Dilemma # 3: Human Rights and Integrated Schooling

In the United States we have a very diverse culture consisting of people of different races and religions and ethnic backgrounds. A challenge that can exist in these types of diverse environments is how to put policies in place that allow individuals to maintain and honor their rich and unique cultural traditions without isolating themselves from the benefits of full participation in the larger culture. To think about this a bit more, imagine a situation in which Native Americans in some community in the American West ran schools for their own children. In these schools the children were taught about their heritage and history. They were also taught to speak their own tribal language and to understand their ancestors' religious traditions. Only Native Americans could attend these schools, and consequently the children who went to them had very little contact with the nonnative community in the larger culture. Some people felt that these schools worked to put the Native American children at a disadvantage when, as young adults, they tried to find jobs in the mainstream culture. Because they had been so isolated and had so few social contacts with those outside their own group, it was quite hard for them to leave their own communities.

Imagine now that as a remedy to this, some people proposed that the Native American children should be moved from their tribal schools and placed in public educational institutions outside their communities. They would be given new nonnative names like Jack or Jennifer and they would have full access to all of the schools' instructional resources. Even more importantly, they would be able to make friends and bond with students, teachers, and other mentors at these schools who could help them later in life to integrate into the mainstream culture.

The question is whether the above "integration proposal" is a good idea. Would being forced to attend these public schools enhance these children's lives by giving them a right to an educational experience that would benefit them later, or would it harm them and be a violation of their rights in some manner?

Construct arguments in support of both sides of this issue. What position seems most fair to you in an ideal world? Why?

1. Would it make a difference in how you think about this if you knew that the parents and/or the Native American students themselves could choose whether or not to attend these types of public schools? Why or why not?
2. What if statistics showed that the Native American children who did attend these types of public schools were able to secure significantly higher paying jobs after graduation than the children who stayed in the traditional tribal schools? Should this fact be important as you think about this?
3. What if we learned that if these policies were put in place that over time the number of individuals who would be able to speak the old tribal language and who remembered the old traditional religious practices would be significantly diminished? How should this be taken into account as we try to decide if any rights have been violated by this integration policy?

Summary

In this [reading,] a review of "societal justice" or the relationship that should exist between the individual and the larger state was presented. The framework we used here is based, in part, on a secular notion of human rights that emerged during the period of the French Enlightenment. Particular attention was paid to a document called the *Universal Declaration of Human Rights* that was written after the end of World War II. In this document, which was signed by multiple nations of the world, an Enlightenment view on the types of universal rights that should be protected in just and civilized states is presented. Although it has had considerable impact on how human rights are thought about, some scholars have criticized it as being overly Western in tone, and not truly universal in character.

Rights can vary on numerous dimensions. Some rights specify things that the state must do in a just society, and others specify things the state must refrain from doing. Rights can also address different economic, social, political, civic, religious, and cultural life domains. Rights that the state should guarantee to all its citizens can emphasize tangible outcomes, such as adequate food and shelter, and/or types of participatory processes, such as the right to assemble in public places. Each of these different kinds of rights can be more or less stressed in different types of governing structures, and great debates have taken place on which type are the most essential component of a just society. Some, in fact, have questioned the centrality of individual human rights at all to conceptions of societal justice. Alternatives to this rights-based model of justice emphasize the importance of individuals' fulfillment of duties and obligations to others, or of the fundamental place of religious prescriptions for a moral life.

Group rights can also be distinguished from individual rights. Group rights emphasize the importance of the individual embedded in the larger whole, as opposed to the individual standing alone. These rights consist of guarantees to groups to protect and uphold the traditions, moral codes and rituals that sustain them and contribute to their heritage and identity.

A key question in all of this is whether any human rights are truly universal, or if all are bound to certain unique cultural situations. Those who support a culturally relativist perspective would say that all rights must be viewed and evaluated in terms of the context in which they are practiced. Proponents of a more absolutist position would disagree and say that some rights transcend all cultural boundaries and are universal in nature.

Finally, an issue can be raised about the impact that these attempts to formally codify our understanding of universal human rights have actually had on the lives of individuals around the world. Some would suggest that because the enforcement mechanisms for these types of rights documents are not strong, their impact has been minimal. Others would assert that, to the contrary, attempting to define human rights in a formal way sets the stage for important dialogues about the meaning of justice at a global level.

References

Baderin, Meshood. 2003. *International Human Rights and Islamic Law.* Oxford, England: Oxford University Press.

>Bietz, Charles. 2001. "Human Rights as Common Concerns." *American Political Science Review.* 95 (2): 269–282.

Binion, Gayle. 1995. "Human Rights: A Feminist Perspective." *Human Rights Quarterly.* 17 (3): 509–525.

Centre for Constitutional Studies. 2013. *Positive and Negative Rights.* Canada: University of Alberta.

de Benoist, Alain. 2011. *Beyond Human Rights: Defending Freedoms.* Artkos Media Ltd.

Donnelly, Jack. 2013. *Universal Human Rights in Theory and Practice* (3rd edition). Ithaca, NY: Cornell University Press.

Hayden, Patrick. eds. 2001. *The Philosophy of Human Rights.* St. Paul, MN: Paragon House.
Howard, Rhoda E. 1992. "Dignity, Community and Human Rights." In *Human Rights in Cross-cultural Perspectives: A Quest for Consensus,* edited by Abdullahi Ahmed An-Na'im, 81–102. Philadelphia, PA: University of Pennsylvania Press.
Humphrey, John P. 1979. "The Universal Declaration of Human Rights: Its History, Impact and Juridical Character." In *Human Rights: Thirty Years after the Universal Declaration,* edited by Bertrand G. Ramcharen, 221–237. Leiden, The Netherlands: Brill Publishing.
Ignatieff, Michael. 2001. "The Attack on Human Rights." *Foreign Affairs.* 80: 1–2.
Jacobson, Michael and Ole Bruun, eds. 2000. *Human Rights and Asian Values: Contesting National Identities and Cultural Representations in Asia.* Richmond, Surrey, England: Curzon Press.
Jones, Peter. 1999. "Human Rights, Group Rights and People's Rights." *Human Rights Quarterly.* 21 (1): 80–107.
Mahoney, Jack. 2007. *The Challenge of Human Rights: Origin, Development, and Significance.* Malden, Mass.: Blackwell Publishing Ltd.
Mayer, Ann Elizabeth. 2007. *Islam and Human Rights: Traditions and Politics* (4th edition). Boulder, CO: Westview Press.
Meijer, Martha. eds. 2001. *Dealing with Human Rights: Asian and Western Views on the Value of Human Rights.* Bloomfield, CT: Kumarian Press.
Melton, Gary. 2008. "Beyond Balancing: Toward an Integrated Approach to Children's Rights." *Journal of Social Issues.* 64 (4): 903–920.
Organisation of the Islamic Cooperation. August 5th, 1990. The Cairo Declaration of Human Rights.
Patman, Robert G. eds. 2000. *A Review of Universal Human Rights.* New York, NY: St. Martin's Press.
Pollis, Adamantia and Peter Schwab. eds. 1980. *Human Rights: Cultural and Ideological Perspectives.* Santa Barbara, CA: Praeger Publications.
Qureshi, Shazia. 2012. "Feminist Analysis of Human Rights." *Journal of Political Studies.* 19 (2): 41–55.
Renteln, Alison. 1985. "The Unanswered Challenge of Relativism and the Consequences for Human Rights." *Human Rights Quarterly.* 7 (4): 514–540.
The United Nations. 1948. *The Universal Declaration of Human Rights.*
The United Nations. 1966a. *International Covenant on Civil and Political Rights.*
The United Nations. 1966b. *International Covenant on Economic, Social and Cultural Rights.*
The United Nations. 1979. *Convention on the Elimination of All Forms of Discrimination Against Women.*
The United Nations. 1989. *The Convention on the Rights of the Child.*
Triggs, Gillian. 1988. "The Rights of 'Peoples' and Individual Rights: Conflict or Harmony?" In *The Rights of Peoples,* edited by James Crawford, 141–157. Oxford, England: Clarendon Press.
UN Regional Asia Pacific World Conference on Human Rights. April 1993. The Bangkok Declaration of Human Rights.

Discussion Questions

1. How do you think our world could change if we started addressing and using social inequalities to change how we handle crime?
2. How would you define "societal justice"?
3. What rights should be universal?
4. Name three things that you would change in our current criminal justice system.